An Outline of
Psychology
as applied to Medicine

John Weinman BA PhD

Reader in Psychology,
Unit of Psychology as applied to Medicine
Guy's Hospital Medical School
London

Second Edition

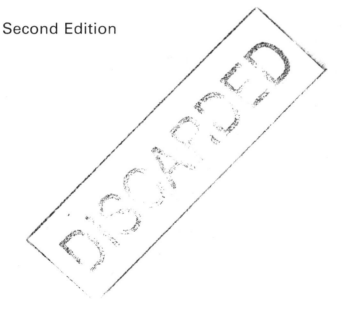

WRIGHT
1987 Bristol

OAK
M

Published under the Wright imprint by
IOP Publishing Limited,
Techno House, Redcliffe Way,
Bristol BS1 6NX, England.

First edition, 1981
Reprinted, 1982
Second edition, 1987

British Library Cataloguing in
Publication Data

Weinman, John
    An outline of psychology as applied to
    medicine.—2nd ed.
    1. Psychology   2. Medicine and psychology
    I. Title
    150'.2461   BF131

ISBN 0 7236 0890 3

20,602

8707193

0012796

WLM120

616.0019

Typeset by
Activity Limited, Salisbury, Wiltshire

Printed in Great Britain by
The Bath Press, Lower Bristol Road, Bath BA2 3BL.

To My Family

Preface to the Second Edition

In planning the changes for the second edition, I have been guided by feedback from students and colleagues both in deciding on what changes to make to the original volume and in selecting new areas for inclusion. I have tried to improve the format of the book by clarifying the text where necessary and by a better use of subheadings and spacing. Many topics have been brought up to date by including references to more recent developments both in the text and in the recommendations for further reading at the end of each chapter. In addition, a number of other topics, which either were missing from the first edition or have developed mainly since that time, are now included. Thus there are new sections on psychological influences on the immune system and on psychological approaches to the management of pain, stress-related disorders and stressful medical procedures.

Two chapters have undergone major structural changes. The chapter on 'Doctor–patient communication' in the first edition is now entitled 'Patients and doctors' and begins with a consideration of health attitudes and behaviour prior to outlining more specific communication issues. The chapter on 'Coping with illness and handicap' replaces the one on 'Psychological reactions to physical illness and handicap' and focuses on the processes involved in coping with physical illness and with chronic and terminal illness. Finally, the last chapter now has an enlarged section on cognitive approaches to treatment and ends with an outline of counselling and its applications.

The changes which have been made reflect the major developments in the field of psychology as applied to medicine and the emergence of 'health psychology' as a separate and substantial specialty. Since health psychology is concerned with the psychological aspects of health and illness, it is hoped that this book will provide both a starting point and a framework for the reader.

J. W.

Preface to the First Edition

Psychology is the discipline concerned with the study and understanding of human behaviour. In recent years it has become an important part of the curriculum for students of medicine and allied health disciplines. This book is intended to provide an outline of the subject for the benefit of those students. In this book I have therefore tried to integrate basic and applied areas by including psychological topics which can be related to medicine as well as looking at psychological aspects of clinical issues. Although the earlier chapters tend to cover the basic topics and the later ones the clinical areas, there is deliberately a great deal of overlap. Wherever appropriate, clinical applications are used to illustrate so-called basic topics and areas of basic psychology are elaborated to clarify and augment the more clinical sections.

References to research findings are supplied in the text. The use of these will be found to be variable between the chapters in that some sections lend themselves to the presentation of a fair amount of experimental evidence whereas in others a general description of the key issues seems more appropriate. Recommendations for further reading are also given at the end of each chapter and these will allow the interested reader to pursue any of the topics in greater depth.

Many areas in psychology can appear complicated, controversial or even poorly resolved. I have attempted to look at some of these areas and to examine the evidence critically so that the reader can be aware of the current 'state of the art' rather than be

presented with an over-simplified view of the
issues. Thus this book has been written in the
belief that the reader will welcome being given
an insight into current issues as well as
complexities inherent in attempting to
understand human behaviour.

J. W.

Acknowledgements

This book originally emerged from a course in psychology for medical students which began at Guy's Hospital Medical School twelve years ago. I am indebted to many students who have provided invaluable feedback not only about the course but also on the first edition of this book. Many colleagues also offered very useful advice and information for the first edition as well as helpful comments for preparing this edition. In particular David Armstrong has continued to provide encouragement and critical discussion.

I would like to thank the following for the use of diagrams and tables which appear in the book: Plenum Publishing Co. for *Fig.* 2; Van Nostrand Reinhold Co. for *Fig.* 3; W. H. Freeman and Co. for *Figs.* 5 and 12; Churchill Livingstone for *Figs.* 6 and 14; Dr C. M. Hawkes and *Medical Education* for *Fig. 15; British Journal of Orthodontics* for *Table* 3.

Many thanks are also due to Carol Butterfield for typing the manuscript so capably and to Tony Hale for drawing the cartoons. Finally, Mary Anne, Anna and Jonathan deserve my warmest thanks for supporting and putting up with me while I struggled to turn my thoughts into words.

Contents

1

Psychology and medicine

In the first part of this chapter there is an attempt to outline the different ways in which psychology can relate to medicine. Following this there is an account of the mechanisms which mediate pain perception. The decision to include a discussion of pain mechanisms in this opening chapter has been made for two reasons. First, it is a fundamental topic in medicine and one in which a psychological perspective forms an integral part. Second, it provides a clear example of the limitations of adopting a narrow biological approach to health and disease. Thus the analysis of pain perception will be used to demonstrate the importance of considering psychological and biological approaches in conjunction.

• 1.1. Psychology in relation to medicine

Psychology is concerned with understanding human behaviour and as such is inextricably bound up with the practice of medicine. In many ways psychology can be seen to have a more diverse relevance to medicine than the traditional preclinical sciences and because of this it is sometimes difficult to grasp an overall picture of the contributions which can be made. Five fairly distinct but nevertheless related areas of relevance can be identified and the reader might find such an overview useful before proceeding with the other sections. These five areas are:

   a. Changes in behaviour associated with such factors as ageing, psychiatric illness and neurological impairment.
   b. The role of psychological factors in the aetiology of medical problems.
   c. Doctor–patient relations.
   d. The patient's response to illness and treatment.
   e. Psychological approaches to treatment.

Each of these areas is covered in detail in different sections of the book but in this introductory chapter a brief summary of each is presented.

a. Changes in behaviour

Identifying signs and symptoms is a basic part of diagnosis and for a wide range of problems this may involve recognizing changes in behaviour. Psychiatric patients occupy the largest number of all hospital beds and it can also be argued that, in the majority of general practice patients, there is a significant psychological component in their illness. Also many of the disorders of development and ageing, as seen by paediatricians and geriatricians respectively, are characterized by changes in such aspects of behaviour as impairments of speech, learning or memory. Perhaps the most striking examples of changes in behaviour are those seen in neurology and which arise from damage to localized brain regions. These areas in medicine, in which the observation of behavioural change is central, should serve to illustrate the importance of understanding aspects of 'normal' behaviour and the relation between neurological structure and function as a basis for investigating and dealing with certain disorders.

It might be thought from the foregoing discussion that this area of relatedness is directly parallel to the relation between, for example, anatomy and surgery in that the understanding of 'normal' functions serves as a basis for dealing with pathologies. Such a conclusion is only partly acceptable since the relation between normality and abnormality in behaviour is neither agreed nor clear-cut. For neurological disturbances of behaviour, a knowledge of psychological processes can be of direct value in understanding the nature of the dysfunction. For example, the sometimes dramatic losses of memory which can follow on from damage to certain brain regions can be more clearly understood with reference to unimpaired memory processes. However, the relation of normal to abnormal cannot really be extended to psychiatry in such a clear way.

Many people imagine that psychiatric illness is abnormal in the sense that it falls far outside the realm of normal everyday behaviour and is therefore easily defined. While this may be true for a small number of bizarre psychological problems, many of the problems seen by psychiatrists or clinical psychologists comprise aspects of behaviour which many people show or feel at times. Anxiety and depression constitute two of the commonest psychiatric problems, yet just about everyone has experienced both of these to some degree at some time. Also there is no clear 'normal' state in relation to the clinical entity of depression and which corresponds to the way in which one might describe normal lung function in relation to a lung disorder such as bronchial asthma.

It is important to bear these points in mind because problems of behaviour do not simply separate off in a simple and universally agreed way from so-called 'normal' behaviour. Normal behaviour is largely socially defined and so definitions of abnormal behaviour vary from generation to generation and from culture to culture. As we shall see, psychological problems are not purely defined by changes within the individual but will depend on the context within which they occur and the ability of the individual to cope. Moreover, with many psychological problems, subjective rather than objective criteria may be used for defining problems.

The first nine chapters of this book present aspects of 'normal' behaviour. Chapters 2–4 are concerned with basic behavioural processes and their neuroanatomical substrates. Chapter 5 examines the nature of emotion and stress together with the links between associated physiological and psychological processes. Individual differences in personality and intelligence are described in Chapters 6 and 7 while the changes in behaviour which accompany child development and ageing are outlined in Chapters 8 and 9. In addition to describing basic aspects of human behaviour, these earlier chapters also present many examples of related clinical issues.

b. Psychological factors as a part of aetiological mechanisms

It is increasingly being realized that many physical and psychological disorders arise directly and indirectly from what people do to themselves rather than solely from external sources such as viruses. There are aspects of human behaviour such as smoking and reckless driving which can result in serious and often fatal medical problems. There are also a range of disorders which are often referred to collectively as 'stress-induced' illnesses which seem to stem from the way people respond to adverse environmental factors. Many major changes in people's lives which necessitate physical or psychological adjustment now appear to be associated with a greater proneness to illness. The recognition of these effects serves to emphasize the importance of maintaining a psychosocial as well as a biological equilibrium in safeguarding health.

The task for the psychologist here is twofold. First, to be able to identify and measure those psychosocial factors which appear to have stressful effects. Second, to incorporate those factors into an aetiological model which provides the links between psychological processes (e.g. moods, behaviours, etc.) and related physiological processes (e.g. autonomic, endocrine or immunological changes). An important question here concerns the role of psychological factors in disease and whether they have a direct causal effect or act as triggers to the onset of disease in certain individuals. These issues are examined in Chapter 5 but also reappear in various forms in other chapters.

c. Understanding doctor–patient relations

The liaison between the doctor and the patient lies at the very heart of all medicine and as such can have profound effects on the way problems present and are resolved. There has been a tendency in the past for this meeting to be regarded in somewhat passive terms whereby information is extracted and treatment imparted. However, it is being increasingly demonstrated that the quality of communication and the nature of the relationship between doctor and patient can determine not only what problems are discussed but also the degree to which patients adhere to treatment.

In view of this it becomes clear that an understanding of doctor–patient relations together with the development of appropriate interpersonal skills is necessary to be able to define the nature of the patient's problems as well as resolving them most effectively. An optimal approach here implicitly recognizes the doctor–patient liaison as a complex interaction and that the patient will respond emotionally both to illness and treatment.

d. The patient's response to illness and treatment

It is hardly surprising that people should respond emotionally to adverse changes in their state of health since these often result in pain, inconvenience or social disruption. This reaction can also be affected by the individual's social environment in a number of ways. For example, it has been shown that the recovery of patients from a stroke can be positively or negatively affected by the amount of understanding and support from their families.

More serious medical problems may result in hospitalization and sometimes in physical handicap both of which require psychological and social adjustment. There can be a tendency among clinicians to regard this psychological component of physical illness as separate and sometimes of secondary or lesser importance. While it may be convenient to discuss the psychological response as separate, for the patient the illness has a psychological and social reality as well as a biological one. The psychological aspects form an integral part of the disease process and may play an important role in determining adaptation to treatment and subsequent speed of recovery.

In short, illness occurs within the context of a person's life and is not merely a pathological process occurring in isolation. The patient has a past and a future and any illness will relate to both. The discussion of psychological aspects of pain later in this section illustrates this point. A description of pain in purely neurophysiological terms fails to account for the range of responses to pain. Likewise the failure to acknowledge the patient as an individual in a social context will result in an incomplete understanding of the whole disease process. Furthermore, it will preclude the possible benefits of psychological aspects of treatment, including the placebo response.

A number of chapters cover these topics. The way in which patients cope with illness and handicap is examined in Chapter 12 and the reactions to hospitalization and particular treatment environments are dealt with in Chapter 13. In addition Chapter 1 includes an account of responses to pain and Chapter 10 begins by looking at attitudes and beliefs about health and illness.

e. Psychological approaches to treatment

Since many medical treatments now consist of methods of modifying attitudes or behaviour rather than administering medication, these are obviously primarily psychological in nature. The most immediate examples of this are the range of psychological treatments in psychiatry, where therapeutic improvements are often brought about by such methods as talk, relaxation, emotional expression and direct behaviour modification.

However, psychological treatment approaches are not only confined to patients with psychiatric problems. Recent years have seen the development of a field known as *behavioural medicine* which is concerned primarily with the application of psychological approaches for the understanding and treatment of physical problems. Some of these have been developed for treating quite specific problems such as hypertension, headache or pain, whereas others are used more as preventive or risk-avoidance procedures.

It is now becoming clear that many problems, which were previously thought of as primarily medical and hence demanding conventional medical intervention, are in fact more appropriately solved by changing attitudes and behaviour. It is also apparent that the incidence of some problems, such as respiratory and cardiovascular disorders, could be significantly affected by altering behaviour such as smoking, exercise and diet. Finally, it will also be seen that the extent to which any medical treatment is adhered to is often a function of a range of psychological factors, including the personality of the patient and the quality of the interaction between the doctor and the patient.

A number of chapters in the book describe psychological approaches to treatment. The fullest account is in Chapter 14 which is entirely devoted to this topic. However, other chapters include descriptions of psychological treatments for pain (Chapter 1), for stress-related conditions (Chapter 5) and for dealing with stressful procedures in hospital (Chapter 13).

This introductory account of the relation of psychology to medicine illustrates the breadth of this field. It has developed rapidly in recent years with the emergence of behavioural medicine and health psychology as specialist areas of psychology. Health psychology is concerned with the study and application of psychological approaches to health and illness. It therefore includes the topics in the latter half of this book as well as many topics discussed in earlier chapters.

● 1.2. Pain as a model

Pain is one of the commonest reasons for consulting the doctor and the following account of pain perception can be used to illustrate the relationship between the biological nature of a symptom and the psychological and social meaning placed on it. In this way it is possible to examine the nature of psychological aspects of pain as well as the importance of looking in more detail at human information processing, which is the concern of the next chapter.

Clearly pain is not all 'in the mind' and usually reflects a certain level of physiological activation. Thus a complete account of pain perception must include a description of physiological mechanisms together with a consideration of psychological aspects.

a. Neurophysiological mechanisms

Pain can be thought of as a type of signalling device for drawing attention to tissue damage or to physiological malfunction; rather like an alarm system in which an unpleasant stimulus inevitably gives rise to the unpleasant subjective feeling which we call pain.

A full physiological account of mechanisms mediating pain perception must include a description of receptors, pathways and cortical mechanisms. Recent evidence indicates the existence of three types of pain receptor responding to mechanical or thermal distortion or to both. Fibres from these receptors run in the peripheral nerves to the posterior root and posterior horn of the spinal cord. These afferent fibres synapse in the dorsal horn of the grey matter in the spinal cord and, after crossing to the other side, ascend to the brain in the lateral spinothalamic tract. Other pain fibres are scattered more diffusely in the spinoreticulothalamic system. Two distinct groups of afferent fibres have been identified:

   i. Myelinated fibres with a fast conduction rate (approx. 10–20 m/sec).
   ii. Unmyelinated fibres with a slow conduction rate (approx. 1–2 m/sec).

Studies involving direct microelectrode recordings of electrical activity in these afferent fibres in animals and in humans indicate that activity in these two types of fibres is correlated with different categories of pain experience. Activation of the faster, myelinated fibres is associated with the clinical entity of 'immediate' pain which is sharp and well localized, whereas slow fibre activation is related to the experience of 'referred' or 'secondary' pain, which is aching or burning, long lasting and poorly localized.

The central mechanisms mediating pain perception are still relatively poorly understood. As we see below, a number of brain areas must be involved not only in establishing the location and nature of a pain but also in determining the physical and emotional responses. There is also growing evidence that there are naturally occurring analgesic substances in the central nervous system (Terenius, 1978). The most widely studied of these are the endorphins which are polypeptides found in both the spinal cord and in a number of sites in the brain. This evidence comes from many animal experiments as well as from a small number of human studies. For example, increases in cerebrospinal fluid levels of endorphins are found in patients with severe persisting pain after they are given peripheral electrical stimulation which brings pain relief. A suggested function for these endogenous opiates is that they provide analgesia and inhibit pain-motivated withdrawal behaviour during coping responses to environmental stress (Bolles and Fanselow, 1982). Other pain modulatory mechanisms have also been found to exist in the central nervous system but the presence of these does not diminish the importance of the psychological aspects to be described below.

Until fairly recently it was thought that once a message was fed into a sensory receptor, it was relayed directly to the brain where it would produce the sensation of pain, warmth, touch, etc., depending only on the physical characteristics of the initial stimulus. However, various parts of the brain stem and cortex exert a descending inhibitory influence on incoming sensory information at the earliest synaptic levels.

b. Limitations of a neurophysiological model

So far pain has been discussed in purely physiological terms as a signalling system; however, this still leaves the critical question of whether a description of these sensory mechanisms is sufficient to fully understand the perception of pain. There is now a great deal of evidence showing that this is not so, and that it is a mistake to equate sensation with perception. There is not necessarily a one-to-one relationship between sensory input and subjective experience of pain. This can be readily demonstrated in many situations where the impact of a noxious stimulus is either much greater or much less than would have been predicted from measured sensory characteristics. The following serve as examples.

i. At one extreme there are patients who feel pain in the absence of any organic damage. This is usually referred to as psychogenic pain in that it is thought to be both generated and affected by psychological factors such as anxiety and depression. Psychogenic pain is not trivial or imaginary, it can be felt intensely by the patient.

ii. At the other extreme are situations in which people sustain significant physical injury and feel relatively little or no pain. This is most dramatically seen in some religious ceremonies in other cultures where there are such procedures as stepping into fire and hookhanging rituals in which hooks are thrust into the small of the back without obvious pain.

iii. There is also the well-documented 'placebo' effect, in which a therapeutically inert substance can be shown to diminish or totally eliminate pain (*see* Chapter 14 for a more detailed discussion).

These examples greatly weaken the case for a simple biological model of pain and suggest that a consideration of higher level processes is necessary for a more complete understanding. In this respect, the perception of pain shares the general characteristics of other perceptual systems such as vision and hearing, which are discussed in Chapter 2. Our present understanding of these processes is based on studies by both psychologists and neurophysiologists. It is now clear that a satisfactory theoretical framework for understanding pain must also be based on both approaches.

c. A combined physiological and psychological approach

One model of pain which has been influential in recent years and which incorporates both physiological and psychological characteristics is the *Gate Theory* (Melzack and Wall, 1965). The central feature of this model is that afferent sensory information can be subject to 'gating' in the spinal cord. This gating mechanism is one which can control the amount of input from the periphery to higher brain centres. It is thought to be located in the substantia gelatinosa, which receives axon terminals from large and small afferent fibres. The relative amount of activity in these two types of fibres will determine the degree of gating which occurs. Activity in the large, myelinated fibres tends to inhibit transmission from the spinal cord transmission cells (i.e. closes the gate) whereas small fibre activity tends to facilitate transmission. The spinal gating system is also subject to descending influences from the brain.

When the output of the spinal cord transmission cells exceeds a critical level, the action system activates all the brain areas involved in pain perception. The output from the spinal transmission cell ascends mainly by way of fibres in the anterolateral spinal cord and projects to two main brain systems:

    i. To the ventrobasal thalamus and somatosensory cortex via neo-spinothalamic fibres.

    ii. To the reticular formation, medial intralaminar thalamus and limbic system via medially coursing fibres.

It is postulated that three quite separate types of activity ensue. First, there is purely perceptual registration of the sensory information, which defines the physical characteristics of the pain stimulus. Second, there is an emotional and motivational response to the stimulus, generated by the limbic system. Finally, there is an interpretation of the meaning of the pain in terms of the present context and past experience. This high level interpretation is assumed to be carried out in neocortical regions and can exert control over the sensory and motivational processes. The perception of pain is assumed to depend ultimately on interplay of all three activities.

The Gate Theory is by no means universally accepted and has had to be revised to account for some of its original weaknesses (Wall, 1978). Even though it is now generally held to be incorrect in some of its fundamental details (Nathan, 1976), there is general agreement that gating mechanisms of some sort must operate in the perception of pain and that cortical centres can determine the degree to which incoming information is processed and attended to. In this way those cortical areas which subserve such processes as attention, memory and emotion can exert an influence on incoming sensory information.

d. Psychosocial influences on pain perception

There are many findings which highlight the role of various psychological or social influences on the experience of pain. Perhaps the broadest of these are the *cultural differences* which have been shown to influence the response to pain. In a study of cultural subgroups within the USA, differences have been reported in the response to and the interpretation of pain (Zborowski, 1952). It was found that 'old Americans' shared an accepting, rather stoic attitude and did not respond so overtly as Jewish or Italian Americans. However, these last two groups differed with respect to their attitudes towards the pain; the Jews being more concerned with the meaning and implications of the pain and the Italians with obtaining immediate relief. Dramatic cultural differences can be seen in the reactions of women to childbirth, which is associated with pain in Western culture but not in all other cultures; there are even some tribes in which it is the men who experience the greatest pain during childbirth. It should be mentioned that there is no strong evidence of cultural differences in sensory thresholds which would explain these findings in purely sensory terms. These differences are in pain tolerance and appear to reflect different cultural attitudes towards specific and general pains.

The ethnic differences point to the role of the socialization process in determining attitudes towards pain and highlight the importance of past experience in the response to a sensory stimulus. Hence Melzack (1973) has concluded that 'significance or meaning of environmental stimuli acquired during early experience plays an important role in pain perception'.

Within our own culture there is also evidence of a differential expectation of pain threshold for men and women. It has been shown that women in hospital are routinely given more powerful analgesics than men, whose requests for analgesia tend to be overlooked more often by staff. This expectation, that men should be able to tolerate more pain than women, is also derived from cultural values within our society and will in turn be reflected in the different socialization procedures for boys and girls.

Not only past experience but also the *present context* can influence pain responses. In a frequently cited study, it was found that the request rate for pain relief among soldiers, who had received war wounds, was found to be very much lower than that of a civilian group with equivalent injuries (Beecher, 1959). Thus the psychological impact of tissue damage sustained within the context of the battlefield can be quite different from equivalent damage sustained in a situation not normally associated with injuries. The influence of the context may be partly due to the extent to which the individual's attention is focused on the pain and the extent to which he or she is prepared for the pain. A well-directed kick below the dinner table may be excruciating but a kick of the same intensity received while scoring a winning goal may hardly be felt at the time.

The possibility of providing *distraction* from a pain indicates that attention is limited and that attention to one sensory source can reduce or abolish awareness of another source. The selective quality of attention is discussed in some detail in the next chapter. It has also been found that *preparation* for pain can reduce some of its impact. As will be seen later, this can have practical implications for the doctor since the provision of clear information about likely postoperative pain levels can also reduce requests for analgesia and make it easier for patients to cope on their own. Preparation may also help to increase an individual's feeling of control over a painful stimulus. The more someone perceives that he or she has some control over a potentially painful stimulus, the less painful it is likely to feel.

The *emotional state* and the *personality* of the patient can also play an important part in pain perception. Anxiety commonly results in a lowering of the pain threshold which means that pain tends to be felt earlier and more intensely and to have a greater effect on behaviour. In a group of women with carcinoma of the cervix it has been found that pain-free patients were rated as less emotional and more sociable than a group who felt pain but did not complain (Bond and Pearson, 1969). Those patients who were rated both emotional and sociable were those who complained of the pain and also received more medication. There is also evidence that pain tolerance may be related to extroversion, as measured on personality tests. In laboratory studies extroversion has been associated with higher pain tolerance and introversion with a greater sensitivity to pain. Similarly, in studies of pain in childbirth, more introverted mothers have been found to feel pain sooner and more intensely but to complain less.

Finally, the potency of the '*placebo*' effect provides very strong evidence of a major psychological component in the experience of pain. A belief that a substance will relieve pain can apparently be enough to do so. Not a great deal is known about the mechanisms underlying the placebo reaction but there is increasing evidence that this must involve the activation of endorphins in the brain. Even so, the magnitude of the placebo response has been found to vary enormously from individual to individual and within the same individual, depending on the characteristics of the situation in which the placebo is administered (Ross and Olsen, 1982). Similarly the behaviour and attention of the doctor may substantially influence the extent of a placebo response since enthusiasm on the part of the doctor has been shown to enhance the placebo response. This may partly explain the 'wonder drug' phenomenon, in which a new drug may be found to be particularly effective only during the initial period of its use. Although our understanding of placebo effects is still limited, they seem to be due to the individual's expectations that a therapeutic change will come about. Placebo effects in pain relief may also reflect a reduction in anxiety and the related effects on both endorphin production and spinal gating mechanisms.

This relatively brief summary of some of the psychosocial factors in pain perception serves to confirm the importance of moving away from a simplistic sensory model of pain to one which embraces higher level influences. A pain stimulus is usually indicative of localized organic damage but its impact on the individual can be greatly determined by many psychosocial factors. Moreover, this approach can be extended to all symptoms in that, whatever the biological parameters of the symptom, they alone may be insufficient to explain the patient's response.

e. Psychological approaches to the management of pain

With the increasing realization that pain is a psychological as much as a biological phenomenon, a range of psychological approaches to management has been developed. These are aimed at different aspects of pain. Some aim to change pain behaviours, others aim to modify an individual's perception or interpretation of pain and others are concerned more generally with reducing anxiety or helping the individual to cope with stressors which give rise to specific types of pain such as headache.

Attempts to change pain behaviour are based on principles of *operant conditioning*, described in Chapter 14. Simply, these aim to reduce 'pain behaviour' (e.g. complaining; requests for analgesia) and increase 'well behaviour' (e.g. physical activity) by using systematic social responses. Thus staff and family members are instructed to ignore pain behaviour and to praise or attend to healthy behaviour. Although fairly widely used in clinical settings, the efficacy of this approach is not yet strongly proven but seems to be promising.

Attempts to change the way in which patients perceive and think about their pain are generally described as *cognitive treatments* (*see* Chapter 14 for a more detailed account of this approach). The cognitive approach typically begins by finding out how patients think of their pain experience. Treatment then comprises an attempt to challenge and modify these thoughts in order to enable patients to interpret their pain in a less negative and more adaptive way. Thus chronic pain patients may be helped to distract or distance themselves from the pain or to relabel the pain sensations in a less distressing way. Psychologists working in pain clinics often begin by providing patients with a model of pain, such as the Gate Theory, in order to allow patients to understand how psychological factors can influence pain perception. This, in turn, seems to provide a good basis for psychological intervention, particularly the cognitive treatments.

The more general psychological approaches are based on techniques for reducing anxiety and for stress-related pain. Relaxation training (*see* Chapter 14) has been found to reduce pain in chronic pain patients and since it has been shown that anxiety can significantly affect pain threshold, it must be assumed that this therapeutic effect is due primarily to anxiety reduction. However, its efficacy may also be due to an increased sense of control on the part of the patient (i.e. patients now feel that there is something which they can do to cope with or reduce their pain).

A somewhat specific variation of this approach is based on biofeedback techniques which make use of monitoring equipment to feed back to patients the levels of activity of a specific physiological process (e.g. brainwave activity; localized muscle activity). Chapter 14 gives a more detailed account of the nature of biofeedback techniques and their application to a wide range of clinical problems. Most of the work on biofeedback for pain control has been for the treatment of headache using feedback of fontalis muscle activity. Although studies have shown that this can be effective in reducing headaches, it would now seem that the effect is a non-specific one due to the effect of relaxation rather than biofeedback *per se* (Turner and Chapman, 1982).

Finally in this section on psychological approaches to pain management, it is worth mentioning the various interventions which are used with patients undergoing stressful medical procedures such as surgery. These interventions, which may consist of either supplying preparatory information about the various medical procedures and the likely types of postoperative sensations, including pain, or providing the patient with a way of coping with the pain, have been found to be successful in reducing postoperative pain. A fuller description of these techniques is given in Chapter 13.

It is hoped that the reader is now aware that there are many direct parallels between this outline of the psychological aspects of pain and the issues which were discussed in the first part of this chapter. Psychological factors alone can give rise to the experience of pain. More commonly these factors can determine the amount of pain which is felt and what action is taken. The patient's response to a noxious stimulus can be of critical importance not only in determining the degree of unpleasantness but also whether a medical opinion is sought. Finally, psychological approaches may be used in the management of pain, particularly chronic pain, in the clinical setting.

- ## Recommended reading

Psychology and medicine
Gentry W. D. (ed.) (1984) *Handbook of Behavioural Medicine.* New York, Guilford Press.
Steptoe A. and Mathews A. (ed.) (1984) *Health Care and Human Behaviour.* London, Academic Press.
Stone G. C., Cohen F. and Adler N. E. (ed.) (1979) *Health Psychology.* San Francisco, Jossey Bass.

Pain
Melzack R. and Wall P. (1982) *The Challenge of Pain.* Harmondsworth, Penguin.
Pearce S. and Richardson P. H. (1986) Chronic pain: psychological approaches to management. In: Lindsay S. J. and Powell G. E. (ed.) *Handbook of Clinical Psychology.* London, Gower.

2

Human information processing

The previous section on pain perception brought out the important point that sensory information is not all automatically processed to the level of conscious awareness in a mechanical fashion. There is a range of factors which will determine the degree to which sensory information is attended to and its ultimate effects on behaviour. Having recognized this, it is possible to examine human information processing in more detail both as a basis for understanding human behaviour and in order to be able to look at the effects of neurological lesions. In this chapter those processes involved with the uptake, selection, processing and storage of information are outlined. An attempt is also made to indicate the extent to which these processes are dependent on experience and the way in which they can be affected by neurological damage.

● 2.1. Attention and perception

a. 'Seeing where' and 'seeing what'

As the result of some recent observations on patients with damage to the primary visual cortex and many animal studies, there are good grounds for postulating that there are at least two functionally distinct visual systems. One system is based on the visual cortex and the other on the superior colliculus (*Fig. 1*).

The system which projects from the eyes to the visual cortex, via the lateral geniculate nucleus, appears to be primarily concerned with the detailed processing of visual images which are fixated by the central, foveal regions of the retina (i.e. 'seeing what'). There is neurophysiological evidence that this type of sensory information is processed by specific types of retinal ganglion cells ('sustained' cells) which are particularly suited to detecting the fine details of a visual scene. Furthermore, information from these cells is projected to specific regions of the visual cortex by slow-conducting afferent fibres. In contrast, another class of retinal ganglion cells ('transient' cells) are more sensitive to temporal changes and the detecting movement, particularly in the periphery of

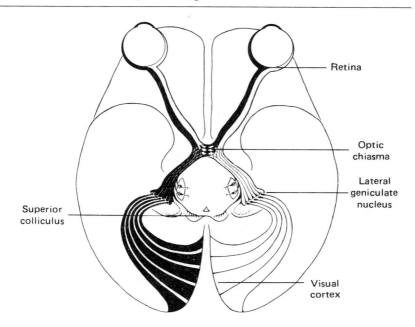

Fig. 1. Diagram of the human visual system showing the projections from the retinae to the left and right visual cortex. (Adapted from Polyak S. (1975) *The Vertebrate Visual System.* Chicago University Press.)

the visual field. These cells project via fast-conducting fibres to the superior colliculus as well as to parts of the visual cortex (Ikeda and Wright, 1974).

Neurological damage to the primary visual cortex produces a blindness to part or all of the visual environment, depending on the location and extent of the damage. For example, damage to the whole of the right visual cortex, sparing the left side, would result in a blindness to the left half of visual space in front of a person (*Fig.* 1). However, there is evidence that cortically blind patients retain some basic attentional capacities, which operate at a preconscious level and provide information about the position of objects, particularly in the periphery (Perenin and Jeannerod, 1975). Animal studies indicate that these 'seeing where' capacities are mediated by a phylogenetically more primitive visual system based on the *superior colliculus* in the mid-brain (*Fig.* 1). Damage to the superior colliculus in humans has been shown to disrupt eye movements but without affecting the perception of objects.

In everyday perceptual processing these two systems must act in unison since visual perception is an integrated activity involving both attention to peripheral stimuli and detailed processing of information currently in focus. It is only when selective damage occurs to either system that their separate contributions can be observed or inferred. However, it does indicate the value of separately considering attentional aspects of perceptual processing from those processes concerned with the identification of attended information. In the section which immediately follows, a brief account is given of the uptake and

nsory information by the visual system, which can be seen most
the nature of eye movements.

vements and perception

e focus of attention changes from moment to moment in an organized
fasi. and the pattern of eye movements demonstrates this sequential aspect of
selective attention. Vision is sharp only within the small foveal region of a few
degrees (the whole visual field takes up approximately 210°) and visual acuity
decreases markedly in the periphery of the retina. Eye movements are used to
place the image of a target on to the fovea where it can best be seen. The
'scan-paths' of eye movements indicate how purposeful they are since observers
can be seen to centre most of their fixations on informative features of a display.
Two distinct types of eye movement exist:

i. *Saccadic*. Most eye movements are saccades, rapid jumping movements which are planned in advance and are executed without continuous control
during the movement itself. They occur about 3–5 times every second.

ii. *Pursuit*. This is a smooth movement which only happens when the eye
follows a moving object in the environment. The eye cannot be moved slowly
from one place to another except during the pursuit of movement.

The principal function of the eye movement system is the rapid foveal
localization of a stimulus and the pursuit of any movement of it. The study of eye
movements while subjects are scanning pictures has shown that fixations tend to
concentrate on the most informative or unusual areas. It has also been shown that
when the subject is asked to make an inference about the picture (e.g. the ages of
the people in the picture), then the pattern of eye movements will depend on the
type of information the subject is trying to extract. In this way eye movements can
provide a basis for inferring about higher order processing of visual stimuli. They
show that sensory information is not passively received but that we actively select
out for detailed processing (i.e. via the fovea) information that is most relevant to
our current behavioural needs (*Fig. 2*).

Apart from saccadic and pursuit movements, the eyes are in continual
motion (normal nystagmus). Quite a bit of research has been directed to the
question of what happens if these small tremors, minor drifts and small saccadic
flicks are eliminated by stabilizing the retinal image. When this is done by use of
optical correcting systems, special contact lenses or after-images, then the
stabilized image fades and disappears after a few seconds. These findings have led
to the notion that the visual system primarily transmits information about stimulus
change and that these continuous eye movements are necessary to maintain
information input.

Even when information is processed by peripheral receptors this still does
not imply that it will reach conscious awareness and be attended to, as was seen
most clearly in the previous section on pain perception. Attention is a complex,
selective process and a separate consideration now follows.

c. Selective attention

During the whole of our waking lives we are constantly bombarded by a
very large number of stimuli and it can be shown very easily that we are only
actually aware of very few of these messages at any one time. The processes
concerned with ignoring unimportant information and for seeking out and

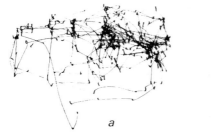

Fig. 2. Eye movement patterns made when looking at the picture depend on whether the viewer is asked to judge the material circumstances of the people in the picture (scanning pattern *a*) or their ages (scanning pattern *b*). (From Yarbus, 1967.)

concentrating on the information we need are usually referred to as *selective attention* mechanisms.

Many experimental studies of selective attention are based on the 'cocktail party' situation, in which we have to concentrate on one message and ignore others which may be as loud. We are surprisingly good at this and can ignore all but the most gross characteristics of rival messages except in situations where a rival message contains subjectively important information (e.g. one's name) when attention switches automatically. Findings like this show that selective attention is not just a question of blotting out rival messages but more a system of monitoring a whole mass of inputs and focusing on the most appropriate at any particular moment.

Selective attention has been most extensively studied using a 'dichotic listening' paradigm, in which separate messages are presented simultaneously over headphones to each ear and the subject's task is to follow one message only. These studies have shown that attention is not absolute since certain features of the 'unattended' message still get through (Triesman, 1966). Sources of evidence for this are experimental findings which have shown that it is possible to:
—hear one's own name in the 'unattended' message;
—hear words in the unattended message which fit into context in the attended message;

—notice that a delayed unattended message has the same meaning as the attended message, even when it is in a different voice.

The current view of attention has shifted from the older idea of a passive filter to one of attention as a control process for the flow of information (Keele and Neill, 1978). As such it plays a very dynamic role in determining not only what is attended to but also the way in which information is processed. The control process can preset itself for expected information and can inhibit or distort the processing of unexpected or conflicting information. Thus attentional processes operate in conjunction with the memory system and can be modified by learning.

That perceptual processing is selective is also apparent when the neurophysiological mechanisms of perception are considered, since there is now a good body of evidence which shows the existence of 'gating mechanisms' in the nervous system at a number of levels from the periphery to the higher centres. There is earlier evidence, particularly from the somatosensory system and referred to in the section on pain, both of feedback at the efferent level and of descending cortical inhibition. Both of these features would necessarily modify the nature of incoming messages or possibly 'reject' them altogether.

The breakdown of attentional processes has been observed in both psychiatric and neurological disorders. There are a number of studies in which schizophrenic patients have been shown to have difficulty in blocking out unwanted stimuli (Frith, 1979). Some authors have also suggested that this is the basis of the 'over-inclusive' type of thought disorder which occurs in some patients and in which there is great difficulty in forming appropriate concepts. Neurological lesions can produce similar deficits. Lesions in the right or left occipital cortex can produce partial or total inattention to the corresponding contralateral part of the visual field.

This account of attentional processes has illustrated that human information processing is organized, selective and subject to disruption in some psychiatric and neurological patients. Similarly, recent studies of the visual system based on the visual cortex have revealed a great deal of information about its normal mode of operation and the nature of associated neurological damage.

●   2.2. Perceptual processing

a. Processing in the visual cortex

Considerable advances have been made in recent years in understanding the way the visual cortex decodes the information it receives. Much of this stems from the work of Hubel and Wiesel (1979) and other experimenters who have studied the responses of single cells in the visual cortex. Their experiments followed a similar, quite simple pattern. An anaesthetized cat would be placed facing a screen on which patches of light of various shapes and sizes could be presented. These stimuli would be moved about the screen and responses recorded from a single cell in the cat's visual cortex, by means of a microelectrode, until the receptive field characteristics of the cell could be determined (i.e. what type of stimulus the cell responded to maximally and in which area of the visual field).

The first striking observation that they made was that many cells in the visual cortex responded to straight lines or straight edges of specified orientations in well-localized parts of the visual field. These responses contrasted with the more peripheral cells (i.e. retinal ganglion or lateral geniculate) which showed greatest responses to small round spots of light. Cortical cells did show some response to small light spots but they seemed especially tuned to detect line segments, which suggested that they were the building blocks from which more complex percepts were derived. This became even more plausible when other cells were found with higher level response patterns. Hubel and Wiesel called these 'complex' cells since they showed less specific response patterns (i.e. that would fire when a particular line stimulus was presented anywhere in the visual field). Probing further into adjacent areas of the visual cortex, they found cells with even greater abstracting powers ('hypercomplex' cells). Microelectrode and morphological studies have demonstrated that these cells with specific response characteristics (e.g. only to horizontal or vertical lines) are organized into columns throughout the primary visual cortex.

More recently there has been a move away from the view that visual cortical cells operate exclusively as 'line-segment detectors' or specific feature analysers. This has arisen from a growing body of neurophysiological and psychophysical evidence that these cells operate as spatial frequency analysers (Maffei and Fiorentini, 1973). Just as the output of an electronic or audio system can be characterized in terms of its frequency response for time-varying signals, visual stimuli can be characterized in terms of their component spatial frequencies. Thus it has been proposed that the visual system analyses stimuli by transforming and representing retinal images in terms of the different spatial frequencies which are present. It has been argued that neurons in the visual cortex have a selective frequency response and the combination of these provides the 'picture in the head' which corresponds to the image on the retina.

Although there is no direct evidence that the human visual cortex is similarly constructed there is indirect evidence from studies of after-images. The distortions in the after-images produced as the result of fixating stimuli (e.g. tilting or moving lines of specific spatial frequencies) are consistent with the possibility that cells in the human visual cortex also respond selectively to specific features (Chapter 4 in Frisby, 1979). Moreover, direct electrical stimulation of cells in the visual cortex in blind humans has produced direct visual experiences in that the people involved report 'seeing' small lines out in front of them (Brindley and Lewin, 1968).

Having established that an initial representation of the retinal image is made possible by the selective responsiveness of cells in the primary visual cortex, the problem remains as to how all this information is organized to provide us with a conscious awareness of our external environment. This problem is summarized by the object which is represented in *Fig. 3*. When one first looks at this it may appear to be a collection of odd black shapes on a white background. As soon as you see the object (a Dalmatian dog), then this is immediately seen as a whole against an undifferentiated background. How does the visual system make the enormous jump from detecting all the lines, edges and spatial frequencies present in an image to seeing actual objects? The answers to this question are still fragmentary and are based on neurophysiological, neurological and psychological evidence.

The neurophysiological evidence of stimulus analysis beyond the primary visual cortex indicates that there are adjacent areas which carry out separate analyses of different stimulus attributes (e.g. colour, movement, orientation) in

Fig. 3. The perception of whole objects is more complicated than the identification of the components. (Photograph by R. C. James, taken from Thurston J. and Carraher R. G. (1966) *Optical Illusions and the Visual Arts*. New York, Litton Educational Publishing.)

parallel (e.g. Zeki, 1978). The output from these separate analyses appears to be combined in the inferotemporal region of the brain at the back end of the temporal lobe. This area does appear to be directly involved with the recognition of whole objects. It has neurons with very large receptive fields and some of these have a high degree of stimulus specificity. For example, some cells in the monkey have been found to respond maximally to the shape of a monkey's hand (Gross et al., 1972). It should be pointed out that the evidence for the existence of such cells is still rather meagre and as yet their significance is unclear. It may be that these cells would exist for familiar stimuli and allow very rapid recognition of these, possibly bypassing the earlier stages of analysis.

Such conclusions are essentially speculative but it is also known that patients with damage to the inferotemporal regions may have disorders of visual recognition in which they may be able to see all the components of a stimulus but still not be able to recognize it (visual object agnosia). The visual experiences of these patients have been described as percepts stripped of their meaning. This raises the critical question as to how we make sense of visual images and are able to know with great accuracy what information is present. This process of assigning meaning to a visual image has been a preoccupation of psychologists studying perception and this is the next approach to be considered.

b. Psychological aspects of pattern recognition

The way in which our visual systems are able to combine all the elements of a visual stimulus into meaningful units was extensively studied by the Gestalt school of psychology which flourished in the earlier part of this century. They demonstrated that there were certain basic organizational tendencies in perception which make the parts of the visual world form the units which we are then able to recognize as complete objects (e.g. the Dalmatian in *Fig.* 3). They were able to demonstrate that if components of an image were close to each other (proximity) or had a similar texture or colour (similarity) then those components were automatically grouped together. They also showed that the overriding tendency of the visual system to form perceptual units in this way was facilitated if the figures were simple and regular (goodness). Once this initial organization has taken place then the perceived objects have an immediate salience or presence against an undifferentiated background (figure/ground resolution).

These Gestalt principles of early perceptual organization have remained influential although current theories of these early pattern recognition processes are much more complex. Current theories have been based largely on computer models of visual processing and many incorporate the idea that an important early stage in perception consists of creating a 'primal sketch' or crude representation of the visual world prior to detailed pattern recognition (Marr, 1980). The 'primal sketch' would therefore be a fairly automatic procedure based on the interpretation of incoming sense data and providing something corresponding to figure/ground separation. This sketch would then have to be interpreted by higher level visual processes in order to create conscious awareness of what objects are present. The interpretive process which proceeds from the early line detecting and object identifying stage has been described as a 'top-down' process since it must make use of stored knowledge and experience. It would appear that the actual recognition of objects depends on detecting certain salient features rather than on matching the whole shape with a stored image in memory. Developmental studies of perception which are described below and in Chapter 8 also provide some evidence for the role of stored knowledge for actual object recognition.

Depth perception

This also appears to be made possible by detailed analysis of sense data together with the use of stored knowledge. Such factors as texture, lighting, perspective and overlapping all provide immediate information which can be computed about the relative distance of objects in the visual field. Knowledge of the relative size of a specified object provides a further source of information about its distance from the observer. The latter is not particularly accurate in that there is not anything like a 'one-to-one' correspondence between the retinal size and perceived size of a familiar object, as is discussed later on.

Possibly the most powerful source of depth information arises from the fact that we have two eyes with slightly differing views of the world. These two images are combined giving rise to stereoscopic vision and neurophysiologists have provided clear evidence that this retinal disparity can be detected directly by neurons in the visual cortex (Pettigrew, 1972). These neurons are driven by inputs from the two eyes and play an important role in binocular depth discrimination by responding to the degree of disparity of the same stimulus in the two eyes. By presenting apparently meaningless pairs of patterns in a stereoscope and finding that these are combined to produce a single image in depth, it has been shown experimentally that stereopsis is an automatic process which is not dependent on one's knowledge of the stimulus. However, if the two retinae are not properly aligned, such as in people with a squint, then stereopsis is not usually possible.

Movement
Movement can be perceived over the whole visual field, unlike pattern recognition which seems to depend on central or foveal vision. Recordings from individual retinal ganglion cells and from cortical cells in animals have shown that many of them respond to movement in one direction only, regardless of the identity of the moving stimulus. These cells have also been shown to respond transiently, in contrast with the more sustained responses of the centrally located cells which are involved in the detection of shape. These cells are also triggered by 'apparent' movement (the type used in 'moving' neon lighting displays). Human studies of apparent movement indicate that perception of movement depends on the sequential detection of crudely matched features at proximal points in space. Movement after-images provide further confirmation of the existence of cells in the human visual cortex which selectively respond to movement in one direction.

• 2.3. Pathologies of perception
Perhaps the most startling perceptual abnormalities are hallucinations. These can occur as the result of hallucinogenic drugs but may also occur in some types of schizophrenia and in certain neurological conditions, particularly those associated with temporal lobe damage. That hallucinations can occur is not surprising when the study of perception shows it to be a higher order process and that visual, auditory and somatosensory experiences can be produced by direct stimulation of the appropriate cortical areas.

Damage to the primary visual cortex produces blindness in corresponding portions of the contralateral visual field. Direct stimulation of these areas in people who have lost vision in adult life has produced visual sensations of small spots of light in the appropriate area of the visual field. These findings have led to the attempt to develop prosthetic devices for blind people based on implanted electrodes (Brindley and Lewin, 1968). Equivalent sensations have been produced with other sense modalities by direct stimulation of the appropriate cortical areas.

Higher level perceptual disorders, involving difficulties in the integration or interpretation of information from the primary receptive areas, are found in patients with lesions in the parietal, temporal and occipital areas surrounding the primary sensory areas. Disturbances of identification, recognition, discrimination or classification are called 'agnosias'. For example, patients with visual agnosia may be unable to identify drawn objects even when they can copy them and when neurological examination shows that their visual fields and visual acuity are quite normal. One recent writer has described the visual world of the agnosic as comprising 'percepts stripped of their meaning'. From this it is clear that any perceptual processing must involve higher level brain regions which identify and interpret sensory input using stored information, which indicates the importance of learning and memory in information processing.

•   2.4. Perceptual learning

As with many other psychological functions, there has been considerable debate as to whether perceptual abilities are acquired or innate. However, psychologists now recognize that this is not an 'either/or' question and that the problem is to determine the nature of the interaction between innate mechanisms and environmental influences. At one time it was thought that the study of people who had been blind from birth and who had sight given to them in adult life by removal of congenital cataracts, would provide the answer to this question. Studies of these people showed that their immediate visual capacities are very minimal and that a great deal of effort and relearning is necessary to get even a small amount of useful information from the eyes. However, these studies do not necessarily throw any light on the normal development of vision. Experiments with new babies have shown that a considerable degree of organization exists and that the visual world of the baby is probably not the total confusion it was once thought to be.

a. Neurophysiological evidence

An obvious question for the vision neurophysiologist is whether the properties of 'feature-analysing' cells in the visual cortex, described earlier, are present from birth or are dependent on learning. In the cat it has been found that these response characteristics are present when the kitten's eyes first open although they are somewhat sluggish and coarse in comparison with the adult. However, if during the first 2–4 months, the kitten's visual environment is systematically distorted by occluding one eye or by surgically inducing a squint then marked differences in cortical cell responsiveness are found since cells are no longer binocularly driven.

These results go some way to suggesting a mechanism by which environmental factors can influence a genetically determined structure. It was found that there was a 'sensitive period' for this plasticity since environmental changes had no effect if they followed a few months of normal development (*see* Chapter 8 for a more detailed discussion of 'critical' periods in development). These findings have been substantiated by evidence from studies in which kittens were reared in environments with only vertical or horizontal stripes. After several months it was found that single cells in the visual cortex only responded to lines corresponding to their previous environment (i.e. all the cells now only responded to vertical or horizontal lines). This was also evident at the behavioural level since a kitten reared in an environment consisting only of vertical lines will eventually only be able to perceive vertical lines and will be effectively blind to horizontal lines.

These experiments show the relationship between inborn and acquired attributes in the visual system. The basic cell response system is inborn but is open to modification for short periods during the early months or possibly years in the case of the human. In this way the visual system develops functional connections that are appropriate to the features of its environment. These studies also help to indicate why people with congenital cataracts often fail to derive any significant visual competence when the cataracts are removed in adulthood. This appears to be because they have failed to receive appropriate stimulation during the early years (*see* Chapter 8, p. 123).

b. Human developmental studies

Studies of infants have shown that the ability to perceive depth and a preference for complex stimuli is present very early on. However, differences in perceptual ability between adults and children have been well demonstrated and suggest the type of perceptual learning that does occur. For example, children of 6 years have been shown to have less organized patterns of eye movements in that they are less consistent in their scanning and less skilful at selecting informative areas of pictures. It has also been found that younger children need more information in 'incomplete' line drawings in order to recognize the objects which are depicted in the drawings.

Perceptual abilities undergo adaptive changes which may be qualitative as well as quantitative and some of these are described in more detail in Chapter 8. Basic capacities become more efficient and organized but at the same time there is sufficient flexibility to be able to adapt to marked changes in the visual environment. This dependence of adult perception on previous experience has some important consequences.

c. Some consequences of perceptual learning

i. Visual constancies

These are situations in which we continue to perceive objects more in terms of their original size, shape and brightness after changes in the retinal image have occurred. For example:
—Regular shapes continue to appear quite regular when tilted.
—Familiar objects continue to appear approximately the same size as they move towards or away from you.
—Familiarly coloured objects still seem to be the same colour even when the reflected light from them is very different (e.g. pillar boxes still look quite red at night).

Constancies are not complete in that we do perceive some changes in the stimulus features, but the final percept tends to be a compromise between the retinal change and the original stimulus. Constancies are a basic feature of the visual system but their dependence on experience can be inferred from the fact that constancy increases with age and is greater for more common objects. However, constancies can be found to a degree in infants, indicating that factors other than experience must also be involved.

ii. Expectations

It can be fairly readily shown that what we actually perceive can depend on what we expect to see since perception is directly related to previous experiences and therefore becomes to some extent an 'assumptive' process. Expectations can also be set up for short-term situations by telling a person about what they will be seeing or priming them in some way.

iii. Capacity for relearning
If our environment suddenly changes as the result of wearing goggles which distort the visual world by inversion or lateral displacement, then it has been found that we can adapt to this after a period of time. Successful adaptation is dependent on continuous motor feedback since it does not occur if subjects cannot see their own limbs moving in relation to the displaced visual image.

iv. Individual differences
Some changes in perception occur in the same individual with changes in mood or motivational state. For example, detection thresholds can be raised with monetary rewards and the apparent size of objects (e.g. food or coins) can vary as the consequence of a prior state of deprivation (of food or money). Some recent experimental studies of anxious and depressed patients have indicated that they will selectively attend to and notice more anxiety-related or depression-related stimuli than control subjects, indicating that their underlying emotional state biases their processing of incoming information. Some psychologists have also demonstrated enduring differences in modes of perception between individuals.

v. Recovery from early blindness
As was indicated earlier, if perceptual development is significantly restricted during the early years then adult perception may be impaired to varying degrees from slight inefficiency to almost total incapacity. There is no specific indication as to whether there is a fixed 'sensitive period' in human perceptual development but it is certainly suggested by the studies of patients with congenital cataracts removed in early adulthood. This issue will be discussed in more detail in Chapter 8 in the section on early environmental influences on development.

vi. Pain perception
The role of learning in perception also makes it easier to understand the origin of individual and cultural differences in response to pain, described in the previous chapter. Early socialization appears to play a very important part in determining how the growing child reacts to and copes with a painful experience. Parental reactions can range from the unruffled and stoic to the demonstrative and emotional. These responses can be transmitted to the child who in turn is likely to respond to pain in a correspondingly similar fashion.

•   2.5. Memory

a. The structure of memory: boxes or levels?
What happens to information after it has been perceived is usually

discussed under the general heading of memory. It is clear that some information is forgotten almost immediately whereas some might be retained for seconds, hours, years or even for a lifetime. This variability of retention has led to the idea that memory is not a unitary system but contains a number of subsystems with different capacities and durations. In fact most contemporary discussions of memory functions tend to subdivide memory into three distinct systems or 'boxes' which are outlined a little later.

Many factors will ultimately determine how well something is remembered or conversely how readily it is forgotten. These include the nature of the information (i.e. how familiar, salient, etc. it is) and the way in which it has been processed (i.e. the degree to which it has been attended to). In this sense it is quite arbitrary to discuss memory as something quite separate from perception since they are both stages in information processing. Thus some psychologists now maintain that memory should not be considered in terms of separate storage systems but as a direct by-product of perceptual processing. Within such a framework, the fate of any information is determined by the 'level' to which it is processed (Craik and Lockhart, 1972).

This notion of level of processing becomes clear if a hypothetical experiment is presented. Imagine a study in which three groups of subjects are presented with identical lists of words, each for one second, and have to make different decisions about the words on the following lines:

Group A—have to decide whether each word is typed in upper or lower case.

Group B—have to decide whether each word rhymes with a selected word.

Group C—have to make a decision about the meaning of each word.

Subjects do their tasks as quickly as possible and do not know beforehand that this is a memory experiment. When afterwards they are unexpectedly asked to recall as many words as possible, it is found that Group C perform better than Group B who in turn are superior to Group A.

The results from experiments of this type indicate that when subjects have focused on only the physical characteristics of verbal information (i.e. its typeface), then it is subsequently processed to a relatively superficial level and is easily forgotten. Similarly when subjects have focused on the meaning of words then processing of the same words takes place at a 'deeper' semantic level and is correspondingly better remembered.

A number of quite stringent criticisms of this level of processing approach have been offered (Baddeley, 1978). It is arguable as to whether a description of human memory in terms of different 'levels' of processing is really so different from the more conventional 'boxes' models except that it offers a more flexible approach. On the other hand, the neurological disorders of memory outlined below can currently be more readily described and understood in terms of damage to particular memory stores. Thus an outline of the more conventional three-stage model now follows.

b. A three-stage memory model

The majority of experimental psychologists appear to accept that a three-stage model provides the best current description of memory processes. This is based on the evidence that there seem to be three distinct types of memory store for processing information and these are shown diagrammatically in *Fig.* 4.

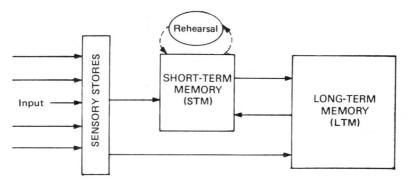

Fig. 4. A three-stage model of memory.

A description of the storage and processing characteristics of each of these three memory stores now follows.

i. Sensory stores

These are large-capacity stores which hold sensory information in a relatively unprocessed form for very brief durations. Experimental evidence indicates that separate auditory and visual peripheral stores exist and which are often referred to as 'echoic' and 'iconic' memory respectively. These stores are described as 'precategorical' in that they appear to hold a representation of a stimulus in a physical form. Thus subjects can select information from the sensory stores on the basis of physical characteristics such as the spatial position and colour but not in terms of the meaning.

The evidence for the existence of sensory stores was originally based on a series of careful experiments by Sperling (1960). He presented 3 × 4 letter matrices to subjects for very brief periods and when they were asked to recall as many items as possible then it was found that about four items could be reported. However, if subjects were required to recall only the top, middle or bottom row of the matrix test and were not actually told which row until just after the matrix had disappeared, then it was found that they could often report all four items in the particular row. This and a number of other similar experiments have indicated that potentially all the information from the sensory stores can be accessed but since it fades rapidly (usually within 0·5 sec) there is not normally time for subjects to report more than a few items.

The function of the sensory stores is probably to hold a representation of a stimulus so that at least parts of it can be attended to, processed and held more permanently. This may be of particular importance in the visual system in which eye movements are made every few hundred milliseconds and a persisting representation of the visual field would therefore provide continuity of perception. The biological basis for sensory memory is unclear and it is uncertain as to whether neurological impairment can specifically interfere with its functions.

ii. Short-term memory

This is a kind of 'working memory' with a limited capacity and from which information is lost within about 15–20 sec, although it may be retained for longer periods through rehearsal. Things like the last few words of a sentence you have just heard or a telephone number can just be retained in short-term memory since its capacity is limited to something like five or six items. A number of psychologists now believe verbal items are held in short-term memory in terms of their sounds rather than their meanings. However, studies of patients with brain damage also suggest that there are two separate short-term memory systems for verbal and for visual information, located respectively in the left and right hemispheres. It is currently held that part of the short-term store has a storage function while another part plays a more active role in active rehearsal using subvocal speech (Baddeley, 1983).

iii. Long-term memory
Information which is selected for more permanent storage enters long-term memory. In contrast to short-term memory this has a very large capacity and stores information principally in terms of its semantic-associative characteristics. Forgetting from this system is relatively slow and may be due either to actual loss of information or to an inability to retrieve. Information does not appear to be stored faithfully in long-term memory but is reorganized and distorted, sometimes in very subjective ways.

A useful distinction has been made by Tulving (1972) between episodic and semantic memory components of long-term memory. The former is taken to refer to the memory of events and episodes specific to the individual, whereas the latter refers to such things as knowledge and language which are common to many individuals. The importance of this distinction becomes clear when patients with neurological amnesia are considered since, although these patients are able to converse adequately, their memory for specific events may be greatly impaired so that something which happened just a few minutes previously might be completely forgotten.

c. Variations in memory capacity
Box models of memory can give rise to the misleading conclusion that the capacity of the memory stores is totally invariant. However, many factors can affect memory and some of these are of direct relevance in medicine:

i. Level of processing
As was indicated earlier, the way information is processed will determine how much can subsequently be remembered and for how long. Thus if people are given more time to remember a list of words, they may be able to generate rehearsal strategies which facilitate memory.

ii. Individual differences
Although short-term memory is often described as a fixed capacity store it is clear that a range of short-term memory ability exists within the population and which is partly but certainly not wholly related to intelligence. Moreover long-term memory ability varies enormously both between and within individuals. The extreme examples here are the so-called 'memory freaks', a very small group of individuals whose long-term memory capacity is greatly in excess of the majority and sometimes apparently limitless. These individuals are particularly adept at processing and organizing information so that it can be easily retrieved. Some rely

strongly on the ability to associate all information and others on developing complex visual images. They have also been shown to be able to access information in short-term memory very rapidly.

iii. Depression
Another example of individual differences in memory can be found in some psychiatric patients. Patients with depression have been found to recall relatively more negative or depression-related information than non-depressed controls. These findings provide support for cognitive theories of depression (*see* Chapter 14). In more general terms they illustrate that information processing mechanisms are closely related to many other aspects of behaviour.

iv. Ageing
Ageing produces decrements in memory after about the age of 50. Age-related impairments are described more fully in Chapter 9 but it must be remembered that these are not absolute since there is a great range in memory capacity among the aged.

v. Treatment effects
Medication affecting the central nervous system can also have a direct or indirect affect on memory functions. For example, it has been claimed that L-dopa has a specific beneficial effect on memory but this is much more likely to be an indirect effect related to the arousing properties of the drug. More recently it has been claimed that piracetam does have a specific effect on cognitive functions including memory, particularly in older age groups, but this is still open to debate.

On the other hand, electroconvulsive therapy usually has a detrimental effect on memory as is described below. Also it has been found that anaesthetic agents can disrupt a range of performance skills, including memory, for some hours postoperatively.

d. Biological basis of memory
The findings from both animal and human lesion studies implicate the temporal lobes and hippocampal regions as brain areas involved with memory. The exact nature of the storage of memory still remains something of a mystery, although a picture is beginning to emerge. The general picture at the moment is that short-term memory is mediated by electrical activity and that more permanent storage takes place through chemical or structural changes, or both.

Most of the evidence on the electrical basis of short-term memory comes from the many studies showing that perturbations of the electrical activity of the brain (e.g. by electroconvulsive therapy) can disrupt consolidation of memory. A suggested underlying mechanism is that of the 'reverberating loop', which would comprise a specific closed network of cells corresponding to a single memory. Once stimulated, reverberations could continue for a short period of time holding the information active. Deliberate or accidental administration of large electric shocks disrupts this process.

Long-term storage would have to involve a more permanent structural change of the neural circuit. This could be achieved by specific chemical changes, probably in the synapse or in the growth of new synapses. These two possibilities are not mutually exclusive and some evidence for both exists, but the chemical theories are currently more favoured. There are now quite a number of studies implicating RNA in memory storage, although the grossness of these studies often leaves room for doubt. It seems most likely that storage will be found to involve growth, atrophy or change in the metabolism of transmitter substances at synapses.

e. Disorders of memory

Specific memory deficits are seen most strikingly in patients with localized brain damage and these are briefly described below. Memory impairment, particularly of short-term storage, is also seen in patients with generalized organic dementia and is usually the first of the cognitive functions to decline (Chapter 9). Anxiety has also been shown to disrupt short-term memory and a number of psychiatric patients have been described as showing 'hysterical amnesia' (a selective or sometimes total memory loss for past events which has a psychological rather than a neurological basis). Specific neurological disorders of memory can be conveniently subdivided into long- and short-term deficits.

i. Long-term memory deficits

Poor learning and retention of ongoing events are the main features of the amnesic syndrome; this may range from an almost total memory loss for day-to-day events to relatively mild conditions where the patient is able to function relatively normally in spite of an unreliable memory for recent events and a slowness in learning new material. Retrograde amnesia, the loss of memory for events antedating the onset of the illness, is a constant feature though it may be variable in duration. In contrast one aspect of memory is intact, namely short-term memory, as tested by immediate span and forgetting over durations of up to 20 seconds.

These amnesic states are fortunately relatively rare and are usually associated with bilateral lesions, either of the hippocampal regions or of diencephalic structures, particularly the mamillary bodies. They have been found in patients with Korsakoff's syndrome and following encephalitis or severe head injuries. Although it has been thought for some time that these deficits were the result of failure to consolidate, or to pass information from short-term to long-term memory, there is some good evidence which indicates that the problem may be as much one of retrieval as of storage (Baddeley, 1976).

ii. Short-term memory deficits

Memory deficits, particularly of short-term storage, have been associated with damage to the temporal lobes. More specific experimental studies have clarified the nature of these deficits. It has been found that in patients who have undergone left anterior temporal lobectomy, there is an abnormally quick loss of information in short-term memory. Recent research has also suggested the possibility of anatomically distinct visual and auditory short-term stores, on the basis of patients who have shown selective auditory or visual short-term defects. Moreover, some of these patients with short-term deficits have normal long-term storage, providing further evidence for the separateness of long- and short-term memory and indicating that information does not necessarily have to pass through short-term memory in order to be held in long-term memory.

● **Recommended reading**

Perception
Bruce V. and Green P. (1985) *Visual Perception: Physiology, Psychology and Ecology*. London, Erlbaum.
Frisby J. P. (1979) *Seeing*. Oxford, Oxford University Press.

Memory
Baddeley A. (1976) *The Psychology of Memory*. New York, Harper & Row.

3

Brain mechanisms and behaviour

In this chapter there is an outline of some of the known relations between brain areas and behavioural functions. In an outline of this sort it is not possible to do more than provide a fairly crude picture of what is currently known. There are still many uncertainties and gaps in the evidence and care must be taken not to fall into the trap of thinking that all psychological functions can be neatly and exclusively localized to specific brain regions. The picture that should emerge from the following account is that these regions are somehow important but not exclusively involved in the behaviours concerned.

Much of the animal evidence and nearly all the human evidence is derived from observing deficits following lesions or damage to particular brain areas. This approach can give rise to gross errors of interpretation if findings are taken too literally. It must be remembered that localized lesions not only remove a defined area of tissue with related loss of function but also disrupt the overall unity of the brain. Fortunately there is now a sufficient correlation between many of the findings from the lesion studies and those using other approaches, such as direct electrical stimulation or recording procedures, to help justify the general conclusions presented below.

● **3.1. Hemisphere differences in function**

In contrast with other mammals, there is now both anatomical and psychological evidence that the cerebral hemispheres of humans do not share mirror-imaged functions. Detailed anatomical studies comparing the two cerebral hemispheres have revealed significant enlargements in a region called the planum temporale, which lies on the upper surface of the temporal lobe hidden within the Sylvian fissure (*Fig.* 5). This area is known to be involved in linguistic functions and as these studies found it to be significantly enlarged on the left side in the majority of adults and babies, this has strongly suggested the presence of a preprogrammed language area (Geschwind, 1979).

Neurologists have known for a long time that unilateral damage to equivalent areas in the two cerebral hemispheres does not always result in similar

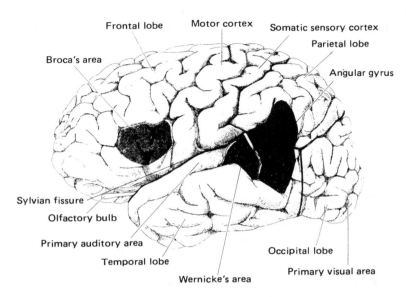

Fig. 5. The map of the human cortex. (From *Specializations of the Human Brain* by Geschwind N. Copyright © 1979 by Scientific American, Inc. All rights reserved.)

functional impairment. The most consistent evidence for this is that left hemisphere damage, particularly to the inferior frontal and posterior temporal/parietal regions, produces various disorders of language whereas damage to the corresponding regions in the right hemisphere rarely does so. Originally such findings gave rise to the notion that in the majority of individuals the left hemisphere was dominant since it contained language functions. However, more recent evidence has shown that each hemisphere contributes different but complementary functions. There are three quite distinct sources of this evidence.

a. 'Split-brain' studies

These involve the investigation of psychological functions in patients with surgically separated hemispheres for the treatment of intractable epilepsy (i.e. the cerebral commissures are sectioned to prevent the spread of epilepsy). Using procedures which involve unilateral presentation of stimuli (i.e. to one hand, ear or visual field), the functions of each hemisphere can be tested separately.

b. Experiments on normal subjects

Again this involves taking care to present information unilaterally but here the approach involves comparing the relative efficiency of the hemispheres in processing different types of information.

c. Studies on patients with unilateral brain damage

These are patients with damage restricted to the right or left cerebral hemisphere. A careful assessment and analysis of their behavioural deficits can provide evidence as to the different behavioural functions mediated by the two hemispheres. For example, damage to the temporal lobes often results in impaired learning and memory but the exact nature of this depends on the side which is damaged. Damage to the anterior left temporal lobe specifically impairs the learning and retention of linguistic material but tends to leave unaffected the learning and retention of visuospatial information. However, the reverse pattern of deficits is found when the damage occurs in the equivalent area on the right side.

Taken as a whole the findings from these three quite different approaches has yielded a pretty consistent picture in the great majority of individuals. The left cerebral hemisphere is more rapid and accurate in processing most language and sequentially ordered stimuli whereas spatially organized information is more efficiently handled by the right hemisphere. Two related points must be made here. First, although there is evidence that some aspects of hemisphere differentiation may be preprogrammed from birth, there appears to be considerable plasticity in the first few years of life. Equivalent areas on one side may take over behavioural functions normally subserved by areas which are damaged in childhood. This point is dealt with in Chapter 8 on child development. Second, it must be remembered that most behavioural functions are to some degree represented in both cerebral hemispheres with one hemisphere showing a greater specialization. This is certainly true for language functions since there is increasing evidence that the right hemisphere can carry out some aspects of language processing, as well as taking over all language processing in the event of early left hemisphere damage (Krashen, 1976).

In the normally functioning brain, the hemispheres obviously work together and the above section has not really dealt with the problem of how the two cerebral hemispheres interact. However, much less is known about hemisphere interaction and the role of the corpus callosum than is known about the differences in modes of processing observed in the two hemispheres.

● **3.2. Localization of functions**

Until fairly recently there has been a widely accepted subdivision of the cerebral neocortex into three functionally distinct areas, namely the sensory, motor and association areas. Sensory areas were deemed to be solely involved with the reception of sensory information, motor areas with the organization and execution of responses and the association areas with functions lying between these, particularly those concerned with higher cognitive processes such as memory, language and problem solving. Although this subdivision is still widely accepted and will be used here, it should be noted that recent findings make it increasingly difficult to accept this three-way classification of cortical areas. Hence the following statement which appeared in a review of brain functions.

We now know that neural activity in the sensory cortex does not just mirror reception activity, nor is the motor cortex the keyboard of the mind. Furthermore we know that association takes place both in animals with little or no association cortex and in animals in which the normal complement of association cortex has been surgically removed. (Masterton and Berkeley, 1974)

Following the account of cortical functions, there is a brief outline of the behavioural functions of selected subcortical areas.

a. Sensory and motor areas
The functions of the sensory areas have been partly covered in the previous chapter in which a description was given of single-cell activity in the visual cortex. Damage to this area in humans gives rise to partial or total loss of pattern vision depending on the extent of the damage. However, there is recent clinical and experimental evidence that some very basic capacities, involved in attention and eye movement control, may still exist following cortical blindness, albeit at a preconscious level. This has led to the idea that the main visual pathway (retina → lateral geniculate nucleus → visual cortex) is primarily concerned with feature extraction and pattern detection and that a subcortical visual system based on the superior colliculus mediates aspects of the attention process. A gross oversimplification of the relative roles of two such systems can be described in terms of 'seeing what' and 'seeing where', as described in Chapter 2.

Single cells in the visual cortex have feature-analysing properties (i.e. respond to specific types of environmental stimuli), are organized in columns and are susceptible to early environmental modification although at least some of their response properties are present from birth. Information from this region is relayed to the visual association areas, particularly the inferotemporal region, for higher level processing.

The auditory system has not been so intensively studied as the visual system. Electrophysiological studies have also revealed a variety of feature-analysing cells organized in columns. However, ablation of this area still leaves some basic auditory functions intact (e.g. auditory thresholds). The main impairments here are related to sound localization and to the discrimination between more complex sounds.

Cells in the somatosensory cortex have also been shown to have specific feature-analysing properties in that they do respond to specific somatosensory stimuli. These also have a columnar organization but, as with the auditory cortex, their functional significance is not really understood.

A complete understanding of motor functions can only be derived from a consideration of all the areas known to be involved in the control of movement, namely the motor cortex, cerebellum and basal ganglia. A great deal of this is more the province of neuroanatomy and only a very brief description is given here.

Motor commands are generated in the cortex as the result of information processed in the sensory, association or motivation areas. The intricate timing of rapid movements is now thought to be preprogrammed in the cerebellum whereas the basal ganglia appear to be involved in the generation of slow voluntary movements. For movements needing a complicated analysis of tactile objects, the output patterns of the cerebellum and basal ganglia are further processed in the motor cortex (Kornhuber, 1974).

b. Association areas

The main association areas are the frontal regions and the parietal-temporal-occipital regions. These areas are most developed in humans and, as their name implies, they are involved with correlating and elaborating intracortical events, particularly in such aspects of behaviour as memory, learning, language and the timing and organization of responses.

i. Frontal regions

One of the most consistent deficits in monkeys following dorsolateral frontal lesions is in tasks requiring delayed responses. This deficit appears to be due to lack of attention rather than a memory loss since these animals tend to be distractable and unable to inhibit incorrect responses even after long training periods. Repeated errors are also a characteristic of patients with frontal lobe damage who tend to perform poorly on tests involving planning ahead and the ability to change from one approach to another.

Frontal damage can also give rise to impaired visual scanning and disorders of expressive aspects of language (e.g. difficulties in articulation and fluency). These disorders of language were noticed by neurologists in the last century and were related to damage involving the inferior paracentral area of the frontal cortex in the region of the third frontal gyrus, now often referred to as Broca's area (see Fig. 5, p. 31).

From the diverse evidence available there is a tendency to ascribe an executive role to the frontal lobes and to think of them as co-ordinating and sequencing various cortical processes. This view is consistent with both the behavioural data and the neuroanatomical findings. Moreover, it has been suggested that the tremendous development in the control and organization of cognitive functions, which is seen up to the age of seven years, reflects the maturation of the frontal cortex during this period (Mackworth, 1976).

ii. Temporoparietal regions

Neurological disorders of language are also found following damage to the temporoparietal regions, particularly to the superior parts of the temporal lobe described earlier in the section on hemisphere differences. These language problems are usually of a receptive type (i.e. difficulties in understanding spoken or written language) and, as with the frontal impairments, are more commonly, but not exclusively, found with left-sided lesions. Corresponding damage involving right temporoparietal regions commonly gives rise to such specific visuospatial and constructional deficits as poor route-finding and the inability to do simple drawings.

In primates there is now good evidence that the inferotemporal area is concerned with higher aspects of visual perception. Damage here does not usually interfere with such basic visual processes as threshold judgements or pattern discrimination but can result in the failure to recognize whole objects even when all the component details are perfectly 'visible' (agnosia). These findings, together with the neurophysiological studies of single cells in this area, suggest that it is involved with the integration and interpretation of visual information which has been detected and processed by the visual cortex.

Lesions in the more anterior regions of the temporal lobes have been consistently associated with disorders of memory and learning. A functional asymmetry has also been found here in that left temporal damage is more commonly associated with problems in the learning and retention of verbal information whereas right-sided damage causes greater problems with visuospatial information. However, it should be pointed out that in many of these patients damage was also found in the mamillary bodies and in parts of the limbic system, particularly the hippocampus.

c. The limbic system

The limbic system consists of a group of structures forming a ring on the inner surface of each hemisphere; the septal area, the cingulate gyrus, the hippocampus and the amygdala (*Fig.* 6). Phylogenetically these are among the most primitive of the cerebral regions and are associated with olfactory functions in lower order animals. Research over the past 30–40 years has shown that this area is involved in a range of behavioural functions from memory to emotions.

In humans, damage to the *hippocampus* has been traditionally associated with disorders of memory. Patients find it difficult to retain information for any reasonable period of time and this in turn impairs learning of some new information and skills. For example, one patient with hippocampal damage could read a magazine article repeatedly, each time believing that it was new material. More formal testing of this patient showed that he always forgot when his attention was distracted. This ties in with recent theories which have stressed the

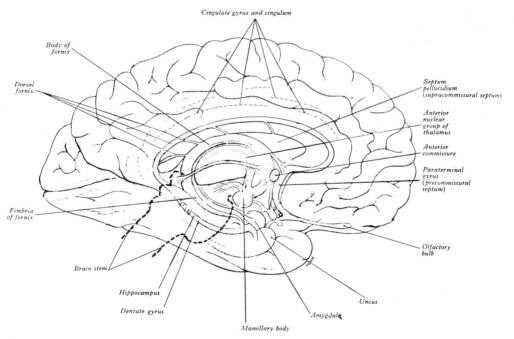

Fig. 6. Diagram of the medial aspect of a cerebral hemisphere showing the majority of structures in the limbic system as well as other structures and the approximate position of the brain stem. (Adapted from Williams and Warwick, 1975.)

role of the hippocampus in focusing attention. Rats whose hippocampi have been removed are easily distracted and less able to ignore irrelevant or redundant stimuli in test situations. These results have also given rise to the notion that the hippocampus is involved in focusing attention by a mechanism which filters out irrelevant stimuli.

Removal or electrical stimulation of the *amygdala* typically changes emotional and motivational states. After a brief period in which an animal's activity is reduced, amygdalectomy often results in increased activity which may be reflected in general behaviour or in such specific activities as eating or sexual behaviour. Lesions in the amygdala can also produce a range of emotional changes. For example, wild animals can become quite tame and docile whereas other studies have described an increased aggressiveness. Moreover fear and rage can be produced by stimulation as well as by lesions of the amygdala. In general terms the amygdala appears to control emotional and motivational aspects of behaviour. A more specific conclusion is that the amygdala is primarily involved in actively suppressing motivated approach behaviour.

The other parts of the limbic system have also been implicated in emotional behaviour, particularly the cingulate gyrus which, it has been suggested, might underlie the experience of emotion. One theory of the limbic system has suggested a functional division between the upper and lower regions of this area; the lower part (amygdala and hippocampus) is concerned with those emotional states associated with biological survival (fighting and eating) and the upper part (cingulate gyrus) with emotions related to sexual and social behaviour (Maclean, 1975).

It is clearly unwise to think that the control of emotional behaviour is exclusively located in the limbic system. The limbic system has major connections with other cortical areas and with the reticular formation. Emotional behaviour involves many areas of the brain since human emotional responses depend on the degree of arousal and the interpretation of the situation giving rise to the emotional change (*see* Chapter 5). In recent years, there has been an increased interest in surgery of the limbic area for the treatment of chronic emotional disturbances such as severe aggressive behaviour. Needless to say, the scientific validity and the ethical considerations surrounding this still rather crude approach to behavioural changes are much disputed.

d. The hypothalamus

One key to understanding the functions of the hypothalamus is its position between the higher regions and the brain stem, below the thalamus and close to the pituitary gland and the limbic system. It has connections with many other brain regions and with sensory pathways and has a very rich blood supply.

The hypothalamus plays a vital role in regulating and integrating a range of behaviours. It is involved in the control of water balance and in regulating body temperature, the activity of the autonomic nervous system and various endocrine processes.

The hypothalamus and related areas, particularly the medial forebrain bundle, have been shown to be prime sites for 'electrical self-stimulation' studies. In these brain regions electrical stimulation appears to have a very strong rewarding effect. In a typical experimental situation, an animal with a stimulating electrode placed in the region of the hypothalamus is allowed to roam round a cage. In the cage is a small lever which, when pressed, activates the electrode. It is found that the animal not only quickly learns that pressing the lever turns on the current but continues to press it, sometimes almost continuously, for hours on end. This, together with the related finding that electrodes in other areas produce the opposite effect, leads to the rather simplistic notion of the existence of reward and punishment centres in the brain, particularly in the hypothalamic region. The functional significance of these 'self-stimulation' areas is still open to debate but results certainly suggest that this brain region is directly involved in motivated behaviour and probably in emotion.

As with the limbic system, observations of emotional changes following electrical stimulation or induced lesions have led to the conclusion that, if the posterior hypothalamus is stimulated, sympathetic activity is evoked together with such behavioural changes as increased arousal and rage. In contrast, stimulation of more anterior areas tends to evoke parasympathetic activity resulting in such changes as decreased arousal and lowered heart rate. This suggests that the posterior hypothalamic regions are associated with 'fight and flight' type reactions to threat situations and the anterior regions with more vegetative functions. More recent research has confirmed and refined these findings and supports the idea of two discrete hypothalamic controls over emotional aspects of behaviour. This dualism, an opposition between excitatory and inhibitory functions, can be seen in other behavioural investigations involving this area, including studies of the role of the hypothalamus in the control of eating and drinking.

Lesions placed in the ventromedial part of the hypothalamus consistently lead to overeating (hyperphagia) and therefore to obesity, whereas lesions in the lateral part of the hypothalamus produce the opposite effect: animals stop eating (aphagia) and would starve if not force-fed. These complementary effects give rise to a dual-centre theory of feeding involving a 'feeding centre' and a 'satiety centre' which exert a reciprocal control on each other (*see* Blundell, 1975, pp. 73–80). These separate systems for initiating eating and for satiation are located in the lateral and ventromedial areas of the hypothalamus respectively.

Other brain areas can be shown to be involved in eating, but not so directly. For example, interference with the limbic system has an effect on food intake, rarely as dramatic as interference with the hypothalamus, but sufficient to confirm the notion that the hypothalamus plays a central rather than an exclusive role in the control of eating. A few clinical observations with humans, involving either damage or stimulation of these hypothalamic areas, are also consistent with the general view that they are involved in hunger motivation. Moreover, there is now good evidence that the separate centres associated with initiating and terminating hunger are activated by specific neurochemical systems. It has also been shown that separate neurochemical pathways are involved in eating and drinking since direct injections into rats' hypothalamic regions have shown that feeding is activated by noradrenaline and drinking by acetylcholine.

e. The reticular formation

A great deal of evidence has accumulated in the past few decades implicating the importance of the brain stem reticular formation in the control of arousal and wakefulness. Approximately one-third of our lives is spent in sleep and even while we are awake there are many intrinsic and extrinsic factors which produce variations in our state of arousal, as is discussed in the next chapter. The reticular formation is a core of neuronal tissue located in the centre of the brain stem and connecting at its upper end with the hypothalamus and thalamus. It receives branches or collateral inputs from all sensory pathways and can therefore provide a barometer of sensory activation. Within it there are two distinct subsystems:

i. *The Descending Reticular System* (DRS) comprising cells with axons which project down to the spinal cord.

ii. *The Ascending Reticular Activating System* (ARAS) comprising cells with axons which project to higher levels in the brain stem. This pathway connects to a group of nuclei in the thalamus and then by various routes to the whole cortex.

It has been demonstrated that, if the brain stem is sectioned at its base, the resultant brain waves recorded from an experimental animal still show an appropriate evidence of wakefulness but sectioning at the top leads to an almost persistent state of sleep. Electrical stimulation of the brain stem either produces or increases the brain-wave indications of arousal. More specifically, cutting the sensory afferents in the brain stem but sparing the ARAS has been found to have no effect on the sleep–wakefulness pattern, whereas the reverse process, cutting the ARAS and sparing sensory afferents, results in sleep. The most usual interpretation of these and similar findings is that the ARAS has a diffuse, activating effect on the cortex rather than a role in relaying specific sensory messages. However, there is a reciprocal side to this process since paths descending from cortical areas have also been demonstrated and these are thought to mediate changes in arousal level that are internally generated, such as those due to motivational or emotional factors. There is also some evidence to suggest that in addition to regulating the organism's general level of wakefulness, the reticular formation may be involved in selective attention.

The following general conclusions can be summarized from the very selective review of brain functions presented above:

i. In humans the two cerebral hemispheres have differences in structure and function. The left side is more competent at processing linguistic and sequential information, the right side at processing visual and spatial information.

ii. Within each hemisphere there are clearly defined areas set aside for sensory, motor and higher cognitive (association) functions, although this strict subdivision may well be outliving its usefulness.

iii. Subcortical regions appear to be largely concerned with more basic functions, particularly emotion, motivation, eating, sexuality and general arousal. However, it should not be forgotten that these areas typically operate in conjunction with higher cortical regions.

This last point is critical since a brief overview of this sort tends to isolate and delineate functions whereas human behaviour depends on the unity of the whole brain and the complex interplay of all the structures involved. A complete understanding of the functions of the brain is still a long way off, but it is hoped that the present review will at least convey a general picture of the current state of some of our knowledge. Even the present limited concepts can be of use in the clinical context in the diagnosis and management of patients with neurological damage to the higher central nervous system. Psychological tests are routinely given to patients with brain lesions in order both to define the nature and degree of psychological deficit and to help to indicate more precisely where damage has occurred, on the basis of the evidence described above. These clinical applications are briefly described in Chapter 6 on intelligence.

●   **Recommended reading**

Beaumont J. G. (1983) *Introduction to Neuropsychology*. New York, Blackwell.

Heilman K. M. and Valenstein E. (1985) *Clinical Neuropsychology*, 2nd ed. New York, Oxford University Press.

4

Arousal, circadian rhythms and sleep

In many ways this chapter follows on conveniently from the end of the previous one which described the role of the reticular formation in controlling the level of wakefulness. It appears to do so by exerting a non-specific activating effect on the whole neocortex via a complex system of diffusely projecting afferent fibres. This activation can be directly affected by the level of sensory input and by the individual's internal emotional state. Thus, the reticular formation is greatly concerned with the control of cortical arousal as evidenced by brain wave activity.

• 4.1. Arousal

A central concept which runs through this and the next chapter is that of 'arousal', which is a fairly difficult one to define because it can be described in a number of ways. In general behavioural terms, the level of arousal corresponds with the level of alertness of the individual and can be anything from drowsiness through to states of intense mental activation. It therefore refers to a continuum of behavioural and underlying physiological states which range from total stupor to hypermania. High levels of arousal may be an indication of a responsiveness to a high level of external stimulation. Increased arousal can also accompany internal changes in motivation or emotion and these are discussed in the next chapter.

Monitoring an individual's level of arousal, activation or alertness is clearly not a simple process since the experience is essentially a subjective one. It is possible to obtain subjective reports by asking individuals to rate themselves on a fixed scale. This can be difficult but fortunately other approaches can be used. First, it is possible to manipulate the level of arousal by modifying external stimulation. Second, there appears to be a natural periodicity in arousal which occurs during the day and this 'circadian' rhythm is described below. Third, it is possible to obtain information about an individual's state of arousal from a number of direct or indirect measurements. Indirect measurements might consist of various performance measures since arousal is known to have an effect on performance. More direct approaches include a variety of physiological measures which can provide an indication of central and autonomic nervous system activation.

The electroencephalogram (EEG) is a technique employed for recording changes in the electrical activity of the brain. Using electrodes attached to the scalp, it is possible to derive a continuous record of the voltage fluctuations which can be detected on the surface of the brain. Although the EEG record is a fairly gross representation of total electrical activity of the brain, it is possible to detect and quantify changes by analysing the amplitude and the frequency of the wave forms. The EEG record can therefore be thought of as a kind of mental barometer which can indicate from moment to moment the type of brain wave activity occurring in the whole brain and in more specific regions (e.g. frontal or occipital; left or right side).

When EEG records are correlated with the behavioural and subjective measures referred to above, some consistencies emerge. In very general terms, when people are relaxed the EEG record consists of larger amplitude and slower frequency waveforms whereas smaller amplitude and higher frequency wave-forms are found in more 'aroused' states. In highly aroused states, such as those associated with strong emotional responses, there is also a tendency for the EEG waveform to become desynchronized. It is not possible or practicable to enter into a more detailed discussion of the use of the EEG or of other techniques for monitoring brain wave activity. For the present, it is sufficient to be aware of the fact that it is possible to detect general changes in cortical activity and that these can give an indication of an individual's level of arousal or alertness.

Earlier work on the regulation of wakefulness tended to be concerned with whether the organism was awake or asleep. This partly stemmed from earlier animal investigations which had shown that damage to different areas of the reticular formation could result in states of almost permanent sleep or wakefulness. However, it is clear from the EEG evidence and from experimental studies that there are many levels of arousal within both waking and sleep states. In the next chapter there is a consideration of the nature and effects of some of the more extreme forms of arousal seen in emotional states and in response to psychological and environmental stresses. The section which follows below is concerned with the 'normal' variation in level of arousal which occurs within a 24-hour period.

● **4.2. Circadian rhythms**

Consider the following situations and reflect on what they have in common:

a. A doctor or nurse misreads the output from a complex patient-monitoring device during the first night of a night shift.

b. A patient shows a large and consistent daily fluctuation in symptom severity and response to treatment.

c. A medical research scientist, making a brief visit from England to the USA to present a paper on recent research, experiences uncharacteristic difficulty in organizing his thoughts and presenting the talk.

One feature which is common to these diverse situations is that each involves some aspect of circadian rhythms. In the first and third examples an individual is forced into a work routine which is shifted in time from the usual daily rhythm and in the second example there is evidence of a daily variation in a disease process. All three examples provide some hints as to what this section will be concerned with, namely the nature of the changes in physiological and psychological processes which follow a 24-hour pattern.

Many bodily processes have been shown to have a fixed periodicity. Some of these cycles can be fairly brief and some, such as the menstrual cycle, take much longer to complete. In recent years claims have been made for the existence of 'biorhythms', apparently naturally occurring cycles which can affect performance efficiency and feelings of wellbeing. Various devices have even been marketed and these are intended to predict the timing of such cycles in order to allow individuals to plan such behaviour as the making of important decisions to coincide with the occurrence of advantageous biorhythms. At present it is far too early to say whether such biorhythms really do exist and those who spend money on any of the prediction devices are effectively buying a toy rather than a well-founded piece of scientific equipment.

In contrast, the various physiological rhythms that follow a 24-hour cycle have been extensively studied. In the following section it is intended to say something about these rhythms and their effect on behaviour, as well as considering their social and clinical relevance. Since one of the most obvious behavioural changes is the transition from wakefulness to sleep, there will be a separate account of sleep.

a. What are circadian rhythms?

The term 'circadian rhythm' is taken to refer to the patterns of biological change which last about, but usually not exactly, 24 hours. Many physiological and metabolic functions in humans show a well-defined 24-hour periodicity, which appears to be consistent and intrinsic since it remains when environmental conditions are radically changed. It is thought that these 24-hour cycles are kept finely adjusted by environmental cues such as light/dark changes. However, these environmental cues do not appear to be critical in controlling circadian rhythms because they persist when the cues are removed or altered. This has been found in studies of volunteers in caves or special experimental laboratories, where no external light can be seen and where clocks, radios and any other indicators of time of day or night are not available. In these studies, where people set their own patterns of sleep and wakefulness, it has been found that they settle into a cycle with something quite close to a 24-hour periodicity. In one of the larger, more recent studies an average cycle of about 25 hours was reported with a standard deviation of approximately half an hour. For the majority of individuals in these studies, all the bodily rhythms change their phase in synchrony but for a few there appears to be desynchronization in that some rhythms appear to get out of step. Thus at the outset it can be seen that there may be a group of individuals who are particularly vulnerable to changes in their pattern of circadian rhythms.

It is not the place of this book to describe all the physiological processes which show a circadian rhythm. The discussion will be limited to one variable, namely body temperature, which is the most extensively studied and is most commonly used in correlating physiological with psychological changes during the

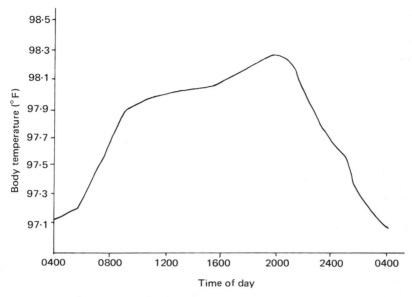

Fig. 7. Time of day and body temperature.

24-hour cycle. Measures of daily changes in body temperature have been recorded in a large number of studies and typically the pattern which is found can be seen in *Fig.* 7.

Hospital records of patients whose temperatures are routinely taken at various times of the day also provide a record of the daily pattern of temperature changes. Patients without fever and non-patients alike show a pretty consistent pattern with temperature at its lowest in the early hours of the morning and at its highest in the early evening. This pattern appears to develop during the first few months of an infant's life and the magnitude of oscillation between minimum and maximum temperature tends to increase during the first 2 years. The fact that this rhythm is found in non-febrile patients who are confined to bed also indicates that it does not depend on the presence of physical activity during the waking hours.

One of the most important practical consequences of these body rhythms in industrialized societies is in relation to shift work. Some 30 years ago about 10 per cent of the British working population did shift work and this figure appears to have doubled since then. There are good claims now that the biological status of the night worker may be sufficient to affect his or her psychological health as well as accident-proneness and job efficiency. The reason is that the person who shifts to night work will continue to show circadian variations associated with working by day and sleeping at night for some time after the change of shift. Most studies of night workers have found that the temperature rhythm adapts relatively slowly to the changing pattern of sleep and wakefulness and can take about 5 or 6 days to fully adapt. This means that, during the early part of the adaptation period, night shift workers will be working at a time when their level of arousal is at its lowest and trying to sleep when they are biologically at their highest arousal level.

Ironically, since many night shift workers resume a 'normal' sleep–wakefulness cycle at the weekends, the adaptation achieved during the working week is lost over the weekend. It is possible that permanent night workers and even those who follow a weekly rotating shift system all through their working lives eventually adapt more rapidly.

The medical evidence on the effects of shift work on health is conflicting, some reports showing a significantly greater incidence of psychological and physical problems and others showing hardly any adverse effects, as compared with day workers. There are problems with such comparison studies, particularly since any observed effects may be due to sampling or to the occupational factors associated with jobs necessitating shift work. One thing is clear and it is that, given the usual pattern of circadian rhythms, psychological efficiency is greatly reduced at night. This can be understood more clearly by considering the relation between circadian rhythms and performance.

b. Circadian rhythms and performance

If performance measures are obtained at different times of the day by testing individuals on a battery of psychological tests, then it is possible to see the extent to which human performance shows a circadian variation. Typically such studies involve the use of fairly simple tasks, such as mental arithmetic and letter cancellation (going through a block of text and crossing out defined letters), both of which have the advantage of being repeatable and provide measures of speed and accuracy. Other measures which are used in these studies of performance efficiency include short-term memory tasks (e.g. memory span), reaction-time tasks, vigilance (monitoring a screen and responding to the occurrence of a faint and infrequent target) and reasoning tasks. Practically all these aspects of performance show a pattern of circadian variation which is surprisingly close to that found with body temperature (Marks and Folkard, 1984). The highest levels of performance are found in the late afternoon and early evening when body temperature reaches its peak and when circadian arousal is at its highest. Correspondingly psychomotor performance appears to be at its worst in the early hours of the day when body temperature is also at its lowest level. Readers might be surprised to see this result when reflecting on their own daily pattern of efficiency since by the early evening most of us are tired after a day's work. However, when these fatigue effects are controlled for by studying people only working at certain times of the day, then the reported circadian periodicity in performance is found. This general picture has been complicated more recently by evidence indicating that there may be a number of different circadian performance cycles with different phases and peaks.

Why should such a relation between body temperature and performance exist, and is it a causal one? Taking the questions in reverse order, it appears that the relation is not a causal one. In other words it does not appear that the body temperature *per se* directly affects performance level although some workers have claimed that the associated increases in metabolic activity would have this effect. If time of day effects are controlled for, then no particular correlation between temperature and performance is found. Also, if body temperature is increased or decreased artificially, no direct effects on performance are detectable. All of this suggests that a third and still unknown factor, which shows a circadian variation, carries body temperature and performance with it. Temperature and performance changes therefore appear to be a function of an intrinsic biological clock.

Returning to the question of shift work it can now be seen that there are good reasons why night work is associated with significantly lower performance levels. It is sad but probably true to note that the majority of night shift workers are engaged in relatively mundane tasks and are therefore susceptible to a circadian effect, especially during the first couple of days of a new shift. Moreover, some of the largest circadian effects have been found with vigilance tasks and since jobs involving monitoring and checking are becoming more common with increased automation in industry and medicine, this is potentially a large problem area.

c. Clinical implications

It seems appropriate to ask whether there is any clinical significance of this analysis of circadian rhythms. In considering this, four different areas are now discussed briefly.

i. Shift work in medicine

From the point of view of the doctor or nurse who is having to work night shifts it is clear that there are associated problems and that both may be prone to making certain sorts of errors before their circadian rhythms have managed to adapt to night work (e.g. *see* Wilkinson et al., 1975). This may well be compounded by the added burdens of sleep loss and fatigue. There is equivocal evidence as to whether shift work is more likely to give rise to health problems than daytime working. It is something to bear in mind when looking for causes of illnesses in the individual patient, especially if he or she may be one of the small group of people who experience difficulty in shifting the phase of their circadian rhythms.

ii. Diseases

Many diseases exhibit rhythmic activity and the majority of these are circadian. These include bronchial asthma, diabetes, leukaemia and pulmonary oedema and for the majority there is a tendency for attacks to occur from 3 a.m. to 4 a.m. or at the time of rising. Many factors may contribute to this periodicity and these may interact with endogenous circadian factors. For example, some of the variation in bronchial asthma attacks may be due to the fact that the patient is lying down at night. However, the periodicity still continues when patients are not in bed at night or when they cross time zones. Even so, a whole range of biological and social factors may determine or modify the circadian variation in disease processes.

iii. Treatment effects

Just as the incidence of attacks of various diseases has peaks, so the sensitivity to treatment can also be cyclic. For example, oral histamine lasts nearly three times as long if given at 7 a.m. than at 7 p.m. whereas patients are considerably more sensitive to insulin at night than during the day. Many other drugs have been reported to show a circadian variation in sensitivity or excretion and these include amphetamine, cortisone, digitalis, librium and a range of narcotic agents. Clearly it is important for doctors to be aware of these differences and to make use of this knowledge in treatment. The administration of drugs like corticosteroids, insulin and antibiotics, which are given in maintenance doses, could be timed to coincide with those times when excretion is slowest. In this way it may be possible to reduce the quantity of maintenance doses.

iv. Pain

It has also been shown that there is a significant circadian variation in pain threshhold. In the first chapter there was an outline of some of the factors which can affect the perception of pain and it was concluded that pain could not be thought of as a fixed response to a given level of sensory activation. In one study of patients with intractable pain, the reported intensity of pain was found to increase consistently throughout the day and to peak in the early evening (Folkard et al., 1976). This was found across a group of patients with different organic causes and appeared to reflect a change in the sensitivity to a continual pain rather than a periodicity in the disease process. Interestingly, the same study also indicated that those who went to work reported less pain than a comparable group who were at home, indicating that the distractions of working may also modify the pain response. From a practical point of view, such studies indicate that patients may require different levels of analgesia at different times of the day and that personality and social factors must also be taken into consideration. Patients could be made aware of the circadian variation they may experience in the intensity of their pain and they could be encouraged to plan their use of analgesics accordingly. Finally, it should be noted again that although circadian variations in psychological processes can be demonstrated these do not necessarily have an absolute effect in that they can be modified by social, motivational and personality factors.

● **4.3. Sleep**

The most obvious behavioural change which occurs during the circadian cycle is the transition from wakefulness to sleep. For most of us approximately one-third of the 24-hour period is spent in sleep and so a separate consideration of its nature seems appropriate. Moreover, sleep disorders are among the commonest symptoms seen by doctors and to some extent these can be understood more easily with reference to the 'normal' pattern of sleep.

a. What is sleep?

It is probably not too surprising to find that sleep occurs at a time in the circadian cycle when body temperature and arousal level are at their lowest. A common-sense interpretation of the functions of sleep would therefore be in terms of a recovery process in response to the activities of the preceding day and as a preparation for a new day. However, the notion of sleep as the natural response to a hard day's activity can be seen to be too limited since the amount of sleep may be relatively unaffected by the variability in waking levels of activity. It seems as if sleep constitutes a very basic part of the overall circadian pattern which is laid down in the early period of development and persists throughout life. One further misconception about sleep is that it is a somewhat passive state and corresponds to an absence of wakefulness and mental activity. It is now known that there are brain regions which give rise to cortical rhythms associated with the onset and maintenance of sleep.

Sleep is by its very nature a private event and relatively inaccessible to research investigation. In general terms, sleep is indicated by loss of awareness and a decreased responsiveness to the environment. Before the advent of electrophysiological monitoring it was thought of as a fairly unitary event, a period of inertia which varied only in its depth. This picture has radically altered with the development of equipment to monitor brain wave activity (the electroencephalogram or EEG), eye movements (the electro-oculogram or EOG) and muscle tension (electromyogram or EMG). Continuous polygraphic records of a whole night's sleep obtained in sleep laboratories have revealed that sleep consists of a number of fairly distinct phases which follow each other in a regular pattern.

There is now reasonable agreement that there are two quite different states of sleep and that these can be defined primarily in terms of EEG, EOG and EMG characteristics as follows:

i. Rapid eye movement (REM) sleep

This sleep stage derives its name from the characteristic bursts of conjugate rapid eye movements which occur during it. During REM sleep, brain wave activity is similar to that seen while awake and at a reasonable level of arousal since the EEG pattern is of low voltage with rapid frequencies. The sleeper also appears to be in a state of intense physiological activity at this time since cerebral blood flow is greater than when awake and autonomic functions such as heart rate and sweating are active and highly variable. In contrast, muscles are relaxed. This contrast between apparent high levels of physiological and mental activation and complete muscular relaxation has given rise to one of the other names used to describe this sleep state, namely paradoxical sleep.

When subjects awake from REM sleep they will frequently report dreams. It has been suggested that the conjugate eye movements actually correspond to the visual scanning of the images experienced during dreaming but for various reasons this is most unlikely. As *Fig.* 8 shows, the phases of REM sleep tend to occur about every 90 minutes throughout the sleep period and increase in duration

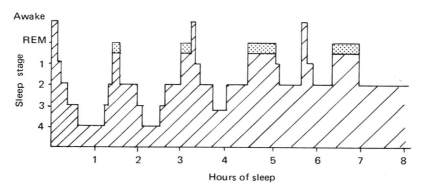

Fig. 8. The profile of sleep stages.

later on. Approximately 20–25 per cent of total sleep of 7–8 hours is usually spent in REM episodes.

ii. Non-rapid eye movement (NREM) sleep

This is sometimes referred to as orthodox or quiescent sleep and as the name suggests is characterized by a virtual absence of eye movements. NREM sleep can be classified into four further stages of increasing depth in which it becomes progressively more difficult to wake the sleeper. The stages are as follows:

Stage 1 is the lightest stage which the sleeper first enters when falling asleep and is characterized by a relatively low-voltage, mixed frequency EEG pattern. Approximately 5 per cent of the night is spent in Stage 1 and it appears to be something of a transitional state between wakefulness and deeper sleep levels.

Stage 2 contains the presence of runs of fast EEG waves in the 12–14 Hz band which are imposed on a background of relatively low-voltage activity. These runs of fast waves have a characteristic spindle-shape tracing on the polygraph record and are usually referred to as 'sleep spindles'. About half the total sleep is spent in Stage 2.

Stage 3 and Stage 4 are often referred to as 'slow wave sleep' because the concomitant EEG record contains high-voltage, slow-wave activity. In Stage 3 these large slow waves are present for approximately 20–50 per cent of the time whereas in the very deep Stage 4 sleep they are predominant. Stage 3 takes up about 7–8 per cent and Stage 4 about 10–16 per cent of the night's sleep.

In NREM sleep there are no consistent conjugate eye movements and the only EOG activity which tends to be recorded are slow oscillating movements which occur during drowsiness and the lighter stages. Bodily functions tend to be at rest and cardiac and respiration rates are steady and slower than during periods of relaxed wakefulness. The sleeper appears to be fully relaxed and on wakening does not usually report mental activity or dreaming.

The typical sleep pattern for a healthy individual is shown in *Fig.* 8. As the sleeper becomes drowsy and the muscles relax, the EEG pattern becomes desynchronized and the sleeper drifts into NREM sleep. Between 30 and 40 minutes after falling asleep, Stage 4 is reached and the first REM episode appears after about 90 minutes. This 90-minute cycle of slow wave and REM sleep continues throughout the night but Stage 3 and Stage 4 sleep tend to be concentrated in the earlier part of the night. This pattern is only an approximation based on records of a large number of records taken mainly from young healthy volunteers. It can vary, but the overall pattern appears to be fairly widespread.

b. The functions of sleep

From the foregoing account it is evident why many sleep researchers tend to think of sleep as an oscillation between two distinct states, namely slow wave sleep (i.e. Stages 3 and 4) and REM sleep. It is perhaps unfortunate that orthodox sleep is referred to as NREM sleep as this tends to suggest that REM has some sort of primacy in the sleep process. Any such conclusion would be quite inaccurate as it now appears that slow-wave sleep (SWS) and REM sleep both have important and separate functional roles. These two states also appear to have different physiological substrates.

An indirect indication of the relative importance of different sleep states comes from studies in which volunteers are selectively deprived of one or other state. The earlier studies tended to be concerned with REM deprivation and showed that following a period of REM deprived sleep, there would be a rebound effect. Thus in the nights immediately following the REM deprived period there is a greater proportion of REM sleep. A similar rebound effect is also found with patients who have taken sleeping pills, many of which have the unfortunate side effect of radically diminishing the amount of REM sleep. Coming off the pills leads to a dramatic rise in the proportion of REM sleep and often to rather florid dreams.

The REM rebound phenomenon provides a clear indication of the importance of this stage of sleep and a similar effect is found if SWS is reduced experimentally. It is more difficult to deprive volunteer sleepers of SWS without waking them but where this has been done then a marked rebound effect is found. Indeed, if volunteers are totally deprived of sleep for a few nights it appears that there are large increases in the proportion of SWS during the initial recovery nights whereas REM does not show such a large increase. The REM rebound does not take place fully until the SWS rebound has been completed. These increases in SWS and REM following partial or total sleep deprivation appear to be at the expense of Stages 1 and 2 sleep. From these studies it is possible to infer that both sleep states are vital and possibly that the replenishment of SWS takes precedence over REM recovery. However, the latter conclusion may be misleading in the light of the fact that the majority of SWS normally occurs earlier in the night whereas most REM occurs later on and this time difference may determine the order of the two rebound processes.

At one time it was thought that loss of REM sleep could have severe disrupting effects on waking behaviour and health, but this view has been greatly modified by more recent research. It has become apparent that REM deprivation has no serious detrimental effects in humans in the short term. Although REM deprived volunteers tend to report feeling more ill at ease or irritable, their performance on various psychological performance tests is not particularly affected. In contrast, SWS deprivation does appear to have effects on waking behaviour in that there are reports of subjects becoming depressed and lethargic.

The evidence discussed so far for the functional roles of SWS and REM has been rather indirect since it has been concerned with the effects of the absence of the two states on sleep and on behaviour. More directly, there have been attempts to assign functional roles to different sleep states and these can be briefly summarized. First, it is suggested that SWS has a particular role in the restitution of bodily processes, especially as human growth hormone is released in large quantities during this sleep state. Consistent with this notion is the finding that there is an increased proportion of SWS following strenuous daytime exercise or at times when the body is physically stressed as the result of such procedures as starvation. In contrast, it has been suggested that REM sleep is particularly important for synthetic processes in the brain. The increased cerebral blood flow which occurs during REM sleep cannot be related to coping with the demands of the external environment and so it is surmised that internal metabolic needs are being dealt with during this sleep stage. The fact that REM sleep increases proportionally in young animals during periods of most rapid brain growth and decreases proportionally during the cerebral deterioration accompanying senility can also be taken to provide some indirect support for this idea.

This rather neat dichotomy of REM and SWS functions associated with the restitution of brain and body processes respectively is very attractive but should be treated cautiously. At best it may provide a loose framework for conceptualizing different functional aspects of sleep but at worst it may be a grossly simplified and misleading picture of the complexities of the whole sleep process. Also, by focusing on the separate roles of these two sleep states it is possible that any links between them may be overlooked. For example, one theory has proposed that SWS might be a sleep phase when macromolecules (i.e. proteins and/or RNA) are synthesized, particularly in the central nervous system, and that these macromolecules could be used in the processes which occur during REM sleep (Hartmann, 1973).

c. Dreaming

The links between REM sleep and cerebral processing hold some additional attractions when the role of dreaming is considered. The temporal association between dreaming and REM sleep was mentioned earlier and so this section on the functions of sleep will be concluded by considering the possible significance of dreams. Since there are far too many theories of dreaming to allow a full discussion here, this account will be limited to two major viewpoints.

First, the psychoanalytic view of dreaming is that dreams are a key to subconscious mental processes. In waking behaviour, subconscious ideas do not emerge very easily since they are repressed by the controls exerted by consciousness but in sleep the controls are removed and these ideas are allowed to surface. It is also argued that some of the strange symbols or allegories that appear in dreams are disguises for worrying or stressful issues for the individual. Disguising these issues in this way is thought to be important since their impact will not be alarming and sleep will be protected. Indeed, some psychoanalytic theorists have argued that dreaming is the major function of sleep and that interpreting dream contents is one way of understanding subconscious fears or preoccupations. Dream analysis is therefore an important part of some psychoanalytic procedures but as with many aspects of psychoanalytic theory there are all sorts of problems with the validity of dream interpretations (*see* Chapter 7 for a more detailed account of the psychoanalytic approach). Even so, it is generally agreed that daytime worries can manifest themselves in the contents of dreams and that the proportion of REM sleep can increase after days of stress, worry or following events of a particular emotional significance to the individual. Shakespeare may well have got it right without the benefits of EEG technology when he wrote of 'sleep, that knits up the ravelled sleave of care'.

The second major viewpoint ascribes dreaming a role dealing with memory and learning. This view has been expressed in many forms but all tend to include the notion that in dreams the memories and experiences of the preceding day or recent past are incorporated into long-term memory. A number of these theories have used computer analogies and envisage sleep as a time when the human computer is taken 'off-line' from the environment to allow memory to be updated by processing and assimilating newly acquired data. It is also possible to combine these two types of explanation of dreaming since it has been suggested that the memories which are processed in dreams are emotionally charged ones and that by processing them during REM sleep, they may be prevented from being dealt with at a conscious level.

It is left to the reader to choose between these various explanations of dreams. One word of warning which can be offered is that evidence for any particular viewpoint is necessarily very inferential since it is pretty well impossible to produce any conclusive proofs at present. Returning to the question of the function of sleep, it can be concluded that while sleep has an essentially restitutive function this may not be of a unitary nature since the different phases of sleep appear to be involved in different aspects of restitution.

d. Factors affecting sleep

So far we have discussed the pattern of a night's sleep as if it is somehow universal and immutable. Nothing could be further from the truth as there appear to be many variations on this basic theme and these are due primarily to individual differences and to situational variables.

Although the average length of a night's sleep is usually given as somewhere between 7 and 8 hours, there is a wide variation between individuals in both the duration of sleep and in its distribution over the 24-hour period. Approaching 10 per cent of a healthy population sleep regularly for less than 5 hours and some people sleep for 3 hours or less without any complaint. Correspondingly some 15 per cent of the population appear to need 9 hours or more sleep each day.

The total amount of time spent in sleep declines from early to middle adulthood and then tends to increase. This increase in sleep from the late fifties and early sixties onwards appears to be due to a redistribution of the sleep cycle. Taking naps in the middle of the day increases with age and there are more nocturnal disturbances in 60- and 70-year-old sleepers. It is not too clear why this should be and it is probably a combination of at least two inter-related factors. There does appear to be an increase in nocturnal disturbances with age but the reduction of social and occupational pressures in retirement means that compensatory naps can be taken more easily during the day. It is quite possible that taking these naps will in turn give rise to a less sustained nocturnal sleeping pattern. From all this it would appear that with advancing age the fixed sleep/wakefulness pattern becomes slightly eroded and may be replaced by a more polycyclic one with bouts of sleep being spread throughout the day.

Environmental changes or disruptions can also have an effect on sleep patterns. In laboratory studies of sleep there is a well-known 'first night' effect in which a disrupted sleep pattern is observed on the first occasion a volunteer is studied. This manifests itself as a delay in getting off to sleep combined with more nocturnal awakenings. A similar picture of sleep disruption is seen on admission to hospital and which may persist for the first few nights after admission. In the latter situation sleep disturbances are probably due to a range of factors over and above the unfamiliar surroundings of the hospital ward. These factors include the unusual noises, changes in the routine of going to bed and the anxiety which patients often experience as a function of illness or hospitalization. Moreover, the pain and discomfort accompanying many diseases may give rise to difficulties in getting to sleep and to more awakenings than usual.

Many drugs including hypnotics, alcohol, stimulants and analgesics can affect sleep. These changes are most prominent when the drug is first taken and with continued use they may diminish or disappear as tolerance develops. However, on withdrawal from the drug, sleep may be quite radically affected. The

REM rebound phenomenon, discussed earlier, appears to be involved in many cases here since hypnotics, for example, significantly diminish the proportion of REM sleep which in turn increases in frequency following the end of drug treatment. After discontinuation of stimulant and depressant drugs there may also be an increased difficulty in getting to sleep together with broken sleep and sometimes nightmares. Normal sleep patterns may not be restored for up to 6 weeks afterwards. With alcohol, which is a common form of self-medication for sleep difficulties, the onset of sleep may be quick but there is likely to be an increased restlessness during the night combined with an early awakening.

e. Problems with sleep

It is rather misleading to find that sleep problems tend to be collectively referred to under the heading of 'insomnia'. Although the latter term implies sleeplessness or absence of sleep it usually refers to three particular problems, namely a difficulty in getting to sleep, a difficulty in staying asleep and failing to feel refreshed after sleep. Clearly the definition of insomnia cannot be based on the length of time spent sleeping since there is a considerable range in sleep duration, as was described above. Each patient's problem may vary considerably in its severity or nature but the critical factor is that there is a reported complaint of problems with sleeping. In the region of 15 per cent of all general practice patients complain of a sleep disorder and this proportion increases with age. Sleep problems tend to be commoner in women and one fairly recent survey showed that about 15 per cent of men and 25 per cent of women over 45 years of age are regularly prescribed hypnotics.

Sleep problems are pretty widespread and the reasons for them appear to be somewhat varied. Occasionally there is evidence of a physical cause, such as a respiratory problem, but the majority appear to have a psychological component. One valuable source of evidence about sleep problems has been the sleep laboratory and in particular the reported differences in sleep patterns between 'good' and 'poor' sleepers. A number of important points have emerged from studies of this type and these can be summarized as follows:

i. Although poor sleepers do take longer to fall asleep they tend to over-estimate the time they take to do so. For example, in one study, subjects' estimates were in the region of 1 hour but the sleep records showed the actual range to be about 15–20 minutes as compared with about 5 minutes for a good sleeper. This discrepancy raises an important point. It is not that poor sleepers should be dismissed as exaggerators but that they appear to be disproportionately stressed by their sleep difficulties. Similar discrepancies can also be noted in the assessment of sleep duration.

ii. Poorer sleepers have a smaller proportion of REM sleep and this is probably due to the shorter sleep duration.

iii. More spontaneous awakenings are experienced by poor sleepers and they take longer to get back to sleep after waking. The result is that they spend something like 15–20 per cent of the night awake as compared with about 5 per cent for a good sleeper.

iv. Poor sleepers spend a relatively large proportion of the night in Stage 2 sleep, which indicates more time is spent in a lighter sleep stage.

v. More body movements during sleep are recorded in poor sleepers indicating an increased restlessness.

Fig. 9. A psychological approach to sleep problems!

vi. In poor sleepers body temperature, blood pressure and pulse rate do not fall normally during sleep.

This pattern of findings from laboratory studies can be related to the earlier description of the circadian cycle of arousal since it would appear that people who complain of sleep difficulties have a higher physiological level of arousal during sleep. As a result, their sleep is lighter, more restless and with an increased probability of waking. Although the majority of this group may not have overt psychological difficulties, laboratory and clinical evidence indicates that they are more aroused and anxious and that this is manifested in a disrupted sleep pattern. In this sense their sleep problems may be a symptom of other psychological problems and it has been shown that as these problems become more intense then sleep disturbances generally get worse.

Sleep difficulties are relatively common in people with more overt psychiatric problems. The commonest reported problems are that of great difficulty in getting to sleep in anxious patients and of early morning awakening in moderate or severe depression. A small proportion of depressed patients report longer sleep durations than usual and this is typically combined with a difficulty in getting up in the morning. One complicating factor in determining the association between sleep disturbances and psychiatric problems is that many of the patients studied are receiving psychotropic medications, all of which are also known to give rise to changes in the sleep pattern.

In contrast to these various sleep difficulties, some people occasionally complain of excessive sleep (hypersomnia). The actual length of sleep time may not be the critical factor, given the normal variation in sleep duration, but the deciding factor is the complaint by the patient. There is a range of problems which can give rise to increased sleep durations and these include cerebral diseases involving the reticular formation and certain metabolic and toxic disorders. Included in the latter are hypoglycaemia, hypothyroidism, uraemia and hepatic encephalopathy. There is also a small group of specific syndromes which may involve cerebral dysfunction in the mid-brain, hypothalamus or brain stem and in which significant increases in sleeping are a characteristic feature.

Among the more dramatic disorders occurring during sleep are sleep walking, sleep talking and the so-called 'night terrors'. Sleep walking may occur at least once in approaching 15 per cent of children between 5 and 15 years, but is only recurrent in a much smaller group. Episodes take place during SWS and typically the sleeper moves around in a trance-like fashion and is unaware that anything strange has happened when questioned either immediately afterwards or the following morning. Sleep walking does not appear to be associated with psychological problems and tends to disappear with increasing age. Sleep talking often accompanies sleep walking and may also occur independently, most usually during the lighter stages of orthodox sleep. Night terrors are, as the term suggests, very frightening episodes often accompanied by screaming. Although they are immediately preceded by a state of SWS early in the night, the episode does not appear to take place during a sleep state. The EEG pattern is one of arousal and there is a great deal of autonomic activation but the individual appears to be unresponsive to environmental stimuli. Although these are very frightening and alarming experiences there is no strong evidence of concurrent psychological difficulties which might explain what has happened.

With the more common sleep problems involving reduced or interrupted sleep there is accumulating evidence that these are indicative of overt or underlying psychological difficulties. This gives rise to two important final points. First, it is becoming apparent that symptom-based treatment of sleep problems may ultimately be of relatively limited value and may actually be counter-productive, in that a drug dependence may be induced with the underlying problem still unresolved. It is being increasingly recognized that underlying problems should be dealt with and that if hypnotic medication is resorted to then it should be as a pharmacological aid over a crisis period rather than as a complete treatment approach. Requests for repeat prescriptions may therefore be regarded as an indication of a wider distress.

The second point is related, but a more general one, and it is that sleep is an integral part of the 24-hour biological and behavioural cycle. There are many links between the sleeping and waking states. The physical and behavioural activities of the day may often be reflected, either positively or negatively, in the quality of a night's sleep. Similarly, the quality of sleep can play a part in determining the mood and efficiency of the individual during the subsequent day.

- ### Recommended reading

Hartmann E. L. (1973) *The Functions of Sleep*. London, University Press.
Marks M. and Folkard S. (1984) Diurnal rhythms in cognitive performance. In: Nicholson J. and Bellof H. (ed.) *Psychology Survey No. 5*. Leicester, British Psychological Society.

5

Stress, emotion and illness

It is not uncommon to hear patients say that they feel their illness has been brought on by stress in their lives. What they usually mean by this is that they have been under a certain amount of pressure at home or at work and that this has affected them mentally or physically. Doctors, too, may report that certain symptoms or illnesses are triggered or exacerbated by stress factors.

What is really meant by such statements? Is it possible to characterize stressful situations and how can psychosocial pressure have an adverse effect on bodily processes? As we shall see, the answers to these questions are complex and, as yet, very incomplete. One fundamental problem lies with the use of the term 'stress' since it can be taken to refer not only to aspects of the environment but also to the individual's behaviour and to underlying physiological responses. As Lader (1979) has accurately observed, stress has become 'a convenient non-technical shorthand term which communicates our ignorance, not our knowledge'. In view of these conceptual problems, a major aim of this chapter is to examine what is meant by the term 'stress'. The concept of stress is discussed and some of the related physiological and psychological responses are described. Following this there is an outline of the relation between the psychological and physiological aspects of the emotional changes in response to a stressor. Finally, these findings are used as a basis for discussing the way in which stress factors might be associated with illness.

● 5.1. The nature of stress

a. Stress: what is it?

One of the primary problems with the term 'stress' is that it is used in a number of quite different ways. Thus it can be used to describe various unpleasant situations or events which are considered to be stressful. Alternatively, it may be used to describe the behavioural or physiological responses which occur when an individual is confronted by an unpleasant situation or stressor. A third view of stress regards it as a reflection of an incompatibility between the individual and his or her environment. This last approach combines elements of the first two since stress is thought to arise from the inappropriate or inadequate responses to certain environmental demands. Each of these three approaches is now considered.

i. Stress as a stimulus

Stimulus-based approaches to stress are concerned with identifying aspects of the environment which have an adverse effect on the individual. This view tends to be a rather simple mechanistic one which attempts to equate human stress with definitions arising from physics or engineering. Metals can withstand a certain amount of stress but they all have a threshold or 'yield point' and if this is exceeded then permanent damage will result. Correspondingly, stimulus-based definitions of human stress incorporate the idea that people also have a fixed capacity to withstand stress and if this is exceeded then adverse changes will occur.

This type of approach is therefore concerned with identifying stressful situations and determining how and why they have adverse effects on psychological and physiological processes. Many of these studies have focused on work environments and on various physical characteristics (e.g. ambient noise, heat, etc.) as well as job demands. Situations where work is under constant time pressure and where a large amount of information has to be processed are generally rated as stressful. Monotony and isolation also have unpleasant effects and situations in which the individual has little control over events are also found to be rated as stressful.

There are a number of problems in this type of approach. First, particular situations are not inherently stressful since there are large variations in the effects of environmental stressors. There are large individual differences in response to such environments (i.e. some people are disrupted by quite low levels of 'stress' whereas others have much higher 'yield points') and there are also variations within the same individual (i.e. on some occasions disruptions occur but on others there is no response to the same environmental demands). Logically, then, an environment can only be rated as stressful if the individual reacts to it in a particular way and specifying an environment's demand characteristics is not sufficient to classify it as stressful. We therefore need to examine the response-based definitions of stress.

ii. Stress as a response

Here stress is thought of as the response which is shown to an adverse or 'stressful' situation. This type of definition has developed from the work of Selye (1956) who viewed stress as the organism's response to environmental demands. On the basis of clinical observations and animal experiments, Selye maintained that the stress response is an inherent mechanism which comes into play whenever demands are placed on the organism and is therefore a defence reaction which has a protective and an adaptive function. He has described a three-stage process, referred to as the General Adaptation Syndrome (GAS), which is a general physiological reaction to all forms of stress. Some of the specific details of the physiological processes involved in this response are presented below. For the present it is sufficient to note that it involves an initial 'alarm' reaction followed by a 'resistance' stage, which represents a functional recovery to a level superior to the pre-stress state. If the stressor continues through the resistance stage then this will result in the final stage of 'exhaustion' in which there is a depletion and breakdown of the recovery processes which are activated in the first two stages.

The problem with Selye's model is that it is too inflexible and mechanistic. The stress response is viewed as a non-specific and automatic response to all stressors, including all illnesses but, as we shall see in later chapters, psychological reactions to physical illness can take many forms depending on the nature of the individual and the context within which an illness occurs. In focusing on physiological responses, the GAS provides a possible framework for understanding the way in which stress can result in physical illness but it more or less ignores the role of psychological responses to stress. The latter point is increasingly recognized as a serious weakness of the GAS model since human studies tend to show that the psychological responses to a stressor are determined by its psychological impact on the individual, as is now discussed.

iii. Stress as a perceived threat

This view of stress combines both stimulus and response elements and deals with many of the weaknesses of the two views described above. The best known proponent of this approach is Lazarus (1976) who maintains that stress occurs when there are demands on an individual which he or she cannot cope with or adjust to. Thus stress is not associated with a specific stimulus nor a specific response but arises when an individual perceives and evaluates a situation as threatening. This evaluation is based on an assessment of the demands of the situation and of the individual's capacity or 'coping mechanisms' for dealing with these demands. This can explain the individual variation in response to stressors since the individual's evaluation of the situation now becomes the key factor. Thus the intensity of any threat will depend on how well the individual feels he or she can deal with the situation. Situations which are perceived as threatening will give rise to emotional arousal, behavioural attempts to 'cope' and a range of underlying physiological changes.

This type of model seems a far more satisfactory basis for understanding human stress since it places an important emphasis on cognitive factors. Human beings do not appear to react automatically and invariantly to specific environmental stimuli but use perceptual and higher order mechanisms to interpret and evaluate their situation, as we saw in Chapter 2.

Lazarus has provided a number of sources of evidence to support this view. Among the most striking are studies in which he monitored psychological and physiological responses to some very grisly films with differing soundtracks or prior descriptions. For example, in one study, three separate groups watched the same film of industrial accidents showing a number of extremely nasty incidents (e.g. fingers being cut off and much worse). The first group was informed that the film was a mock-up involving actors and that the blood was not real. A second group was told that the events were real but the emphasis was placed on the importance of industrial safety and hence the educational lessons which could be drawn from the film. The third group was not given any prior information about the film. It was subsequently found that physiological stress responses were much lower in the first two groups who were able to cope with the horrors of the film either by denial (i.e. 'it's not really happening') or by rationalizing (i.e. 'it's important to learn from these mistakes').

The lesson which can be drawn from these studies is that specific situations or objects are threatening to the individual because they are perceived as such rather than because of some inherent characteristic. This view has been summarized by Cox (1978) and also provides a convenient guide to the remaining contents of this chapter:

> Stress, it is argued, can only be sensibly defined as a perceptual phenomenon arising from a comparison between the demand on the person and his ability to cope. An imbalance in this mechanism, when coping is important, gives rise to the experience of stress and to stress response. The latter represents attempts at coping with the source of stress. Coping is both psychological (involving cognitive and behavioural strategies) and physiological. If normal coping is ineffective, stress is prolonged and abnormal responses may occur. The occurrence and prolonged exposure to stress *per se* may give rise to functional and structural damage. The progress of these events is subject to great individual variation.

b. Physiological and psychological responses to stress

A great deal of the earlier work on stress, stemming from Selye and others, has been based on animal studies and has investigated neuroendocrine and other physiological changes to stress. In addition to developing this research, more recent work has also begun to investigate the effects of stress on behaviour, particularly in response to psychosocial stressors. As we observed above, more recent emphases in this area are on the individual's appraisal of his environment rather than on the automatic response to specific threatening stimuli. In this section there will therefore be a separate consideration of physiological and psychological processes but it is important to point out that these are not separate aspects of the response to stress. They are different levels of analysis, which ultimately need to be seen and understood in conjunction.

i. Physiological responses

It is now generally accepted that the adrenal gland plays a central role in regulating the responses of an animal to the threats or demands imposed on it. Situated above the kidney, the adrenal gland consists of two separate areas, the adrenal medulla and the adrenal cortex, which appear to be involved in different aspects of the stress response. The adrenal medulla is mainly, but not exclusively, concerned with the more immediate responses whereas the changes produced by the adrenal cortex are more involved in long-term responses, such as those corresponding to Selye's resistance stage of the GAS. This division may have been overstated in the past since there is now evidence that the adrenal cortex may also be important for bringing about changes occurring during the initial or 'alarm' stage of stress response.

The initial responses to a stress situation appear to be brought about by increased activity in the sympathetic nervous system which acts in conjunction with the catecholamine secretions of the adrenal medulla. In such a situation the adrenal medulla releases adrenaline or noradrenaline, or both, into the bloodstream. There is evidence that the relative amounts of adrenaline and noradrenaline released may be determined by different types of stressor (Frankenhaeuser, 1975). Increased sympathetic activation brings about a rapid change in cardiovascular activity which allows immediate physical exertion, which in turn can be supported by the catecholamine secretions and the resultant changes in metabolic activity. The physiological responses to the catecholamines include increases in heart rate and blood pressure, peripheral vasoconstriction and the mobilization of the liver energy store through the release of glucose stored as glycogen in the liver. More recently it has been recognized that the endorphin/encephalin system may also play a role in the initial, active responses to a stressor by providing analgesia and inhibiting pain-motivated withdrawal behaviour (Bolles and Fanselow, 1982).

These initial responses have been collectively referred to as the 'emergency' or 'alarm' reactions which rapidly prepare the organism to deal with the demands placed on it and therefore seem to be associated with stressful situations in which active coping is required (*see below*). This rapid mobilization of bodily resources was described by Cannon as preparing the body for 'fight or flight' (i.e. for an immediate physical response). As we shall see later, there are indications that such a response may not necessarily be most appropriate for many psychosocial stressors.

Although this immediate response system has been mainly investigated in animals, a range of psychosocial situations appear to bring about similar sorts of changes in catecholamine production and these include taking exams, admission to hospital, car driving and working in both over-stimulating and under-stimulating environments. Moreover the general pattern of findings shows that the level of catecholamine excretion can be equated with the degree of emotional arousal reported by the individual.

If a stressor is relatively minor or of a short duration, there may be little further physiological response over and above these immediate ones. However, if the stress situation is very intense or continues over a period of time, then the response system involving the adrenal cortex will be increasingly involved. The activity of the adrenal cortex is largely regulated by the blood level of adrenocorticotrophic hormone (ACTH), which is released by the anterior pituitary. When information concerning a sustained or intense stressor has been processed by the central nervous system, it is then passed on to the hypothalamus (*see* Chapter 3). The hypothalamus secretes a substance called corticotrophin-releasing factor (CRF) which stimulates the anterior pituitary to release ACTH, which in turn has a direct effect on the endocrine activity of the adrenal cortex. The latter produces three groups of steroid hormones, namely the mineralocorticoids, the glucocorticoids and the androgens. The release of ACTH appears to have its primary effect on the production of glucocorticoids, the main one of which in humans is hydrocortisone. In response to stressors, the glucocorticoids bring about a number of discrete physiological changes including blocking the inflammatory response and raising blood sugar levels. Many of the changes following on the release of glucocorticoids are believed to play a primary role in what Selye referred to as the 'resistance' stage in the GAS.

In humans the activity of the pituitary–adrenal system can be monitored by measuring the plasma and urine levels of 17-hydroxycorticosteroids (17-OHCS). Elevated 17-OHCS levels have been found in response to a range of psychosocial stressors, including hospitalization, exams, driving and during the anticipation of a perceived stressful event such as surgery. Hence one of the key workers in this area, Mason (1968), has concluded that raised 17-OHCS levels are not related to well-defined emotional states but 'appear to reflect a relatively undifferentiated response state of emotional arousal or involvement, perhaps in anticipation of activity or coping'. As an integral part of this reponse, glucocorticoid release stimulates glucose metabolism by various means and in doing so increases the availability of blood glucose for muscle and brain cells. In this way, the pituitary–adrenal system can provide fuel for physical and mental activity. However, it is not fully understood how these hormones facilitate the various coping processes which are used for dealing with sustained stress. This is a convenient point for turning our attention to the nature of the behavioural or psychological responses which are subsumed under the general heading of coping.

ii. Psychological responses
In very general terms the reactions to stress involve the following stages:

    1. An initial alarm and shock state which results in the endocrine and physiological changes outlined above. These changes are accompanied by emotional reactions such as feeling anxious or threatened.

    2. Coping strategies are activated as the individual attempts to find a way of dealing with the subjectively harmful or unpleasant situation.

    3. If these strategies are successful, the alarm reaction and anxiety state subside.

    4. If these strategies fail and the stressor continues to affect behaviour, a range of psychological reactions, including depression and withdrawal, may occur.

When viewed in these general terms, it is clear that the consequences of failing to cope can be serious. As a result individuals need to develop ways of adapting to and dealing with stressful situations. This section will therefore be primarily concerned with looking at the nature of these coping processes. This concept of coping derives from the work of Lazarus (1976) who identifies two broad categories of coping. The first category involves actual behaviour which attempts to change the individual's unsatisfactory relationship with his or her environment (problem focused). The most obvious example of this type of coping is to escape from the unpleasant situation; however, this may not always be possible. Failing this, the impact of a stressor may be minimized or even eliminated by prior preparation for it. This preparation may consist of increasing one's skills or knowledge, which may be effective for dealing with the threat of an event such as a future exam. Alternatively, it may involve thinking through various aspects of a stress situation and its likely impact, thereby preparing oneself adequately for the reality of the event. As we saw in the first chapter on pain, there is evidence that providing appropriate information prior to surgery appears to be helpful for patients in coping with the subsequent pain and discomfort and may even help in the recovery process.

The second group of coping processes identified by Lazarus have been described as 'palliative' or emotion focused since they are concerned with softening the impact of a stressor. Thus they have an analgesic type of function and may involve either psychological or artificial means. The former includes such responses as denial, in which the individual refuses to acknowledge all or some of the threat of a situation, and intellectualization, in which the individual somehow detaches himself or herself emotionally from the situation. Both these responses can be seen in the psychological reactions of patients to physical illness as will be outlined in Chapter 12. Up to a point, such strategies may serve a protective function and may enable an individual to maintain a reasonable equilibrium through a difficult period. However, there is the danger that they may make it more difficult for the individual to resolve a problem situation and hence prolong or exacerbate the threat.

Non-behavioural palliative responses include the use of alcohol, tranquillizers and relaxation techniques, all of which may reduce the impact of a stressor on the individual. There are also advantages and disadvantages of responding in this way. If an individual is debilitated by the worry and tension associated with a stressful situation, minimizing the emotional responses may then make it easier to employ more direct coping strategies to deal with the problem. Again there is a danger that direct action may be delayed or prevented by resorting to palliative means. However, there are some stresses for which no clear solution may exist (e.g. the problems of looking after someone with a chronic physical or psychological problem) and palliation may be the only way for an individual to cope.

A very large number of different coping strategies are included in these two broad categories of coping (i.e. problem focused and emotion focused). Studies of the way people cope with stressful life events have shown that both types of coping are used by the same individual. Moreover people are generally able to change their way of coping to fit the demands of a particular situation. Thus some situations, such as work problems, are more commonly associated with higher levels of problem-focused coping whereas others, such as health problems, give rise to more emotion-focused coping.

Marked emotional changes may take place following chronic exposure to stress. If various coping strategies fail, the individual may begin to feel both hopeless and helpless. Thus he or she may regard the situation as one for which there is no solution and increasingly see himself or herself as unable to control the events in his or her life. Hopelessness and helplessness are both likely to give rise to depressive feelings and in the extreme may lead to suicidal thoughts and actions. Following the stress of a chronic illness, some patients may literally give up hope and when this occurs they become not only emotionally disturbed but also appear to be more vulnerable to further physical illnesses.

For the individual the most obvious aspect of the occurrence of stress will be what he or she feels at the time, and this would probably consist of one or more of a number of such emotional changes as anger, depression or anxiety. Indeed these negative emotional states have been described by Lazarus (1976) as the stress emotions since he sees them as arising primarily from stress situations. Although this may be too much of a generalization, it does nevertheless indicate that it is necessary to consider the nature of emotion and this is done later in this chapter. Before that, there is an outline of the many factors which can mediate or modify the response to stress.

c. Factors mediating the response to stress

The preceding section has presented a very general account of the physiological and psychological responses which are taken to occur as part of the response to stress. It is important to note that this is not a fixed pattern of changes which inevitably follows the impact of a stressor. For any individual the nature of the response may be determined by many factors including personality, previous experience of similar or related situations and the context within which the stress is experienced. Some of these factors will be outlined now.

i. Prior experience

In Chapter 8, the importance of early experience in child development is emphasized and similar conclusions also seem to hold for the response to stress. Experimental studies have shown that rats, subjected to a certain amount of stress early in life, could 'cope' much better with later stress than rats who had not received this early stimulation. One clear differentiating characteristic between these two groups of animals was found in their physiological responses. The former animals showed a prompt response whereas the non-stimulated animals responded more slowly and less effectively. From such studies and related observations on child development it has been concluded that infantile stimulation produces various advantages in later adaptation to stressful environments (Levine, 1975).

More specific experience with stressful situations also appears to result in an improved ability to cope. In a study of parachutists, it was found that experienced and inexperienced parachutists showed quite different reactions prior to a jump. The experienced ones reported becoming increasingly less fearful from the time of the decision to jump up to the actual jump, whereas the reverse was found for the inexperienced group. It is as if experienced parachutists are able to anticipate and deal with the stress of the jump in advance so that, by the time of the jump, they are less likely to experience anxiety that would interfere with performance. Specific experience of this type therefore provides knowledge about a situation and places the individual into a more predictable position where he or she can be aware of how his or her own behaviour will affect and be affected by a potentially stressful environment.

ii. Information

This arises directly from the last point made above, since experience can provide the individual with information about an impending event. It is also possible to provide people with information in order to facilitate adaptive reactions to stress. In a series of studies of surgical patients, Janis (1958) has shown that preparatory information describing the operation and postoperative pain can aid the recovery process. However, it would now appear that the success of providing information is partly dependent on the style of coping adopted by the patient. Thus there are variations in the amount and type of information that will be beneficial to patients for dealing with the stress of surgery. It may be necessary to consider the role of personality differences in determining the overall response to stress.

iii. Individual differences

As we shall see in Chapter 12, people can differ quite radically in their response to the stresses associated with illness. While a large number attempt to cope with the demands and inconvenience of physical illness in a realistic fashion, there are still individuals who react in ways which may appear puzzling to those who deal with them. Some people try to protect themselves from the full impact of the stresses by denying, playing down or emotionally detaching themselves from the situation. With these patients, providing information may not always have a particularly beneficial effect and in some cases may actually increase their anxiety level. Other patients may become excessively critical or even outwardly aggressive in their attempts to cope with the stresses of an illness or a surgical procedure. These specific reactions may be partly determined by the context of the stressor but are more likely to arise from the underlying personality of the patient.

Personality differences have also been found to influence the impact of life stress on health. One useful personality measure used in this area has been the concept of 'locus of control'. This refers to the degree of control which individuals think they have over what happens to them (*see* Chapter 7 for a more detailed account). There is evidence that individuals who see themselves as having control over their environment are less likely to be emotionally disrupted by mounting stress (McFarlane et al., 1980).

It has also been claimed that there are consistent individual differences in the pattern of physiological responses to stress and emotion-provoking stimuli. Some individuals may show a greater cardiovascular response whereas others might show a more marked change in gastric activity. It is further claimed that stress-related illnesses will be more likely to affect these more active response systems. Thus the 'gastric responders' may be more prone to gastric ulcers whereas 'cardiovascular responders' might be more prone to high blood pressure as the result of sustained stress. It has been argued that these response specificities can be detected early in life and are a consistent characteristic, but the evidence is not totally convincing since not everyone appears to have a dominant response system of this type. Moreover, people also appear to vary in the relative responsiveness of different systems. Even so, it is an interesting notion, which may be applicable to some individuals and may provide a way of identifying vulnerability to specific disorders.

iv. Perceived control
Since situations which are perceived as stressful are ones which the individual feels he or she will have difficulty in coping with, it is not surprising that control or perceived control appears to be an important factor. The evidence from studies of patients rated in terms of their 'locus of control' has been mentioned above. In addition to this there are a number of human and animal studies indicating that lack of control over unpleasant or stressful stimuli is associated with a greater vulnerability to physical illness. Weiss (1972) has shown this using an experimental situation in which two rats are given electric shocks but where only one can control the number of shocks and the other merely receives them. The rat which has control over shocks by learning to avoid them is found to develop significantly fewer ulcers than the passive rat, even though they both receive an identical number of shocks. Correspondingly many harmful and distressing situations appear to be the ones where individuals feel entirely helpless, believing that nothing they can do will significantly alter the outcome.

v. Social support
All the variables discussed so far are related to different aspects of the individual. Not surprisingly research on the impact of stressful events has also shown that the social system, in which the individual exists, can exert an influence on the reactions to stress. One aspect of the social environment which appears to be important is the support or access to other helpful and empathic individuals. As we see in Chapter 8 on child development, emotional support plays an important

role in early emotional and social development, which in turn can considerably influence later behaviour. There is even evidence that severe emotional deprivation in early life can give rise to specific neuroendocrine changes, such as deficiencies in ACTH and growth hormone. Thus, in general terms, insufficient early social support can give rise to physical and behavioural abnormalities, including a reduced ability to withstand stress.

More specifically, there is evidence that responses to stress can be mediated by the social support available to the individual during a stressful situation. Most commonly this support will come from the family but it may also arise from the community. The recovery of patients from strokes can be significantly affected by the mutual understanding or empathy shown by their families.

In some careful studies of the impact of life stress, Brown (1976) has shown that women are less likely to develop a psychiatric disorder if they have a close and confiding relationship with another individual. This does not appear to be a causal relationship since poor social support does not necessarily increase the risk of psychiatric illness. Social support appears to be a protective factor which somehow lessens the impact of a stressor on the individual. In view of these findings, it is perhaps not surprising to find that the loss of a close relationship, which represents a sudden and severe loss of support, has been found to be rated as the most stressful of all life events and is associated with a significant subsequent increase in both psychiatric and physical illness. The specific effects of bereavement are examined more fully later in this chapter, but for the present it serves to illustrate the possible protective function of a close relationship for the individual.

This account of factors mediating the response to stress makes it clear that this is a complex topic in which many inter-related factors must be taken into account. For any individual the nature and magnitude of a stressful experience will ultimately be determined by these and other factors such as inherited characteristics and specifically learned responses. This complexity makes it apparent why Lader (1979) has called the term 'stress' a convenient short-hand term. It may be easy to say that an emotional response or even an illness is due to stress but it must now be apparent that there are great dangers in oversimplifying in this area.

• 5.2. The psychophysiology of emotion

In stress situations the individual's primary experience will usually consist of the associated emotional changes since the most obvious aspect of stress is what is actually felt by the individual. Someone is more likely to seek medical help complaining of emotional and physiological changes which accompany stress, rather than because of the situation itself. Indeed the doctor's task may consist of attempting to identify the stresses which are giving rise to anxiety and tension as a basis for dealing with the patient. Many people seek help for emotional problems or for associated physical problems (e.g. palpitations; fatigue; tension headaches; sleep difficulties). Thus as part of a general understanding of the nature of stress, it is necessary to examine how emotions are experienced and the nature of the links between psychological and physiological processes.

a. The study of emotion

Psychologists tend to make a broad distinction between emotions which are pleasant and those which are unpleasant and it is the latter which are experienced in stressful situations. The emotion which is experienced under stress therefore represents the individual's own awareness of and reaction to a particular situation. The subjective and private quality of emotions inevitably makes them difficult to describe and investigate. However, it has been possible to investigate emotions in three quite distinct ways.

i. First, we can ask people to describe how they are feeling and these verbal reports provide an account of the individual's subjective awareness of emotional changes. This can be difficult for it is not always possible to find words to capture what one is feeling. Various self-report techniques based on questionnaires or check-lists have been developed and these can give an indication of the degree and type of emotional change which has been experienced. These techniques have been found to be of clinical value in monitoring the progress of patients with emotional problems, particularly in response to different types of treatment.

ii. A second approach to the study of emotions has involved the observation of behavioural changes associated with emotional states. In particular there are quite specific changes in facial expression, body movements and posture which are found with different emotions. This non-verbal 'leakage' of emotional expression can provide useful clues for understanding the emotions experienced by other people and can therefore be potentially valuable in a diagnostic interview. At times there may even be a mismatch between what patients say about how they are feeling and the way in which this is said. A more detailed discussion of these non-verbal messages about someone's emotional state is given in Chapter 10 with particular reference to clinical interviewing.

iii. The third and probably most extensively used approach adopted by psychologists in studying emotions has been a psychophysiological one. This involves the use of electrical monitoring equipment to record the activity of various physiological functions, which can then be related to the emotion which is experienced. As we saw earlier, emotional arousal in response to a stressor will result in sympathetic nervous system activation, coupled with a range of neuroendocrine changes. Many of the bodily changes which are associated with sympathetic activation can be detected by applying electrodes and recording the small voltage changes which occur. In the last chapter we also saw that various brain wave states can be detected using electrodes applied to the scalp and that these states broadly correlate with different levels of alertness or arousal. Similarly it is possible to monitor a range of bodily responses in order to get an idea of the degree of emotional arousal experienced.

Many bodily responses may take place during emotional states and probably the most widely investigated are the following:

i. *Cardiovascular.* Activation of the sympathetic nervous system brings changes in heart rate, blood pressure and blood volume. Specific techniques are available for monitoring and measuring changes in each of these.

ii. *Electrodermal.* Since the sweat glands are innervated by the sympathetic nervous system, they provide a good indication of sympathetic activation. Electrodermal activity is generally measured in terms of the conductance between two electrodes placed on the skin, usually on the hand. In addition to measuring the increases in skin conduction associated with emotional changes, useful information can also be obtained from the latency and recovery time of the change.

iii. Muscle potentials. Muscle tension frequently accompanies emotional changes. This can be detected by using surface electrodes to record the electrical activity of specific muscle groups.

iv. Brain waves. As we saw in the previous chapter, the brain is constantly emitting small electrical potentials which can be recorded by applying surface electrodes on the scalp. The resultant polygraph record is called the electroencephalogram (EEG) and has been found to be correlated with different states of alertness or arousal. It is also possible to investigate specific waveforms reflecting the response to a single stimulus and these 'evoked responses' can be quantified in a number of discrete ways.

Of the above responses, the first two groups provide an indication of the activation of the sympathetic nervous system and the latter two give indirect and direct measures of central nervous system activity. In addition to these a number of other bodily responses are sometimes studied in psychophysiological studies of emotion. These include respiratory changes, general and local temperature changes, pupil dilatation and constriction, salivary output and gastric motility.

Physiological activation seems to provide an indication of the degree of emotional arousal rather than of the exact nature of the emotion which is experienced, since a fairly similar pattern of changes is found in many different emotional states. In order to determine the nature of an emotion it is necessary to ask subjects what they are experiencing as well as relying on the observation of behavioural and non-verbal changes. There are also some situations in which the subjective and the physiological aspects of emotion do not appear to correlate. Some individuals who report marked emotional changes do not show significant changes in the peripheral physiological indices. Also the reverse pattern can be found and this should serve to guard against an oversimplified view of the psychophysiology of emotion, in which subjective feelings are completely equated with peripheral physiological changes. The nature of the relationship between subjective feelings and bodily changes is now examined.

b. How is emotion experienced?

Probably the central issue in the investigation of emotions has revolved around the way in which people experience emotions and the relation between the physiological and psychological processes involved. One of the first formal views of this subject was put forward by William James at the end of the last century. He offered a novel analysis of emotional experience since he argued that bodily changes occurred in response to a particular event and that the subjective awareness or experience of these changes corresponded to the emotion. For example, he argued that a frightening experience, such as an encounter with a wild animal, will produce bodily responses such as trembling and the awareness of these responses will result in our feeling afraid. Thus James (1890) contended that: 'We feel sorry because we cry, angry because we strike, afraid because we tremble'. For James, the subjective experience of emotion is therefore secondary to the bodily responses to an arousing event. Different emotional states were thought to be dependent on different patterns of bodily changes.

A very strong series of arguments against this theory were put forward and developed by Cannon and others in the 1920s and 1930s. Cannon argued that the total surgical separation of the viscera from the central nervous system did not change emotional behaviour. If emotional experience depended on the recognition of different patterns of visceral response, then emotions should be radically affected by such a surgical separation. Even more critically, Cannon argued that the same visceral changes accompany quite different emotional states and even occur with non-emotional states. Furthermore, if specific visceral changes are artificially induced this does not result in the experience of the associated emotion. Finally, Cannon maintained that the viscera were rather slow and insensitive in their mode of response and that the immediacy of emotional experiences could not therefore depend on these responses.

In answer to James' 'peripheral' theory of emotions, Cannon developed a 'central' theory which maintained that both the bodily changes and the subjective experience of emotion are controlled by the activation of particular structures in the central nervous system. He regarded the thalamus as the key brain area which controlled the psychological and physiological changes. Since Cannon's time further research has shown that this conclusion was incorrect and that the limbic system and the hypothalamus appear to be critical areas for the neural control of emotion (*see* Chapter 3).

The 'central' theories of emotion, which are fairly widely accepted now, are based on the notion that different parts of the limbic system and associated brain regions somehow control different types of emotional behaviour. The evidence comes from studies in which different brain areas are either stimulated or lesioned and the effects on behaviour observed. From these studies it is possible to conclude that these structures do have a direct involvement in emotional behaviour but that the control of emotion also depends on the interaction with other brain regions, particularly the cerebral cortex.

Peripheral and central theories of emotion have in common the fact that different emotions are assumed to depend on different patterns of physiological activation. In the case of the former, the patterning of the visceral responses determines the emotional state, and in the latter, specific brain regions directly mediate different emotional behaviours. However, the evidence on this issue is far from conclusive since it is quite difficult to relate different emotions to different patterns of physiological activity. Although earlier research had purported to show that different types of emotion could be correlated with different patterns of catecholamine secretion, more recent evidence has tended to cast some doubt on this. This evidence indicates that while the degree of emotional arousal can be gauged from the levels of catecholamine secretion, these do not specify the nature of the emotional response. Moreover a pure physiologically based theory of emotion inevitably has difficulties incorporating the role of the social environment and the individual's perception of environmental events as a possible determinant of emotion. It is these very factors which have given rise to a third view of the way emotion is experienced. This is the view of Schachter (1975) which places considerable emphasis on cognitive and environmental factors in determining the emotional response.

Schachter (1975) maintains that direct stimulation of brain regions or the experimental production of the peripheral correlates of emotions will only produce emotional behaviour in the presence of appropriate external stimuli. Hence he concludes that any physiologically based theory must specify how physiological processes interact with stimulus and cognitive or situational factors. He has derived some ingenious experiments for substantiating this viewpoint. In these experiments subjects are injected with epinephrine (adrenaline), which stimulates the sympathetic nervous system, causing increases in perspiration, heart rate and rate of breathing, as well as other peripheral physiological changes which normally accompany emotional experiences. Some subjects were informed of the sorts of physiological changes to expect whereas others were not told anything or were actually provided with incorrect information. There was also a control group which was injected with an inert saline solution.

Just before the injection could take effect, subjects were put into a situation which would ordinarily lead to a specific emotional response. They were in a waiting room with one other person who they thought was a fellow volunteer but was actually a confederate of the experimenter. This other person had been instructed to behave in one of a number of extreme ways to elicit an emotional response from the subject. Thus he might start joking and fooling around to amuse the subject or he might get very irritated and angry with the experiment and actively criticize or insult the experimenter and even the subject. The responses of the subjects were observed through a one-way mirror and afterwards they were required to complete questionnaires concerning their emotional state.

The main results have been summarized by Schachter (1975) as follows:

i. Given a state of epinephrine-induced sympathetic arousal, subjects may be manipulated into states of euphoria and anger if they have *not* been provided with appropriate explanations of their bodily state.

ii. Given the same state of arousal, subjects are virtually non-manipulable into such emotion or mood states if they have a proper explanation of their bodily feelings (e.g. 'my heart is pounding because of the injection').

iii. Subjects injected with a placebo (saline) are less manipulable into euphoric and angry states.

Although there have been some criticisms of the validity of these experiments, extensions of the theory have led to further supportive evidence. For example, male subjects who are shown pictures of females and provided with false feedback about their heartbeats report feeling most roused by photographs seen while their heart rate changed dramatically and subsequently rated those photographs as the most attractive. Thus Schachter's theory places a primary importance on the way the experience of emotion can depend on specific situations and on the individual's perception of those situations. When an appropriate stimulus causes emotional arousal, the individual strives to make sense of this both within the present context and in relation to previous similar experiences.

There are two important practical points which arise from Schachter's theory. First, many prescribed medications can produce physiological and emotional side-effects which often come as a surprise to the patient. If these are not expected they may be incorrectly related to environmental events. Thus it is important to keep patients informed not only of the psychophysiological effects of medication but of other bodily changes which may occur in their lives and which could give rise to spurious emotional and behavioural responses. Second, recent approaches in the psychological treatment of emotional problems, particularly depression, also provide links with Schachter's theory. The so-called cognitive therapies (*see* Chapter 14) encourage patients to reinterpret events and experiences more positively as a way of dealing with depressive thoughts. These approaches are based on the premise that an individual's emotions and behaviour are largely determined by the way he or she structures or interprets the world.

Having emphasized the importance of cognitive determinants of emotional experience, it is equally important not to overlook the physiological processes. More recent work has indicated that autonomic arousal during emotions may not be as non-specific as Schachter has claimed and that there may be some specific autonomic and central nervous system correlates of different emotions (*see* Leventhal and Tomarken, 1986, for a good review). Cognitions need to be seen together with peripheral and central physiological mechanisms as integral parts of the whole process. Emotional states appear to be a function both of cognitive or situational factors, and of physiological arousal.

- ### 5.3. Stress and illness

Everything that has been discussed so far in this chapter has been concerned with understanding the physiological, behavioural and emotional responses to environmental demands. We have seen that situations which are perceived as threatening will evoke emotional responses together with coping strategies and that a range of physiological and neuroendocrine processes underlie these psychological changes.

The main reason for outlining this evidence is to provide a basis for looking at stress-related or psychosomatic disease. The term 'psychosomatic' has been avoided up to now as it has some unfortunate connotations. It can be used by people in a rather dismissive way (e.g. someone's physical problems may be dismissed because 'they are all psychosomatic'). Hence psychosomatic illnesses are sometimes thought of as not 'real' illnesses and therefore not worth serious scientific and medical attention. A second problem is that in the past psychosomatic medicine was an umbrella term for a rather diffuse and unproductive approach to certain illnesses, such as peptic ulcers, ulcerative colitis, bronchial asthma and essential hypertension, which were held to be caused by unconscious emotional conflicts. Although this was interesting work which hinted at the importance of psychological factors in certain disease processes, it contained a large number of rather nebulous and fairly untestable propositions. Moreover, it attempted to link psychological factors (e.g. emotional conflicts) to biological changes (e.g. peptic ulcers) without any sound framework for considering the intervening psychophysiological mechanisms. More recent work is based on psychophysiological lines and attempts to elucidate the physiological consequences of psychosocial situations, as outlined earlier in this chapter.

This section will have three broad aims. First, there is an attempt to identify those psychosocial situations which have been statistically associated with increased vulnerability to disease. Following this, there is an outline of some possible mechanisms which could account for the links between psychosocial stress and illness. Finally, some psychological approaches to the treatment of stress-related illness are presented.

a. Psychosocial factors and disease

A great deal of the work in this area tends to be epidemiological. In other words, it makes use of large-scale surveys of the prevalence of defined illnesses in populations and attempts to identify psychosocial factors which appear to be associated with high-risk individuals. A number of psychosocial factors have been found to be associated with increased prevalence of various illnesses and these include the following:

    i. Social class.
    ii. Occupational factors.
    iii. Lifestyle.
    iv. Life change or 'events'.
    v. Bereavement and loss.

i. Social class

Not only are many common fatal illnesses (e.g. cancer, heart disease, etc.) comparatively more prevalent in semi-skilled and unskilled workers (OPCS, 1978), but also there are higher levels of self-reported chronic disease in these groups (OPCS, 1983). The reasons for this are still unclear and are almost certainly very complex. For example, such factors as diet, smoking, housing conditions, employment (and unemployment) and the poorer availability and use of medical resources have all been suggested as contributory. It is beyond the scope of this book to discuss the relation between social class and illness but it needs to be mentioned in the context of the present discussion.

ii. Occupational factors

With some occupations, such as coal mining, there is an increased risk of certain physical illnesses because of the known health hazards involved in the work. These are significant occupational factors in disease but fall outside the present discussion since the emphasis here is confined to the role of psychosocial factors. Among the latter, the type of work as well as the physical and social attributes of the work environment have been found to be associated with higher levels of certain physical and psychological illnesses.

As we saw in the previous chapter, shift work may be associated with increased ill-health, at least partly because it can disrupt circadian rhythms and social behaviour. In addition to this, work involving long hours and in physically adverse conditions (e.g. cramped, noisy and poorly illuminated) can give rise to more time off work for health reasons. Changes in the working environment (e.g. to a different line of work or in the level of responsibility) have been found in association with significantly higher rates of myocardial infarction in the year following such changes. Increased health hazards have also been shown to arise from the extremes of job demands. Those who are engaged in boring, repetitive work suffer more frequently from depression, sleep difficulties and stomach disorders than control subjects. Correspondingly, individuals judged to hold responsible jobs with high levels of demand and pressure are also found to have a significantly higher risk of certain physical disorders, including high blood pressure and gastric ulceration.

A point to note with findings of this type is that they do not inevitably apply to all individuals. Many people can cope quite satisfactorily with adverse or demanding work environments and some even appear to thrive in the most trying conditions. This reiterates the point made at the beginning of this chapter about response-based definitions of stress. Jobs and working environments are not inherently stressful since some people will be unaffected by them. Rather it is the difficulty in coping with the demands, changes or monotony of certain occupations which appears to make those situations unpleasant and increase the risk of ill-health.

Unemployment is also associated with higher levels of physical and psychological complaints. Factors such as the major life change involved and the loss of self-esteem appear to be involved here and these are considered below. For the present, these factors serve to illustrate that work meets not only financial but also social and psychological needs for the individual. Failure to meet those needs, whether through unsatisfactory or non-existent employment, can apparently carry a high personal cost in terms of mental and physical wellbeing.

There are methodological problems with any study investigating the effects on health of either unemployment or specific types of employment. The problem is in finding appropriate control or comparison groups against which differences can be measured. There is always the possibility that certain sorts of jobs may attract certain types of individual either for positive (i.e. by choice) or negative reasons (i.e. no one else would do that job). If this happens then one is not just seeing specific occupational effects on health but a complex interaction of personality, social and occupational factors. The same can be said for the effects of many other variables on health and should be borne firmly in mind when evaluating the evidence in this area. Despite these methodological problems there is now clear evidence from prospective studies of school leavers that unemployment *per se* can have adverse health effects on young adults (Banks and Jackson, 1982).

iii. *Lifestyle*

This refers to certain aspects of an individual's personality and is mentioned because it has been the focus of a fair amount of recent work in relation to coronary heart disease. Most of this work has centred around the Type A/B personality dimension. In a review of the literature, Jenkins (1976) concludes that one of the most significant psychosocial predictors of coronary heart disease is a competitive, striving, time-pressured lifestyle. This is the Type A personality classification which is sometimes referred to as the coronary-prone behaviour pattern. Type B individuals, in contrast, are those with a more relaxed and calm style of living.

Type A behaviour has been consistently linked with increased incidence and prevalence of coronary heart disease. Even when the other risk factors (e.g. smoking, cholesterol level, etc.) are controlled, the incidence of coronary heart disease and the death rate from that disease are twice as high in Type A as in Type B individuals. It is argued that, in addition to responding to environmental demands in a less adaptive way, Type A individuals also create stress for themselves by their time-urgent and competitive lifestyle. While there are all sorts of methodological and conceptual problems with the Type A/B classification, the magnitude of the differences in vulnerability to heart disease cannot be ignored. Moreover, there is increasing evidence that interventions to reduce or minimize Type A behaviour are effective in reducing the risk of further myocardial infarction.

iv. Life change or 'events'

In recent years there have been a number of studies investigating the relationship between changes in someone's life situation and the onset of illness. This follows from the work of Holmes and Rahe (1967) and others who maintain that life changes or life events require adjustments in the life pattern of an individual and that this will be stressful. They have focused on the impact of life changes which would be rated as negative (e.g. divorce) as well as those which are positive (e.g. promotion) and have devised a questionnaire to elicit the number of such changes which have occurred in the 2 years preceding the time of testing. These studies have shown that life events cluster significantly in a 2-year period preceding an illness and that the onset of an illness can be predicted by the total number of life events. Thus they maintain that it is possible to quantify the impact of life changes and that high levels of life change are correlated with the onset of disease.

This earlier work has been subject to a great deal of criticism on methodological grounds (Rabkin and Struening, 1976; Cohen, 1979). It was based on a rather simple stimulus-based approach to stress and has the problem that people have to report life events retrospectively which can introduce all sorts of biases. Also it emphasized the negative effects of life changes and ignores the fact that many people may directly benefit from a life change or may undergo life events without developing a subsequent illness. As a result, recent work on these lines has concentrated more on the impact of events on the individual and this is seen to be a function of the appraisal and coping ability of the individual as well as the social support available (Craig and Brown, 1984). Also there is now a greater focus on negative life events since these have been found to be more correlated with subsequent illness.

Retrospective studies of the occurrence of illnesses over quite long time periods (e.g. 20 years) in someone's life have shown that illnesses do not appear to be distributed at random but often appear in clusters. Furthermore, these clusters appeared most often when a person was experiencing difficulties in adapting to various negatively rated life changes. Many different negative life events were found to be associated with an increase in the occurrence of major and minor illnesses. The association between negatively rated life events and illness is interesting and important but, again, it should not necessarily be thought of as causal. It might be the case that a third and as yet unknown factor could account for both the problems in adapting to life events and the susceptibility to illness. For the present, the most general interpretation of these findings is that negatively appraised life events will result in physiological and psychological changes, which in turn will directly or indirectly give rise to disease (*see* section on some possible mechanisms *below*).

v. Bereavement and loss

The life events which are consistently rated as most unpleasant and requiring most adjustment appear to be those involving a personal loss, particularly of a close individual, such as a spouse. Some research workers in this area believe that a generalized sense of loss (actual, potential or imagined) or bereavement is a significant factor in the onset of disease. They contend that loss and bereavement can give rise to an emotional response of hopelessness and helplessness which results in the individual literally 'giving up'. When this happens, the individual can no longer cope, psychologically and biologically, with environmental demands. If the individual has a predisposition to a disease, then being in this psychological state will make the disease more likely to occur because the body will be made less capable of dealing effectively with the processes which give rise to the disease.

Many studies have shown that the recently bereaved are much more likely to develop physical and psychological symptoms. There is also evidence that the bereaved have a higher mortality rate in the 6 months following the death of a spouse (Parkes, 1975). Bereavement is distressing for many reasons and these will vary from person to person. The grief reaction appears to pass through a number of phases with recurrent pangs of depression and again this varies in its duration. It would appear that those who show a strong initial grief reaction and who are able to express their emotions are able to make the best psychological and physiological adjustment. In contrast, there appears to be a less satisfactory outcome for the bereaved person who has had an over-reliant relationship with the deceased, who has reacted badly to previous separations, who has limited social support or who is experiencing other stresses. These individuals appear to be most at risk in terms of their susceptibility to subsequent disease.

As with other psychosocial stressors, there is increasing evidence that the way in which one copes with loss or bereavement may be more critical in determining vulnerability than their actual occurrence. Loss *per se* may not inevitably produce increased susceptibility to illness, but it is the meaning of the loss for the individual together with his or her coping ability which appears more likely to determine this. This may also explain the apparent success of the counselling programmes which prepare close relatives of dying patients for bereavement. As Parkes (1975) points out, anticipatory grieving of this type does not remove grief following death, but it does appear to help both in avoiding some of the possible adverse reactions associated with bereavement and in coping with the period before the death occurs.

b. Stress and illness: some possible mechanisms

Most of the evidence reported above has shown that there is a statistical association between various psychosocial 'stressors' and the onset of disease. These studies have provoked many criticisms and have also given rise to a number of further questions. The most obvious of these are concerned with the nature of the mechanisms which increase vulnerability to disease as the result of stress. From the outset it is probably fair to say that, as yet, medical science does not have a clear answer to these questions and until such an answer exists, research evidence in this field will always be problematic.

There are a number of models which attempt to explain how psychosocial stressors bring about pathological bodily changes. Earlier models attempted to equate different psychosomatic illnesses with specific types of emotional conflict or with specific personality types. These approaches are not strongly adhered to now as most contemporary psychosomatic models are concerned with explaining disease proneness in terms of intervening psychophysiological and neuroendocrine mechanisms. Some of these models are very general and attempt to provide an overall framework for accounting for a range of diseases, whereas others have been specifically developed to deal with one particular disease. Examples of both general and specific models are presented here.

i. General models of stress and illness

One of the most general models which has been used in this field is Selye's General Adaptation Syndrome (GAS) which was outlined earlier. Selye maintains that the biological changes accompanying the GAS can result in both transient and more long-term adverse physical changes. Diseases which arise in this way are referred to by Selye as diseases of adaptation since they are the outcome of a system of defences against threatening or unpleasant stimuli. During the initial alarm stage of the GAS, the observed biological changes in animals include enlargement of the adrenal cortex, atrophy of the thymus and gastric ulceration. In the second or resistance stage of the GAS there is an increased resistance to the specific stressor but a consequent decreased resistance to other stimuli. If the stressor continues unabated, these bodily changes are prolonged and animals can suffer irreversible body damage or even death. The disease process is therefore held to come about as the result of the adrenal cortical and pituitary hormones, the inflammation processes, or the lowering of bodily resistance. The actual disease which occurs during this weakened state is thought to depend on a range of factors including genetic predispositions, acquired physical weaknesses and specifically learned bodily responses. Thus it is assumed that the GAS will lead to disease if there is a prolonged response to a stressor or if these responses are defective.

Selye maintains that the diseases of adaptation can take many forms depending on the specific predisposing factors in the individual. Most commonly they include cardiovascular and gastrointestinal disorders but he contends that stress could play a role in any disease. Recently he has used the GAS to discuss the role of stress factors in cancer and has presented the following general model as a possible explanation. 'Emotions accompanying stress—fear, anxiety and depression—are reflected in limbic system activity, which directly involves hypothalamic and pituitary function. The pituitary, the body's master gland, regulates all hormonal activity. Furthermore, imbalances in hormonal activity have frequently been demonstrated to be connected in increases in malignant growth. Oversecretion of the adrenal has been particularly noted to affect the thymus and lymph nodes and subsequently the white blood cells. Stress can thus be viewed as having a twofold influence on the malignant process: (1) the production of abnormal cells increases, and (2) the capability of the body to destroy these cells is diminished' (Selye, 1979).

The GAS lends itself as an explanatory model for accounting for the effects of life changes or events on health. Investigators of life changes have argued that they require readjustment by the individual and that this could result in physiological activation. Over time these could have a deleterious effect on the body and result in illness. This would explain why more frequent and more severe life changes have an increased likelihood of preceding the onset of disease. Thus it is argued that sustained and unsuccessful attempts at coping with life changes will lower bodily resistance and enhance the probability of disease occurrence.

Although the GAS can provide a framework for understanding how stressful events reduce bodily resistance and cause organ damage, there is evidence that other mechanisms, not based on adrenal cortical hormones, could lead to disease. A selection of these is now considered.

A very different explanation has been offered by Schmale (1972) to account for the effects of loss on physical health. In contrast to the adaptive mechanisms evoked by stressors in the GAS, he and his collaborators have proposed a second defence mechanism which is characterized by energy conservation and withdrawal from the environment. They have found that the emotional state of hopelessness–helplessness, which may be produced by loss or bereavement, can cause such changes as cardiac slowing, decreased blood pressure and decreases in urinary water and sodium output. They argue that a reduced level of biological functioning promotes internal survival and can protect against some unfavourable environmental factors but may increase vulnerability to other stressors. Although the concept of loss and the postulated biological changes feature strongly in discussions of psychosomatic disease, it is not clear how these bodily reactions can increase vulnerability to disease.

ii. Stress and heart disease

A number of models have been put forward to explain the role of stress in heart disease. Common to most of these is that life situations are thought to produce chronic stress or that personality characteristics and coping strategies result in constant pressured involvements with the environment (i.e. Type A behaviour). These stresses could produce heart disease by bringing about changes in the cardiovascular system or through associated risk factors such as diet and smoking.

Friedman and Rosenman (1974) maintain that the Type A behaviour pattern results in chronically increased catecholamine secretion. This in turn will bring about such changes as increases in blood levels of cholesterol and an increased tendency of the clotting elements of the blood to precipitate out, thereby building up deposits and thickenings on the artery wall and narrowing the passageways. Narrowing of the blood vessels and increased clotting increase the risk of occluding a coronary artery and causing angina pectoris or myocardial infarction.

A variation on this model has been proposed by Carruthers (1969) to account for general effects of stress rather than for the effects of Type A behaviour. He has argued that the sympathetic activation in response to stressors will increase the mobilization of free fatty acids from fatty tissues. If these resources are not called on for use in a physical response (i.e. in fight or flight), they are converted to triglycerides and may be instrumental in forming atheroma. Although he and his associates have carried out studies showing that raised free fatty acid and triglyceride levels do occur after a stressful situation, this model is still a suggestive one with many unanswered elements.

Many animal studies have been used for investigating the biological consequences of stressful environments and some of these are quite compelling. For example, Henry and his colleagues (Henry et al., 1975) have shown that adverse social conditions (e.g. crowding; conflict for food and space) produce significant increases in blood pressure which persist for long time periods following removal from the adverse conditions. Similarly, many animal studies have shown that gastric ulceration is a direct consequence of fearful situations, particularly those in which the animal has no control over the adverse stimuli. While these animal studies allow direct observation of the biological consequences of unpleasant conditions, they are problematic for a number of reasons. With the animal studies the connections between stressors and structural damage are still unclear. Moreover, the complexities of the human situation cannot be adequately duplicated by simple experimental manipulations in the social environment of rats or mice.

iii. Stress and the immune system

There is growing evidence that various stressors can alter the functioning of the immune system and in some circumstances cause significant immune suppression. There appear to be two ways in which this can come about. The first involves the hypothalamico–pituitary–adrenocortical system (*see above*), and the production of increased levels of steroid hormones in response to acute stress situations, particularly those in which active coping is not possible. The resulting corticosteroids are known to be lympholytic and this results in reduced immune system responses. The second mechanism involves the central nervous system since there is a two-way interaction between the CNS and the lymphoid organs and via this the CNS can directly influence levels of immune functioning.

A number of animal studies have shown that environmental stress, such as overcrowding, can produce a significant elevation in corticosterone which, in turn, is associated with increases in tumour growth following experimentally implanted tumours. The same pattern of change is also produced when corticosteroids are directly injected into animals. The extent of these changes can be affected both by the degree of environmental demand and by allowing the experimental animals to make coping responses.

Although human studies have also shown a clear relation between exposure to stress and suppressed immune responses, there is less clear evidence on the role of corticosteroids. Temporal factors are important in humans since it has been shown that acute stress generally provokes immune suppression whereas a more chronic exposure to stress is much less likely to produce changes in immune system functioning and, in some circumstances, may result in facilitation of immune responses. Indeed the available evidence indicates that during the more long-term stress responses, which correspond with Selye's resistance stage, there is often enhanced immune functioning.

In addition to the evidence above that various types of stressor can influence the functioning of the immune system, there is also evidence that it is possible to produce conditioned immune responses. Ader and Cohen (1981) have demonstrated that if animals are given a saccharine solution immediately before an immuno-suppressant on a number of occasions, then the saccharine solution, on its own, will lead to a reduced immune response (e.g. a diminished antibody response). This is an example of classical conditioning (*see* Chapter 14 for a fuller account) and is significant because it indicates that it is possible for a neutral stimulus to provoke changes in immune system functioning provided that the stimulus has been associated with previous immune changes.

The various mechanisms described above provide some indication that certain unpleasant and uncontrollable situations can give rise to immune suppression. Following Selye, it would then be expected that there would be an increased vulnerability to such diseases as cancer. There is now a growing body of evidence to support this and which has demonstrated, for example, stress-induced effects on tumour growth and development (*see* Anisman and Sklar, 1984). Although research in this area is very promising, it is important to point out that it is still very much in its infancy and there is a long way to go in understanding the mechanisms linking stress and tumour growth.

There are many explanatory models for stress and disease in addition to the selection outlined above. While the work in this area is suggestive and interesting there is clearly a long way to go before there is an adequate picture of the possible role of stress factors in the onset of disease. The links between emotional responses and disease processes need to be specified and the possible contribution of many other factors will have to be excluded or incorporated. In addition to this, models will have to take account of individual differences in disease proneness and of various situational and social factors.

The evidence to date has provided a number of interesting correlations between psychosocial factors and proneness to disease. As yet there is no real agreement as to the nature of the processes by which emotions can be translated or transduced into the physiological changes which lead to disease. This fundamental problem for stress research has been well summarized in a comprehensive text in this field:

> Psychosomatic medicine must eventually seek to explain how psychosocial stimuli are translated into acute or chronic changes in structure and in physiological and biochemical function. In spite of all claims to the contrary ... we simply do not understand how non-material, symbolic events—such as the psychological responses to life experiences or events—are 'translated' into material changes—such as the release of pituitary tropic hormones, sustained elevations of blood pressure, alterations in immune processes, autonomic neural discharge, or the induction of enzymes or viruses. There are many unknown links in the chain of events that lead from symbol to physiological change. (Weiner, 1977)

c. Psychological approaches to treatment

In recent years psychologists have developed treatment packages known as *stress management* techniques designed specifically for helping people who are thought to have stress-related psychological and physical problems. Although this sounds a very specific approach it generally consists of a mixture of different techniques, some of which are described below. In very general terms, these treatments are aimed either at dealing with particular symptoms (e.g. high blood pressure, tension headache, etc.) or at preventing the reoccurrence of a particular clinical problem such as myocardial infarction. In addition to this there have been some very specific approaches developed for helping people cope with stressful medical procedures (*see* section 13.3 of Chapter 13) or with the demands of physical illnesses (*see* Chapter 12).

Nearly all the psychological treatments which are described in Chapter 14 have been applied in some way to stress-related conditions with varying degrees of success. A quick read through Chapter 14 would be helpful to have a clearer picture of the treatment approaches which are described below.

Perhaps the most widely used technique in stress management is *relaxation training*, in which individuals are usually taught a muscular relaxation technique and encouraged to use this on a regular basis as well as in countering stressful situations. Although there is a general feeling that relaxation training is efficacious, it is not clear how or why it works. There are some indications that it produces specific physiological and psychological changes but equally it may work by increasing feelings of self-efficacy and control.

Relaxation training is often used as part of a general stress-management package. These vary greatly but usually begin by getting people familiar with the nature of stress. They then have to identify and recognize their current stressors and the symptoms which they produce. Patients are also required to monitor their daily lives for the occurrence of potentially demanding situations and learn how to prevent these or cope with them more effectively. In this way patients can increase their feelings of competence in managing potentially stressful situations.

There have also been a number of specific treatments developed for treating particular symptoms. The best known is *biofeedback* which is described more fully in Chapter 14 (section 14.4). This has been applied to a wide range of clinical problems, including tension headache and hypertension, with some success. A number of studies have shown clear therapeutic changes but few of these studies are carefully controlled and it has not really been established that biofeedback *per se* has produced the beneficial changes (*see* Johnston, 1984, for a good critical review).

Some of the most impressive treatments for particular problems have used a combination of different techniques. A good example of this is a treatment approach for hypertension which produced impressive short- and long-term reductions in blood pressure (Patel et al., 1981). This study made use of a combination of relaxation, meditation, biofeedback and stress-management procedures in a package which also includes a health education component.

The treatment packages aimed at preventing clinical problems, such as myocardial infarction, or minimizing their reoccurrence, have also been quite broadly based. Typically these involve an educational component which focuses on the risk factors involved in the disease and emphasizes the importance of changing behaviour to avoid or minimize these. Also these approaches generally include a varied stress management programme based on relaxation training and behaviour change. Some have also used quite specific interventions such as carefully planned physical exercise or a cognitive coping approach.

There are even a number of treatment packages which have been developed for modifying Type A behaviour, either in a general fashion or by concentrating on specific components such as hostility or time urgency. Again these studies are not always carefully controlled but in some of the larger, prospective studies the results are extremely hopeful in terms of symptom change and reduced reinfarction rate (*see* Langosch, 1984, for a review).

As was pointed out earlier in this chapter, there is still disagreement about the exact nature of the Type A personality style and its role in coronary heart disease. Thus one of the problems for these intervention studies is to know precisely what has been changed and which component of the intervention was instrumental. Nevertheless there is evidence from one good prospective study that psychological treatments can not only produce decreases in Type A behaviours but also reduce the likelihood of reoccurrence of further myocardial infarcts (Friedman et al., 1984). An important feature of this study was the inclusion of a cognitive learning component involving the modification of existing health beliefs and the establishment of more 'healthy' values and goals.

The results from this growing approach to treatment are both exciting and problematic. A wide range of psychological treatments has been applied to stress-related disorders with varying degrees of success. Some of the more positive findings have been very encouraging, particularly as they indicate that behavioural change in the broadest sense can provide a long-term approach to treatment or prevention. However, many of the studies, particularly the older ones, have been inadequately designed and controlled and therefore the results are often rather meaningless. Moreover, the problems identified at the end of the previous section clearly create fundamental difficulties for research in this area. Until we have a fuller understanding of the nature of stress and the mechanisms linking stress and disease, there will always be major questions about the efficacy and mode of operation of new treatments. Despite these reservations, there are many indications that psychological approaches will be increasingly used and that the results from treatment studies may also help to throw some light on the underlying processes involved in stress and disease.

●   **Recommended reading**

Cohen F. (1979) Personality, stress and the development of physical illness. In: Stone G. C., Cohen F. and Adler N. E. (ed.) *Health Psychology—A Handbook*. San Francisco, Jossey-Bass.

Cox T. (1978) *Stress*. London, Macmillan.

McCabe P. M. and Schneiderman N. (1985) Psychophysiologic reactions to stress. In: Schneiderman N. and Tapp J. (ed.) *Behavioural Medicine*. Hillsdale, N.J., Erlbaum.

6

Individual differences in intelligence

So far, the contents of this book have discussed human behaviour without really considering the nature of differences between individuals. The two previous chapters were concerned with variations of behaviour within individuals in response to changing internal and external circumstances. The present chapter is given over to describing some of the ways psychologists have sought to describe and measure individual differences in behaviour. The relation of this to medical practice is in some ways obvious since patients are all individuals who will vary in all sorts of ways. Thus patients will differ not only in the way in which they perceive and present their problems but possibly also in the types of problems they experience, as was suggested in the previous chapter. However, there is a much wider clinical relevance in considering individual differences. For example, intelligence tests are used for diagnostic purposes with many types of patient and one medical specialty is taken up with the problems of a group partly defined by their intellectual capacity, namely the mentally handicapped. From this very sketchy introduction it can be seen that an understanding of the nature of differences between people can be helpful in various clinical contexts.

The problem for psychologists investigating individual differences has been to decide on the best way of defining and measuring these. Over the years two broad distinguishable areas have emerged and have been generally studied quite separately. These are the areas of *intelligence* and *personality*. In general terms, psychologists investigating intelligence have sought to describe and quantify differences in level of functioning of various cognitive processes, whereas those who are concerned with personality have concentrated more on aspects of a person's feelings, motives and social behaviour. As a result, these two areas have tended to develop quite separately which has had some rather unfortunate side effects. Psychologists often appear to fall into the trap of thinking of the personality and intelligence of an individual as two quite separate aspects of their behaviour. In reality it can be easily demonstrated that this separation appears to exist more for the convenience of those who study either area than as an accurate reflection of day-to-day behaviour. As we shall see, intellectual functions can be significantly affected by mood and motivation.

● 6.1. Intelligence: what is it?

If psychologists are asked to define intelligence, the majority will probably give an answer based on certain aspects of behaviour. Many definitions, such as 'learning ability', 'problem-solving ability', the 'capacity for abstract thinking' and the 'capacity to acquire capacity', have been offered. There are countless definitions on these lines, none of which is definitive, but they all have in common the fact that they refer to cognitive processes which are taken to reflect intellectual functions. Cognition is a generic term used to describe all those processes involved in knowing. It therefore covers everything from perception to reasoning.

If one looks at both practical applications and at research on intelligence, it becomes clear that the definition of intelligence which is commonly used is an operational one based on the scores obtained from intelligence tests. The problem with this type of definition is that there are many different sorts of intelligence tests, involving quite different skills and abilities. Even so, there tends to be a reasonable correlation between the scores obtained on this range of tests and this has led some people to suppose that this reflects the general intelligence level of an individual which is manifested on a range of diverse tasks.

One important point which may be apparent from this introduction is that there are two quite different approaches to understanding the nature of human cognitive abilities or intelligence. This is indeed so since cognitive abilities have been studied in two quite different ways which can be briefly described.

a. Experimental approaches to cognition

Since the very earliest days of psychology, towards the end of the last century, experimental psychologists have sought to understand the nature of behavioural processes. Those who have been interested in cognition have therefore experimentally investigated the mechanisms involved in such processes as memory, problem-solving and learning in order to provide universal models of cognitive behaviour. To put it more simply, this approach has been primarily concerned with understanding how these processes work and not with individual differences. If an experimental psychologist is asked the question, 'What is intelligence?', the reply would probably be on the lines that intelligence is a non-specific term which refers to a range of cognitive processes. The experimental approach is therefore valuable in that it can provide a description of the various behaviours that are subsumed under the general heading of intelligence, but it has more or less completely ignored the question of individual differences.

b. Psychometric approaches to intelligence

In direct contrast to the experimentalists, the psychometric approach has been entirely concerned with the quantifying and classifying individual differences by using intelligence tests. For these psychologists, the term 'intelligence' is used to refer to the level of performance on defined tests.

The intelligence test movement grew out of work in France at the very beginning of this century. Binet, who is often referred to as the father of intelligence testing, developed fairly simple test procedures for identifying schoolchildren who would be unable to benefit from elementary education and who would therefore need special help. In doing this, Binet did not seek to derive test scores measuring specific skills but merely used these scores to identify retarded children. His method for doing this consisted of testing large groups of children at different age levels and defining expected performance levels for any particular age group. Thus the score of any child could be evaluated with reference to these expected age levels and it was therefore possible to tell the extent to which any individual fell above or below the level expected for their chronological age. The performance measure which was derived was one of mental age, which did not tell you anything directly about the skills possessed by any individual but merely how they compared with other children of the same age. These tests were adapted for use in the USA and scoring was modified to give an estimate of mental age with respect to chronological age. This estimate was referred to as the intelligence quotient or IQ and was originally derived as follows:

$$IQ = \frac{\text{mental age}}{\text{chronological age}} \times 100.$$

From this simple formula it can be seen that the IQ score is a guide to an individual's relative standing in relation to others of the same age and that an IQ of 100 is the average score for any age level.

There are problems in using mental age as a criterion because intellectual functions do not grow in an incremental fashion and the formula becomes inapplicable with increasing age. As a result, IQ scores are now based on the properties of the distribution of scores of a defined population. When intelligence tests are given to a large number of people there is an approximately normal distribution of scores. By the historical convention outlined above, the average IQ score is 100, and a standard deviation of 15 is generally used. Therefore the distribution of scores takes the form shown in *Fig.* 10.

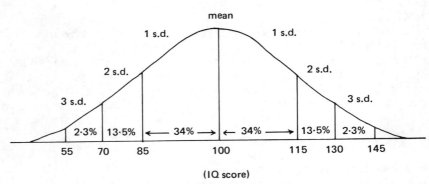

Fig. 10. The distribution of IQ scores showing the proportion of the population falling within one, two and three standard deviations (s.d.) from the mean.

In order to understand more about the nature of skills involved in performing intelligence tests, psychometric psychologists have examined the patterns of correlations between scores obtained on different sorts of intelligence tests. Early studies of this type gave rise to claims that there were high correlations between different intelligence test scores and that this was good evidence for the

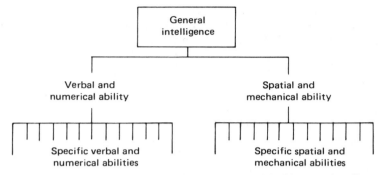

Fig. 11. A diagram illustrating a hierarchical model of human intelligence.

existence of a general intelligence factor. This factor, usually referred to as 'g', was taken to represent some overall level of intellectual competence which determined an individual's level of functioning on all intelligence tests.

The existence of 'g' is now disputed on a number of grounds. First, tests have been found which are not particularly correlated with other tests. This has led to the development of a hierarchical model which can account both for the generality and specificity of various intellectual capacities. This is shown diagrammatically in *Fig.* 11 and is also reflected in the content of some individual intelligence tests, such as the Wechsler Scales which are described later in this chapter. These scales not only provide separate estimates of specific abilities but also give more general measures of verbal and performance IQ in addition to an overall IQ estimate.

A second and less answerable problem with the idea of 'g' concerns the nature of the differences between individuals obtaining different test scores. A model of intelligence based on the idea of general intelligence gives rise to the prediction that individual differences are quantitatively determined on a 'better = more' principle. However, there is now abundant evidence that there are clear qualitative reasons for test score differences. This evidence has come from developmental studies and from comparisons of adults of different levels of test ability. It has been shown that those who score higher are able to do so by using different problem-solving strategies.

It can now be seen that the psychometric approach to intelligence is a very derivative one, dealing with the products rather than the process of cognitive functioning. Level of intelligence is inferred from performance on rather arbitrary collections of cognitive tasks and the structure of intellectual abilities is inferred from correlations between test scores. In attempting to answer the question 'Why is X able to obtain a higher test score than Y?', the psychometrician would be forced into a circular explanation and give the reason that X is more intelligent than Y. Psychometric approaches cannot deal with the question as to what it means, in process terms, to be more or less intelligent.

c. Combining experimental and psychometric approaches

In order to look at differences in cognitive processes which correspond to levels of intelligence, it is necessary to combine the experimental and psychometric approaches to intelligence. Until very recently this has hardly been done since psychometricians have been exclusively concerned with deriving techniques for measuring individual differences whereas experimental psychologists have concentrated on producing universal models of various cognitive functions. Fortunately there are now signs that there is a breakdown in this historical divide between these two approaches. Studies have been carried out on the problem-solving strategies and memory processes of groups of different intelligence levels and these have identified clear differences which help to understand differences in test scores.

From this discussion it can be seen that the traditional concept of intelligence is now being challenged. It is beginning to look as if it will be more meaningful and more useful to describe individual differences in cognitive abilities in terms of strategy differences rather than arbitrary test scores. These strategy differences will therefore refer directly to an individual's capabilities and the way in which they go about solving a problem. Although this may not seem an important change it does have some quite important clinical and educational implications. Some of these are considered in the sections on compensatory education and mental handicap later in this chapter.

• 6.2. Intelligence tests and their clinical applications

a. The tests

The primary aim of nearly all intelligence tests is to provide a consistent estimate of an individual's level with respect to that of a defined population. This is usually expressed in the form of an IQ score or some sort of percentile rating, which will refer to the individual's overall standing in percentage terms (e.g. in the top 5 per cent or in the bottom 20 per cent of the population).

i. Basic criteria for intelligence tests

The acceptability of any new test is therefore dependent on whether it classifies people in a consistent way (*reliability*) and whether it is really assessing what it purports to (*validity*). One way of measuring the reliability of a test is to present it on two separate occasions to the same large group and derive a correlation which provides an estimate of its test–retest reliability. Other techniques for measuring reliability exist but whatever technique is used, the resultant correlation must be very high. Otherwise it is assumed that the test is not classifying individuals in a consistent way and will therefore not be acceptable as a reliable measure.

The validity of a test is a more difficult matter to establish since it usually involves correlating scores with those obtained on an established test, which is known to measure a particular aspect of intelligence. Alternatively, it is possible to provide an estimate of predictive validity by deriving correlations with a 'real-world' intellectual attainment such as an exam taken at a later time. Finally, a psychometric test must also be 'standardized'. This means that the scores for a large population must be available so that the level of any individual's performance can be evaluated. This standardization gives rise to the normal distribution of scores and hence provides the 'norms' or expected levels for a test.

Many tests have different norms available for different age groups in order to take account of the changes in level of intellectual functioning over time.

The majority of tests in routine clinical practice generally satisfy these basic criteria although it might be argued that the validity of some is questionable. However, clinical psychologists can and do use relatively unstandardized tests for quite specific purposes. Certain tests might be used because it is known that they can detect the presence of a specific deficit such as a memory difficulty, a language dysfunction or a disorder of thinking. In using such tests, the psychologist might already have an idea that a patient may have a specific deficit from previously administering a standardized battery of tests and therefore wishes to home in on the nature of a specific problem. In this case the need to derive a differential score disappears since the emphasis is now on the investigation of specific processes. This issue is returned to shortly in discussing the application of tests.

ii. Types of test
Routine intelligence tests differ in a number of specific ways. First, they differ in their mode of administration since some can only be given individually whereas others can be given to a group of subjects. In the latter case, the tests are usually of a fixed duration and the items are of a relatively uniform type. There are some obvious disadvantages with group tests since it might be difficult to check that all the testees have understood the instructions adequately or to determine the level of anxiety of any individual. As we see in the next section, non-intellectual factors such as anxiety and test familiarity can affect test performance. Thus it is not surprising to find that clinical intelligence testing is predominantly carried out using individual tests. Here different types of tests can be easily given and it is possible to see at first hand whether instructions have been understood and whether motivational or emotional factors are affecting test performance. An additional advantage with individualized testing is that detailed timing of performance is possible.

Intelligence tests also vary in the range and type of items which are employed and the measures which can be derived. Many clinical tests consist of a battery of different types of subtest. Using these it is therefore possible to obtain a profile of various intellectual abilities as well as a general measure of overall intellectual level based on an amalgam of the separate subtest scores. Eliciting profiles of separate abilities in this way has proved to be of value in clinical diagnostic testing, as is indicated below. In contrast to the test batteries, some intelligence tests only make use of one type of item and so the resultant measure will tend to reflect a more restricted ability (e.g. verbal reasoning, perceptual problem-solving, etc.). However, some uniform tests claim to provide measures of general intellectual ability since they have been found to correlate with general intelligence measures derived from test batteries.

iii. The Wechsler Scales
Probably the best known and certainly the most widely used tests of intelligence in the clinical context are the Wechsler Scales. There are three separate Wechsler Scales for pre-school children, for children up to about 16 years and for adults. Each of these is individually administered and comprises a range of different subtests which are designed to measure different abilities. There is a broad split into verbal and performance items and separate verbal and performance IQs can

be derived in addition to an overall IQ score. The verbal subtests are ones which primarily involve language skills and include measures of vocabulary, general knowledge, verbal reasoning and verbal memory whereas the performance subtests include measures of constructional ability, visuospatial ability, perceptual ability and coding speed. Performance items tend to be timed and their scoring often makes use of credits for fast working. These items can also be used separately with people with specific language problems, including the deaf, and therefore can provide a measure of fairly basic intellectual skills. In this sense the verbal tests are more 'culture bound' since they can be thought of as measuring skills which reflect the exposure to socializing agents such as schools.

b. Clinical applications

There are perhaps four broad areas of clinical application of intelligence tests and these are briefly described.

i. Specific diagnostic

Here tests are used to throw light on the nature of a specific problem. For example, a child with delayed reading may be referred for psychological testing, which would be structured to determine the child's overall level of ability together with an analysis of specific skills known to be involved in reading. Additional tests might also be involved. This type of assessment is also of particular value with patients with neurological damage for a number of reasons. First, it provides an estimate of the behavioural effects of specific brain damage. Second, using this information it is sometimes possible to localize where the damage is maximal by the nature of the dysfunction. This follows on from the substantial body of evidence on the cortical localization of behavioural functions and which was described in Chapter 3. Finally, and most important, diagnostic assessment of this type provides the basis for therapeutic intervention since an accurate description of specific defects can indicate which aspects of behaviour need specific remediation. In this context it is heartening to see growing links between clinical psychologists and such professionals as speech therapists and occupational therapists.

ii. Baseline data

There may be occasions when an estimate of an individual's overall level of intellectual ability is needed as baseline data because it is envisaged that changes in level of functioning may ensue as the consequence of the progress of an illness or in response to treatment (see iii). Alternatively, it may be necessary to have this information as a basis for helping to make decisions about choice of vocation for an individual or about the best type of environment for treatment.

iii. Assessing the effects of treatment

Two broad and fairly similar applications of tests are relevant here. First, to assess whether a treatment is producing the benefits for which it is designed. Second, it may be necessary to determine whether medication is having negative side effects on cognitive functioning. Clinical impressions can be misleading and, as in other areas of medicine, objective techniques are necessary to determine the magnitude of any changes in intellectual functioning. One obvious problem here concerns the fact that repeat testing with standardized tests is not really possible with gaps of less than a few months in duration. Assessing the response to treatment usually takes place over a much shorter time period and so parallel versions of some tests have been produced and these help to obviate this difficulty. Even with these, there are only usually one or two parallel versions and this may not be sufficient for the rigours of many double-blind clinical trials. One outcome of this problem is that drug trials assessing intellectual changes tend to make use of non-standardized but repeatable performance measures such as reaction time and memory span. Similar measures were described in the discussion of the effects of circadian rhythms on performance in Chapter 4 and it is significant that an increasing use is made of computer-based or other automated procedures for administering these types of tests (Jones and Weinman, 1973).

iv. Assessing mental handicap

The mentally handicapped comprise a group who are defined on the basis of their intellectual capacity as well as on behavioural and social grounds. A separate consideration of the nature and clinical problems of mental handicap is given in section 6.5 and so the present discussion will be limited to the use of tests with this group. Intelligence tests are used to determine whether an individual falls into the category defined as mentally handicapped and furthermore to determine the extent of the handicap. Test criteria were previously the predominant determinants of this classification but now it is recognized that social and behavioural considerations are probably more useful. Batteries of tests can also be used with the mentally handicapped to determine particular strengths or weaknesses of ability for the purposes of remediation. Finally, an accurate assessment of intellectual level may also be of value in making management decisions in determining the most appropriate environment for individuals in terms of their basic capacities.

c. Factors affecting intelligence test performance

Reading the literature on intelligence and intelligence testing one might easily get the impression that these tests are measuring a well-delineated and isolated aspect of human behaviour. This would be rather misleading as a range of factors, other than intelligence, have been shown to contribute to test performance. Among the most obvious of these factors are emotional and motivational ones.

The effects of arousal and anxiety on human performance are well documented. At low levels of arousal and anxiety, performance tends to be poor because people are not sufficiently motivated and therefore tend to operate without efficiency and urgency. With increasing levels of arousal, performance improves up to a point and then decreases in an exponential fashion. Thus at very high and low levels of arousal there is a significantly lower level of performance. Correspondingly, there is an optimum level of arousal for a given task and it is generally found that for simpler psychomotor tasks (e.g. simple reaction-time), optimum levels of performance are found with relatively higher levels of arousal. Similarly, on more complex tasks relatively lower arousal levels produce optimal performance.

These findings apply equally well to intelligence test performance in that motivation and anxiety have been shown to affect the final score. The magnitude of this effect will also depend on the type of task involved, on the lines indicated above. When patients are in states of anxiety or depression they generally obtain lower scores on intelligence test items, especially when performance is timed. The lower scores obtained in these two states may involve a quite different cause. With the depressed patient there may also be associated anxiety but in the absence of this, poor test performance would reflect a combination of low energy and motivation and sometimes even psychomotor slowing. However, very anxious patients would do badly for different reasons in that they might be unable to focus attention sufficiently, may work too quickly and carelessly or may become too preoccupied with making errors. All of these factors would be sufficient to reduce the level of performance on the intelligence test.

In the clinical context it can be useful to recognize these sorts of influences on test performance. A recent decrease in a patient's level of functioning may be indicative of neurological dysfunction but, equally, emotional or motivational reasons may be involved and it is clearly important to determine which is the case for any individual patient. Repeated assessments may be necessary to ascertain the exact cause.

Familiarity with tests and with testing in general have shown to produce specific gains in test performance. With most standardized tests it is recommended that repeat testing should not occur within less than about 6 months to avoid specific learning factors. It would also appear that people who are used to doing tests will tend to perform better than those being tested for the first time. This can be due to a combination of factors including anxiety level and specific learning factors.

• 6.3. Genetic and environmental determinants of intelligence

One of the most fiercely argued questions in the whole of psychology has been whether differences in intelligence are due to genetic or environmental factors. This issue is not just an academic one since there are important educational, social and even clinical implications. At the outset, it is probably worth saying three things which help set the whole question in perspective. First, while it may be straightforward to discuss gene:environment influences on something fairly unequivocal such as height, there are problems in considering the much more complex and less well understood mechanisms of intelligence. Given that the measures involved in such studies will be IQ scores and that, as noted above, many factors can influence test performance, there will be many variables to take account of. Second, there are considerable problems in attempting to separate the genetic and environmental influences on behaviour even with twin studies. Individuals do not develop in isolation and so all behaviour is environmentally dependent. Third, it would appear that factors other than scientific ones can influence the theoretical positions taken by psychologists on this issue. There can be political and social implications of accepting that either genetic or environmental factors predominantly determine intelligence. For example, someone who adopts the genetic view might say that those with poor levels of performance are victims of their genetic endowment and that compensatory social welfare or education programmes are therefore largely an irrelevance. This issue is returned to later in this section and in the two sections which follow on from it.

Up to fairly recently there was a consensus view among intelligence testers that the majority of the individual variation in IQ was genetically determined. In many standard textbooks a gene:environment determinance of 80:20 is accepted. It will be shown from a review of the evidence that this conclusion is clearly no longer tenable.

a. Twin studies

The view that genetic determinants predominate is based primarily on two sources of evidence, namely studies of identical twins and studies of adopted children. Since monozygotic twins are genetically identical it should follow that their IQs should be identical, if IQ is genetically determined. Studies of monozygotic twins have shown very high correlations between their IQs. Moreover, these correlations are generally found to be consistently higher than those for dizygotic or non-identical twins. On its own this evidence is rather meaningless because it can be immediately claimed that monozygotic twins share a very similar environment and one which has a greater similarity than for non-identical twins or siblings. The way out of this problem has been to investigate monozygotic twins who have been brought up in different environments, which is much more difficult to do. However, there are a small number of studies which have done this and these, too, report high correlations, although these are consistently less than the correlations for twins brought up together. In this context it is interesting to note that in one of these studies an average difference in IQ of 14 points was found between monozygotic twins reared apart. This difference is similar to that found in some studies of blacks and whites in the USA and has prompted one influential behavioural geneticist to conclude that the observed racial differences in IQ scores 'can hardly be accepted as sufficient evidence that with respect to intelligence the negro American is genetically less endowed' (Gottesman, 1968). This issue is referred to later.

On the face of it the twin data appear to provide quite convincing evidence that there is a large inherited component to IQ. A more rigorous analysis of these studies, however, shows that this conclusion is premature because the data themselves are problematic in a number of ways. Unless it can be conclusively shown that there is no correlation between the environments experienced by each twin, then it is impossible to rule out environmental influences. A careful inspection of the environments of the separated twins has shown that often the environments were very similar and even sometimes consisted of being with relations in the same family. A second problem is that the assessments given to the twin pairs were not always acceptable and sometimes were not equivalent. Finally, and most disturbing, is the fact that the largest of these studies and the one which also showed the highest correlation has been shown to be totally suspect. The study in question was that reported by Burt (1966) on 53 pairs of twins. Recent analyses of these data have shown beyond doubt that not only were many of the assessments quite dubious and poorly specified but that some of the data had been totally fabricated, even to the extent of inventing fictitious research assistants (Kamin, 1974; Hearnshaw, 1979). It now appears that Burt partly assembled and partly created his own data to fit the preconceived conclusion that intelligence was primarily inherited. The rejection of these data leaves the rest of the twin data in a very weakened state and, if nothing else, reduces the overall estimate of heritability to much less than the 80 per cent which has been postulated for so long.

b. Studies of foster children
      The second line of evidence on this issue has involved the study of foster children and the inferences which can be made either from the IQ correlations between foster children brought up in the same family or from comparing the IQ correlations of a child with its biological parents and with its foster parents. Although these data are again not entirely without flaws and also beset by problems of methodology and interpretation, there is a tendency to find slightly larger IQ correlations between children and their biological parents. These differences in correlations are not large and are fairly variable in their magnitude but they do appear to provide some support for a genetic contribution to IQ differences. Even these results must be regarded with caution because follow-up studies of foster children have shown that they become less concordant in IQ level with their biological mothers over a long period of time.

c. Environmental factors
      Large environmental influences are therefore possible as will become clear after reading the section on compensatory education which follows shortly. In Chapter 8 there is also an account of the environmental factors which can affect cognitive development. For example, it is shown that injury or disease during pregnancy may affect the environment of the fetus and result in temporary or permanent intellectual defects involving either specific or general skills. Such factors as the infant's early diet can also exert an influence on later intellectual as well as physical growth.
      Patterns of child rearing appear to show class-related differences which can influence aspects of intellectual development. Intellectual achievement is generally valued more highly in middle-class homes and hence greater emphasis tends to be placed on success at school. Smaller families, greater material provisions and more parental involvement in early 'cognitive' play are also characteristics of middle-class homes which have generally been found to give rise to a greater capacity to adapt to the demands of the classroom. In these terms, the home environment can exert a number of different influences and that what the middle-class child acquires is likely to be of more use on an intelligence test than the experiences accruing from a working-class home. That is not to say that the knowledge or abilities of the working-class child are in any way inferior since these may be superior in other aspects. Rather it is a comment on the motivation and skills necessary to do well on intelligence tests and the way in which a middle-class environment appears to provide a more advantageous preparation for this.

      An overall evaluation of the evidence on the issue points to the fact that while there appears to be some genetic determinance, significant environmental influences can also operate. Indeed, it may well be impossible and irrelevant to try to assign the exact relative contribution of each. It is probably fair to say that many previous writers have tended to overestimate the genetic basis and that this has had some unfortunate consequences.

A problem with the strict genetic argument is that by postulating a predominant genetic determination of intelligence, any observed intelligence test difference between groups of individuals will be regarded as genetically based. Hence the very emotive debate as to the reported IQ differences between blacks and whites in the USA. For example, Jensen (1969) has argued that the intelligence of blacks must be genetically inferior to that of whites because many studies have shown a difference of approximately 10–15 IQ points between these two groups. He adopts this viewpoint because, in the first place, he believes that intelligence is primarily genetically determined and secondly because he claims that attempts to provide compensatory educational programmes for young black children have failed.

As we have seen earlier, the evidence as to the supposed genetic basis of intelligence is far from conclusive, which rather detracts from the strength of Jensen's central tenet. Even if intelligence were under genetic control, then any differences between populations are not necessarily due to genetic factors. To clarify this point it is instructive to consider the data on height, which does appear to be predominantly determined by heredity. If the average height of urban Indian children in S. America is compared with their rural counterparts, then they are found to be significantly taller. It has been shown that the rural children are smaller because they suffer more from disease and malnutrition, not because they are genetically inferior since both groups come from the same racial stock. Accordingly with intelligence, even if genetic factors are found to have a significant influence, this does not lead to the inevitable conclusion that one racial group is genetically superior if its average IQ scores are higher. Indeed there is good evidence that many environmental factors, including those associated with the test environment itself, provide much more valid explanations of the reported differences in IQ scores.

It is also difficult to concur with Jensen's verdict that compensatory education is ineffective with environmentally disadvantaged children, as will become evident in the next section. All the evidence which has been summarized above, in relation to the question of the genetic and environmental determinants of intelligence, provides convincing evidence of important environmental contributions. There would seem to be relatively little support for a predominantly genetic position. That is not to say that there may be genetic influences on the many complex cognitive processes which are subsumed under the general heading of intelligence. However, these influences do not appear to be as pervasive as some writers have suggested and this is seen most clearly in the importance of early environmental factors in compensatory educational programmes.

• 6.4. Improving intellectual abilities: compensatory education

A number of studies in the USA have shown that, while there is no evidence of marked intelligence differences among infants of different social classes, by the time these children enter school poor white and black children obtain lower test scores. What is more alarming is that this disadvantaged group has been found to fall further and further behind on tests as they progress through school. This adds weight to the discussion in the previous section outlining the importance of early home environment in determining intelligence test perform- ance and school achievement. As a result of these findings, there have been attempts in the USA to develop early intervention programmes to counteract these disadvantages.

Previous evidence had shown that if radical environmental changes are implemented early enough then these can bring about significant improvements in cognitive performance. In one such study, intellectually retarded young infants were transferred from an orphanage to specific institutions for the mentally retarded. Each of these children was assigned to an older retarded girl who was given the task of raising the child. Compared with a control group of children who remained in the orphanage and were adopted later, the individually reared children showed large IQ gains, which averaged 32 points. The children in the control group actually showed significant losses in test performance. A 20-year follow-up of these two groups also confirmed a superiority of school and social competence in the individually reared children.

More specific compensatory programmes have focused on developing learning experiences in very young children within the community. During the earliest period there tends to be an emphasis on providing stimulation and interest. At around the age of 2 years, the emphasis usually changes to more structured teaching approaches which are designed to provide the development of basic educational skills. These programmes work best when the parents are involved and where the children can continue to develop their new skills at home. The results from some of these studies are quite impressive in that the children involved have been found to outscore control children by approximately 20–25 IQ points, which provides considerable justification for such early compensatory programmes.

There are also indications that slightly later intervention can be successful if it is structured appropriately. For example, the provision of intensive individual tutoring in basic problem-solving and specific educational skills for groups of 3–5-year-old children from very poor backgrounds has been found to produce effective IQ and scholastic gains. The authors of one study noted that one important gain which resulted was a growing pleasure in learning and an increased feeling of mastery. They noted that mere exposure to a school environment did not provide the necessary basis for learning but that 'both mastery and enthusiasm for learning will only come when the child can be shown how to become actively involved in the learning process' (Blank and Solomon, 1968).

These results are important because they do indicate that compensatory intervention can be effective if it is early and intensive. At one time it appeared that compensatory intervention did not produce significant gains but these conclusions were found to be based on attempts which were not sufficiently intensive or structured and were given at too late a stage. Improvements tend to be greater when the intervention is earlier and when the active participation of parents is achieved.

● 6.5. Mental handicap: the problem of low intelligence

a. Defining mental handicap

The medical specialty of mental handicap is an area of medicine where the patients are partly defined on the basis of their level of intellectual ability. As was seen in the earlier part of this chapter, there is a wide range in a population's intellectual abilities, as measured by tests, and this forms an approximately normal distribution. The term 'mental handicap' tends to be applied to the 2–3 per cent of the population falling more than two standard deviations below the average IQ score; in other words, those with an IQ of less than 70.

Having indicated that the mentally handicapped can be classified in terms of a low IQ score, it is important to be aware of the following points. First, there is no hard and fast cut-off point involved here in that the IQ criterion is only a rough guideline and is not now thought to be the most useful one. Probably the most important criterion is a social one since a lower intellectual ability only becomes a problem when it gives rise to inadequate social functioning. The second point worth mentioning at the outset is that although the term 'mental handicap' is applied to those with restricted mental and social competences, relatively few of the individuals so classified will actually need hospitalization or systematic medical and psychological help. The majority live within the community and do not need the aid of special services.

There have been various terms used to refer to this group of individuals. Mental handicap tends to be the preferred one in the UK, although subnormality is sometimes used. In the USA the classification of mental retardation is most widely used. Previously mental deficiency was the standard term but this has largely disappeared from use now. In more recent years, there has also been a tendency to make a division between mild and severe mental handicap, where the approximate dividing line is an IQ of 50. The mildly handicapped will have IQs in the range of 50–70 and the severe group have IQs below 50. Workers in this field have also found it useful to subdivide the severe group into three further levels based on approximate IQ criteria.

b. The causes

The categorization of the mentally handicapped into mild and severe groups is not only based on an IQ criterion but also appears to reflect other broad differences. By and large the mild group do not have any demonstrable central nervous system abnormality whereas this is common among the severely handicapped. This is also primarily reflected in the differences in aetiology between the two groups. The causes of severe mental handicap mainly comprise neurological and chromosomal abnormalities. The most common chromosomal abnormality is Down's syndrome (mongolism), which accounts for about 30 per cent of all severe mental handicap in children. There is no social class difference in the prevalence of severe mental handicap. In contrast, there is a social class bias in the distribution of mild mental handicap in that there is a predominance in lower social class groups. This appears to be so for entirely environmental reasons since there is a greater working-class prevalence of such factors as low birth weight, obstetric complications and early environmental disadvantage. Additional factors such as family size and stability, housing and poverty have all been shown to have some influence, which adds further weight to the previously discussed importance of environmental factors in intellectual growth. This division into physically and environmentally caused handicap can be misleading in that it implies that these are totally separate and separable. Even with primary physical causation, environmental agents can increase or lessen the overall impact and similarly many of the environmental factors may operate by bringing about structural changes.

c. Provisions for mentally handicapped people

In the UK there are currently in the region of one million mildly handicapped individuals and about 150 000 people with severe mental handicap. The majority of the former live independently in the community whereas most of the severely handicapped receive special help, which includes residential care or day centres. Only a relatively small proportion of the 50 000–60 000 hospitalized patients are badly handicapped in terms of basic self-maintenance skills. The majority can look after themselves quite adequately, can speak and do not have behaviour problems. The overall number of those who are either incapable of looking after themselves or whose behaviour disorders require a great deal of supervision is probably only about one-tenth of the overall number of the severely mentally handicapped. In view of this, there is an increasing recognition that relatively few mentally handicapped people actually need medical expertise. Moreover, there is accumulating evidence that some of the behaviour disorders seen in this group may have arisen from child-rearing at home or from institutions, which are often restricted, impoverished and understaffed (*see* Chapter 13).

Given that institutions for the mentally handicapped may create rather than solve many problems, there has been a growing commitment to community care. Although this appears, in principle, to be the most acceptable approach, there are still many associated problems. Some of these problems are financial and stem from the very limited resources which are allocated to this group. For the more severely handicapped, the provision of day centres or special sheltered work environments may be necessary and at present such facilities are limited. For the mild group there is the need to find suitable employment and this may bring its own problems. Finally, one major factor regarding the viability of community care is the attitude of the general public, which has been shown to be fairly negative. It is sad but true to note that mentally handicapped people are often treated with disdain, ridicule or worse by the public. To some extent this may be a function of ignorance and the previous lack of integration of this group. Improved community care might help to diminish this unfortunate state of affairs.

Psychological provisions for the mentally handicapped are varied. With very severely handicapped people who are deficient in basic self-maintenance skills such as dressing, feeding and washing, behavioural techniques have been very successfully used. These are described in more detail in Chapter 14. For the present it is sufficient to say they have been used to build up these sorts of skills in many individuals who previously might have been regarded as incapable of performing them. The benefits of this are obvious in that staff can be to a large extent freed from having to carry out these very basic functions and can divert their energies to more therapeutic activities, which will further benefit patients. One important spin-off of the effectiveness of these behavioural techniques has been in rethinking the nature of mental handicap. Previously with the prevailing tendency to think of intelligence as primarily genetically determined, the mentally handicapped were thought to have fixed limitations and therefore not capable of a great deal of improvement. Moreover, we now know from studies of institutionalization (*see* Chapter 13) that if people are treated as incapable their behaviour will mirror this. In this respect the implementation of behavioural techniques provides a very striking demonstration that if tasks are structured correctly and meaningfully, they can be well learned. The evidence from the effects of improving mental handicap hospital environments and the efficacy of behavioural intervention both point to the potency of environmental influences on intellectual functioning, even with a group with restricted abilities.

One further heartening source of evidence concerns the large number of recent studies, mainly in the USA, which have shown that it is possible to improve the intellectual functioning of the mildly handicapped. A great deal of this work has managed to go beyond the test-orientated approach to intelligence and has investigated cognitive processes more directly. What workers in this field have found is that often the mildly handicapped will have difficulty in spontaneously generating appropriate strategies on, for example, memory or problem-solving tasks. Having demonstrated this, these workers have been able to promote techniques for strategy training, with the result that significant improvements in performance have followed. This is perhaps one of the most important reasons for moving away from a strictly psychometric approach to intelligence and towards a conception which concentrates more on the underlying abilities and processes within the individual.

In the first part of this chapter a fairly critical approach to the standard psychometric approach to intelligence was adopted for a number of reasons. Within the specific context of mental handicap it becomes even clearer that providing an arbitrary quantifiable estimate of the level of someone's abilities is not of direct value in specifying the best type of remedial help. In contrast, an experimental approach can more directly identify the cognitive problems of an individual. This, in turn, can provide the basis for individualized remedial programmes. Furthermore, as one worker in this field has observed, this may have wider implications for our understanding of intelligence since he noted 'that the experimental study of the individual is not a development that is being advocated for the benefit of the handicapped populations alone. It is just as relevant for the understanding of cognitive processes in normal children, indeed, this is one way in which the study of handicap can contribute to our understanding of normal development' (Mittler, 1973).

- ## Recommended reading

Mittler P. (ed.) (1973) *The Psychological Assessment of Mental and Physical Handicaps.* London, Methuen.
Sternberg R. J. and Detterman D. K. (ed.) (1986) *What Is Intelligence?* Norwood, N.J., Ablex.

7

Individual differences in personality

When we refer to someone's personality we are really trying to answer the question, 'What is X like?'. We are therefore concerned with consistent aspects of an individual's behaviour which distinguish him or her from other people and allow us to make predictions about his or her behaviour. Wittingly and unwittingly such considerations often enter into one's dealings with patients. The way in which a patient is given information about the severity of an illness may frequently reflect the clinician's interpretation of the patient's personality. Thus, aspects of a patient's personality can play a role in determining whether information is given and, if so, in what detail. It is perhaps worth mentioning that the patient's personality can be used as a rationale for not giving information, even though there is evidence that most patients prefer to be informed about their illness. In the latter case, more is probably revealed about the clinician's personality or at least about the particular approach to patients which is typically adopted.

● **7.1. Personality: an introduction**
When we try to describe people's personality we usually do so in terms of such adjectives as outgoing, impulsive, serious, critical, sensitive, assertive, and the like. In doing so, we are describing various personality *traits* which we feel are somehow typical of their behaviour. Someone is labelled as having a particular trait when he or she is seen to respond in the same way in a range of situations. This labelling probably also takes place with reference to other people we know who respond differently in the same range of situations. Any individual is therefore thought of as having many traits.

Alternatively, we may try to describe people with a single description (e.g. extrovert) which is somehow meant to summarize all the typical aspects of their personality. In doing this we would be attempting to classify someone as being of a certain *type*. The type approach to personality description has a long and varied history with attempts to relate psychological types to 'bodily humours' (Hippocrates) and more recently to body build (Sheldon). Not much empirical support

96

has been provided for these simple typologies and it is probably fair to comment that they have failed because of their very simplicity. Human behaviour appears to be far too complex to be pigeon-holed into one of a few categories. Even though the type approach to personality assessment has tended to give way to the use of trait descriptions, both approaches are still used in assessment procedures.

The great problem for the new reader in trying to understand the nature of personality is that there is no agreed definition. There is no single accepted theory or assessment technique which can be unequivocally accepted and described here. There have been many attempts by distinguished psychologists to describe the nature of personality in terms of the critical characteristics involved and the factors which determine these. The result is that there are many different theories and in this chapter it will not be possible to do any more than give an indication of the diversity of approaches.

One further point worth making in this introductory section concerns the supposed stability and validity of personality traits as revealed by tests. Most personality tests are 'one-off' procedures and there is no way of ensuring that the responses given on one occasion are typical of the individual at all other times. There have been attempts to discover whether personality traits really are stable and these have generally comprised long-term correlative studies of a group of individuals, tested on a number of occasions. Many of these studies have provided moderate evidence for the stability of some but certainly not all behavioural traits. The results of such studies have suggested the possibility that some aspects of behaviour are determined very early on and remain pretty consistent whereas others are more subject to environmental influences. Thus, persisting differences in such personality characteristics as activity level and adaptiveness can be found in very young babies, but many other differences are not seen until much later.

There is accumulating evidence that it is not possible or perhaps feasible to predict behaviour in all situations from a trait description. Although many aspects of an individual's personality appear to remain broadly the same over time, as is reiterated in Chapter 9 on ageing, specific situational factors must also be taken into account. In other words there is evidence that behaviour can vary depending on the situation one is in and personality cannot be considered without reference to specific environmental determinants and constraints. This issue of what has been called 'situationism' in theories of personality has been argued strongly by a number of more behaviourally orientated psychologists (e.g. Mischel, 1969). As we see later in this chapter and in the final chapter, behaviourally orientated theories stress the importance of environmental determinants of all behaviour. They would argue that our behaviour is moulded by our transactions with the environment and hence tend to accept that different behaviours will be associated with different situations rather than thinking of personality traits as consistent.

Trait theorists have responded to these criticisms by maintaining that a trait can be expressed in all sorts of ways and may be more noticeable in certain situations. One other interesting outcome of this trait–situation controversy has been the suggestion that trait consistency is in itself an aspect of personality. Some people appear to be fairly insensitive to different environments and continue to act in the same way regardless. In contrast, others appear to be much more affected by environmental constraints and alter their behaviour much more readily. It would therefore appear to be useful to acknowledge that consistency of a person's behaviour in different situations is an important aspect of their personality. Most psychologists tend to accept an interactionist position on this issue. The person and the situation interact and both must be taken into account in order to understand behaviour.

From this introduction it must be becoming clear that describing and assessing personality is a complex task. It is not surprising to find that there have been many different attempts to do this and some of these differ quite radically in their approach. There will be an attempt to convey an impression of some of these approaches a little later on but before that there is an account of the way personality factors can intervene in various ways in illness and treatment.

● 7.2. Personality differences in response to illness and treatment

Anyone who has dealt with patients, even those presenting with very similar problems, cannot help but notice how differently patients can react to their illness and in the treatment situation. The research literature on this topic provides many examples of these individual differences across a wide range of conditions associated with both illness and treatment. It is possible to delineate five areas where such differences have been observed and these can be summarized thus:

a. Symptom perception.
b. Symptom action.
c. Symptom formation.
d. Response to illness.
e. Response to treatment.

Each of these areas is now discussed.

a. Symptom perception

Symptom perception refers to the way in which people perceive symptoms occurring in their own bodies. The first chapter on pain provided many examples of the variation in response to pain. Some of this variation is situationally and culturally determined but it would also appear that personality can play an important role. For example, it was reported that introverts are found to have a lower pain threshold in that they tend to feel pain sooner than extroverts. Situational factors may also alter pain threshold by affecting anxiety levels. Someone under pressure at home or at work might well be made more anxious and this could amplify the perception of a symptom. People will therefore differ in the way in which they perceive their symptoms and in the magnitude of their subjective experience of pain. This may also determine whether they seek medical help for their symptoms.

b. Symptom action

Symptom action is used to describe what action people take in response to the perception of a symptom and in particular whether they seek medical help. Logically, one might imagine that the only thing which determines whether medical help is sought is the severity of a symptom. However, the evidence confounds such a simple view since there is a well-known phenomenon referred to as the 'clinical iceberg'. This term refers to the fact that the people who present their symptoms to a doctor represent only the minority of people in the community with symptoms. Of the ones who do not present, a large number will have symptoms which could be objectively rated as equally or more severe than many of those presented at consultations. A large number of reasons have been put forward to account for both the help-seeking of those with apparently 'trivial' problems and the failure to seek help by those with quite serious ones. Some of these reasons are situational and reflect previous experiences with doctors but some are clearly determined by underlying individual differences. For example, in one large study of attendance rates in general practice, one factor which correlated with high attendance was the anxiety level of the patient. The higher the anxiety, the more likely the person was to seek medical help (Banks et al., 1975). It may well be that factors such as anxiety have an effect in altering symptom perception (*see above*) as well as in determining whether a visit to the doctor is made.

Other work has shown that differences in a personality trait referred to as 'locus of control' can influence the type of action which follows the perception of a symptom. Locus of control refers to the extent to which individuals feel that the things which happen to them are determined by internal factors (i.e. under their own control) or external factors (i.e. not affected by their behaviour). Some research has shown that high 'E' scorers on a locus of control questionnaire (i.e. with a strong belief in external determinants) are more likely to seek medical and psychiatric help since they feel that they are less able to bring about any effective change themselves and hence rely more on external agents to do so.

c. Symptom formation

This describes the possibility that different types of people might be prone to different types of disorders. The way in which people typically react and behave can have physiological and psychological consequences, which may be the precursors of illness, and was discussed in Chapter 5. Older work on psychosomatic medicine sought to relate certain personality types to specific physical disorders such as migraine or ulcerative colitis. These older notions are now no longer particularly tenable but there do appear to be a number of promising approaches on these lines.

Probably the best known attempt to link personality with a specific disease concerns the recent work which has investigated aspects of coronary heart disease. This stems from the work of Rosenman and his collaborators in the USA. In some extensive prospective studies they have been able to find a strong statistical link between the incidence of coronary heart disease and a behaviour pattern which they refer to as 'Type A'. The Type A behaviour pattern is characterized by enhanced aggressiveness and competitive drive, a preoccupation with deadlines and a chronic impatience and sense of time urgency as compared with the more relaxed and less hurried pattern, which they refer to as 'Type B'. One particularly valuable feature of these studies is that the research has also looked at the effects of many traditional risk factors such as cigarette smoking and diet. They have been able to provide clear evidence that Type A behaviour has an association with coronary heart disease over and above the association which is found with the more traditional risk factors.

While these results appear to be quite clear and acceptable, there are still some difficulties with this work. First, the interview and questionnaire techniques for distinguishing Type A/B behaviour are not particularly sophisticated and it is not really clear as to what aspects of personality are being measured and how consistent these are. Second, there remains the important task of ascertaining why this particular behaviour pattern should be associated with an increased proneness to coronary heart disease.

Rosenman (1979) has argued that heart disease is very much a twentieth-century disease and that Type A individuals are particularly vulnerable to 'twentieth-century stress'. Thus, it is maintained that it is not stress *per se* that is the critical factor but the manner in which Type A individuals respond. He maintains that Type A people show a greater rise in systolic blood pressure in response to physical and psychological demands although no differences in mean blood pressure levels between Type A and Type B subjects are found. It is further argued that these links between behaviour and heart disease are mediated through neurohormonal pathways. To date this work appears to represent the most comprehensive attempt to link personality factors to a particular disease process.

d. Response to illness

The nature of psychological responses to illnesses is dealt with in some detail in Chapter 12 and so will not be elaborated here. Most illnesses require some adjustment on the part of the individual concerned since they are often socially and psychologically disruptive. The way in which people adjust to these demands has been found to vary greatly but in a way which is predictable when the individual's underlying personality is considered. Thus, some people appear to over-react and some appear to under-react or deny the seriousness or inconvenience of an illness. Others become hostile and aggressive whereas some people might actually welcome and exaggerate their illness because it provides an opportunity to express their feelings of dependence on others. These various reactions are examined in Chapter 12 and it will be shown that an understanding of them can be valuable in dealing with patients since these different patterns of response may also be reflected in the response to treatment.

e. Response to treatment

As with the previous category, the question of individual differences in response to aspects of treatment is also dealt with in a number of other sections of this book. People appear to differ consistently in their response to both specific and non-specific aspects of treatment. In the final chapter on psychological approaches to treatment, the importance of the 'placebo' response is discussed. This refers to any therapeutic response which is not directly associated with a specific treatment or medication. Not everyone shows a placebo response and there is a range in the magnitude of the response among those who do. The personality and behaviour of the doctor or person administering the medication also appear to modify the extent of a placebo response.

In more specific terms, it has also been claimed that there are personality differences in response to drugs affecting the central nervous system. One way in which this has been studied has been in relating personality to drug tolerance. In anxious patients a greater tolerance of sedatives is found among the more introverted whereas extroverts are found to be much more sensitive to these drugs (Claridge, 1972). Apparently, the reverse pattern of tolerance to sedatives among these two personality types is found with people who are low in reported anxiety. It has also been shown that aspects of personality, particularly those associated with anxiety levels, can play a more important role than such factors as body weight in determining the amount of intravenous barbiturate which is required to induce sedation.

Finally, it has also been shown that personality factors may play a role in determining the effectiveness of communication between doctor and patient. Again, this topic is dealt with in much more detail later in the book where the importance of providing information to patients is discussed. However, it appears now that different types of explanatory information may be most effective with different groups of individuals. For example, it would appear that those who obtain high 'E' scores on a locus of control rating (i.e. those who believe that they have little control over external events) show best adjustment and are made least anxious by being given fairly general explanatory information prior to surgery. In contrast, those individuals who have a high internal locus of control (i.e. believe that they have some control over external events) prefer to be given quite specific details and show better adjustment when this is forthcoming. This is obviously a fairly specific finding but it does lead on to the more general point that it is useful to be aware of individual differences in the treatment situation and to modify one's handling of patients according to their particular needs and ways of responding. In Chapter 10 there is a fuller discussion of the value of giving patients information appropriate to their needs.

These examples of personality differences in various aspects of illness and treatment have been chosen to give some idea of the range of factors which can intervene rather than as an exhaustive account of the whole area. Hopefully, these examples provide sufficient evidence of the value of acknowledging and understanding something of the nature of personality differences. The problem therefore remains as to how these differences can be best described and measured. In the two sections which follow (7.3 and 7.4) there is a summary of a selection of descriptive and measurement approaches to personality.

• 7.3. Approaches to personality

In attempting to describe and understand personality, psychologists have sought to answer a number of basic questions and these include the following. What is the structure of personality and where does this structure originate? How do personality structures interact with the environment? What is the best way to describe and assess personality differences? Unfortunately for the reader, the answers to these and related questions about personality have been both prolific and varied. The result is that there are many different theories of personality and a bewildering number of assessment procedures. Some of these theories are quite similar in their basic premises and differ only in small detail, but there are very large differences between some of the major theoretical viewpoints.

In this section there is an attempt to give some idea of this diversity by outlining the basic orientations of four quite different approaches. It is not possible to give all the details of each approach, and the interested reader is referred to the recommended readings listed at the end of this chapter. The four approaches to be considered are:

a. Psychoanalytic theories.
b. Behavioural theories.
c. Cognitive theories.
d. Biological theories.

a. Psychoanalytic theories

These stem from the work of Freud who is often credited with having devised the first comprehensive theory of personality. Certainly, Freud's theory coincided with the beginning of the emergence of psychology as an independent discipline and has been very influential since then.

Freud derived his ideas about personality from working with patients with psychological problems. Very early on he claimed that many of these problems were the result of unconscious conflicts which originated in childhood and persisted into adulthood. An important part of his theory is therefore concerned with early psychological development and the way in which this can influence later behaviour.

For Freud, personality consisted of three components or mechanisms which interact and mediate behaviour. He called these the *id*, the *ego* and the *superego* and these three mechanisms serve to handle and control the constant supply of instinctual energy which is thought to drive behaviour. In the newborn, the personality structure consists only of the id, which is the source of most mental energy and responds directly to bodily needs. The id is therefore concerned with the immediate fulfilment of basic unconscious drives and needs. The ego develops a little later on and regulates these drives and needs in relation to the practicalities of the environment. Thus, while the id is thought to operate on the pleasure principle, the ego is constrained by a reality principle and therefore utilizes conscious, cognitive processes to manage the basic drives. The ego also includes mechanisms which can divert conscious attention from underlying anxiety. These include processes such as denial and repression and similar processes appear to come into play during times of stress or illness, as will be seen in Chapter 12. The third mental structure, the superego, develops a little later when children begin to identify with the behaviour of their parents. The superego comprises the internalization of parental codes of behaviour and therefore provides moral and social constraints.

From this brief description it can be seen that the Freudian model is in many ways built on biological and experimental considerations. The biological bases comprise the instinctual energy which drives behaviour and gives rise to the interaction of the three personality structures. For Freud, all behaviour has its roots in unconscious instinctual energy but is ultimately determined by the interplay between the id, ego and superego. The ego and id are thought to be in constant tension with each other and this balance can be upset at any time. A smoothly functioning ego in Freud's system is one which is strong enough to control the id and yet permits sufficient gratification of drives. However, there may be times when the ego is unable to exercise sufficient control and then anxiety and other psychological problems can result.

Biological factors also indicate the nature of personality development for Freud since he postulated a sequence of psychosexual stages in development. The latter are labelled the oral, anal and phallic stages since the young child is thought to become preoccupied with and gain pleasure from these three bodily areas separately. The resolution of each stage must be achieved as part of satisfactory development and failure to do so can lead to specific problems later in adulthood. Different types of psychological problems are held to arise from difficulties at each developmental stage. Resolution of the phallic stage occurs at about the age of 3–5, and is thought to be brought about by identification with the parent of the same sex, which in turn allows for the emergence of the superego. Thus, patterns of early experience dictate the nature of personality development since this takes place through the psychosexual stages.

Freud's theory is very much more detailed than is suggested by this minimal outline. It has been added to and modified by many other psychoanalytic theorists but common to most of these variants is the basic concept of humans striving to reduce the tension created by unconscious drives. Some of the other psychoanalytic theorists such as Erikson have de-emphasized the role of psychosexual factors in personality development and concentrated on the influence of social determinants.

The psychoanalytic emphasis on unconscious factors in behaviour has also dictated the nature of the associated approaches to assessment and therapy. As will be seen in section 7.4, personality assessment makes use of techniques for uncovering unconscious feelings and motives. Similarly, treatment also consists of attempts to allow the patient to go back and discover repressed childhood conflicts which are thought to be giving rise to problems in adulthood. This can be done by describing early memories and through the analysis of dreams as well as with other related procedures. The analyst can help the patient to become aware of these conflicts and to work through them so that they cease to be problematic.

Freudian theory has been attacked on many grounds since it is held to be nebulous, unscientific and based on the detailed observation of a relatively small group of patients. In fairness it should be pointed out that Freud's ideas were developed before the advent of modern psychology and so some concepts are now seen to be fairly untenable. Even so, psychoanalytic theory has had a considerable influence on research and clinical work, particularly in the USA. Some of the concepts, such as the defence mechanisms for dealing with anxiety, have been lifted and transplanted into other theories and some have been rather abandoned and neglected in the absence of any supportive data.

b. Behavioural theories

These attempt to describe the various learning and conditioning processes that shape and determine behaviour. Since behaviourists are not concerned with internal mental mechanisms, they see personality and behaviour as one and the same. For the behaviourist, a person can be best described in terms of what a person does and descriptions of personality are therefore seen as labels for referring to complex patterns of behaviour. If someone is described as assertive, for example, this means that he or she behaves in a particular way towards others. In this sense the theory of behaviour is also the theory of personality.

The basic premise underlying behavioural theories is that learning is the most important determinant of behaviour and that behaviour can change as a result of experience. Thus a human being is seen in a very mechanistic way as a complex collection of responses which are produced in specific situations. By and large, behaviour that is rewarded in specific situations will become strongly associated with those situations and will be produced in that particular context.

Correspondingly, behaviour that is not rewarded or is punished will disappear. Thus the behaviour that individuals acquire is determined by the consequences of their prior transactions with the environment. In attempting to understand someone's personality, the behaviourist therefore tries to establish which environmental determinants are responsible for specific behaviours.

In the same way that Freud used his clinical observations to provide the basis for his theory, the behaviourists have predominantly used animal conditioning experiments to understand the relations between stimuli and responses which lead to the acquisition of new behaviour. Unlike the Freudians, behavioural theorists do not refer to internal mental processes since they believe strongly that a scientific theory should be based only on observable events (i.e. stimuli and responses). So, whereas a psychoanalyst would start to understand someone with a particular problem by a description of his or her personality, the behaviourist would want to identify those environmental factors which were associated with that problem. Taking the example of the compulsive gambler, the behaviourists would not be concerned with the sort of personality which is associated with gambling but with describing those situations which give rise to gambling behaviour.

Behavioural theories have been enthusiastically applied to the analysis of psychological problems, which are seen to be maladaptive learned behaviours. In dealing with these, therefore, a detailed description of the behaviour in question is obtained and this is used to determine treatment. This consists primarily of various techniques which are intended to allow the patient either to unlearn maladaptive behaviour or to relearn a more favourable response. Since there is a fairly full account of behaviour therapy in Chapter 14, no further details are presented here.

The behavioural approach to understanding human behaviour and treatment has an immediate attraction because of its apparent simplicity and straightforwardness. However, this very simplicity would also appear to be a potential weakness since there is abundant evidence that all behaviour cannot be accurately described in simple stimulus–response terms and that internal cognitive processes are not only of prime importance but can also be studied by experimental procedures. It is perhaps significant that a number of behaviourists have now attempted to incorporate cognitive factors into accounts of learning processes and this has enabled them to provide much richer and more flexible explanations of behaviour. In this way behavioural theories can begin to account for the complexity of human behaviour. It is interesting to note that behaviour therapy has also taken on a more cognitive look since many behaviour therapists now acknowledge the importance of describing and changing thoughts as well as behaviours. Although there are still many 'purists' who regret the intrusion of cognitive variables, the work of psychologists such as Beck et al. (1979) provides impressive evidence of the value of adopting a more cognitive approach.

c. Cognitive theories

Cognitive theories of personality have come to the fore in recent years as experimental psychology has become more concerned with cognitive processes and as strict behavioural theories have been shown to be inadequate in explaining individual differences in emotional and social behaviour. Although there is no big name such as Freud or Skinner, there are some interesting new approaches which attempt to describe the ways in which individuals view the world. Thus, just as behaviourists reduce personality to behaviour, cognitive theories see personality in terms of the particular cognitions individuals possess and which explain their feelings and behaviour. By cognitions, what is meant are the thoughts, anticipations, expectations, beliefs and other mental processes that are peculiar to any individual. In many ways cognitivists view the human being as a scientist who is continually trying to make sense of the world and at any one time will have a set of theories which are interpretations based on the data accumulated to date.

The best known of the cognitive theorists is Kelly (1963) who actually refers to 'man, the scientist' since he believes that we all try to predict and understand behaviour. In order to do this we form hypotheses based on the data we have obtained about our behavioural world. New experiences therefore correspond to new evidence for the scientist since these can be used to confirm or disconfirm our hypotheses and this may result in altering our view of the world in some way.

Kelly maintains that behaviour is determined by our perception and interpretation of our interactions with others rather than by the actual interactions themselves. Thus, identical external events may give rise to different reactions because of the particular meaning that an individual will attach to the events. For example, in a married couple, the perception of a statement made by one partner may be interpreted as conciliatory by the speaker and as threatening or patronizing by the other partner. If the statement made by the husband is 'I think I should help more in the housework', he may think of this as a helpful gesture whereas it is possible that the wife might see it as a criticism of her housekeeping ability. The different views of the two individuals involved give rise to quite different interpretations of the same environmental stimulus.

Instead of viewing people as victims of their biological impulses or of external stimuli, cognitive theorists see them as actively trying to make sense of their situation and using their interpretations to guide future behaviour. Kelly has used the term 'construct' to refer to the particular way of categorizing or making sense of the world that individuals use. People differ in both the number and type of constructs which they use for interpreting the world. Rather than attempting to categorize an individual's personality into a preconceived slot or set of traits, Kelly maintains that each person behaves according to their own system of construing. Hence his theory is referred to as the Personal Construct Theory. In order to understand a particular individual it is therefore necessary to know which constructs they use and how the constructs are organized in relation to each other to form the individual's system of construing. Kelly has devised a technique for doing this and this is described in section 7.4.

There are a number of other cognitive approaches apart from the Personal Construct Theory. Some of these have developed from a more behaviourist standpoint and have tried to describe the way in which individuals view the stimulus–response situations which they experience. Thus one approach, referred to as the Locus of Control Theory, attempts to describe individual differences in the perceived control over events in people's lives. Some people feel that they are able to influence events whereas others feel that they have little or no control over things which happen to them. As we saw in Chapter 5, this has been found to be helpful in explaining why some people react more adversely to environmental stress.

Another closely related cognitive-behavioural model attempts to explain depression in terms of learning about one's own apparent inability to effect environmental change. This approach is referred to as the Learned Helplessness Theory, after Seligman (1975), and in recent versions of the theory it is postulated that people who are prone to depression see adverse happenings in their environment as due to themselves whereas good events are thought to be due to chance. According to this theory, an individual's interpretations or attributions of environmental events may be instrumental in generating feelings of helplessness and ultimately depression.

Cognitive approaches offer a number of quite new and valuable ways of looking at personality differences. They are able to deal with the flexibility and complexity of human behaviour and manage to avoid the simplistic pigeon-holing of many traditional approaches. It is possible to derive quite useful data about individuals and the particular ways they have of perceiving the world and coping with problems. This in turn can provide a valuable basis for treatment since it is possible to specify highly individualized aims for a treatment programme by relating to the special needs of an individual. Against this it must be argued that the means for studying and evaluating individual cognitions are still relatively poorly developed and in some ways are rather woolly. Moreover, cognitive approaches can run into difficulties in the research context since there can be problems in comparing individual ways of perceiving the world. However, this difficulty has been to some degree overcome by the techniques evolved in association with the Personal Construct Theory.

d. Biological theories

Biological theories attempt to explain individual differences in terms of underlying physiological mechanisms. In older times efforts were made to characterize personality types in terms of 'bodily humours'. Others sought to differentiate individuals by differences in the size and shape of their heads. Not surprisingly, these rather simple physiological and anatomical correlates do not appear to be related in any consistent way to differences in behaviour. In more recent times there have been attempts to relate personality to body build and although the original research workers claimed a high degree of correlation, more thorough subsequent work has diminished the strength of these claims. However one influential theorist, Eysenck, has attempted to describe dimensions of personality in terms of properties of nervous system functioning.

Eysenck believes that individual differences in personality can be primarily accounted for by three unrelated dimensions which he has called extroversion–introversion, neuroticism and psychoticism. The extroversion–introversion dimension refers to the sociability and degree of caution shown in behaviour. Extroverts are outgoing and impulsive while introverts are more withdrawn and cautious. Eysenck postulates that these differences arise from the balance between excitatory and inhibitory processes in the central nervous system. He suggests that extroverts are characterized by a nervous system which is slower to respond and is more weakly aroused by stimuli than that of introverts. Moreover, the extrovert's nervous system is also reckoned to generate neural inhibition more quickly. These neural differences are held to account for the fact that introverts can be conditioned more easily than extroverts whereas the latter can be characterized as more 'stimulus seeking' because of their higher threshold of activation.

The dimension of neuroticism indicates the extent to which people tend to worry or respond emotionally and this is held to be related to the activity of the ascending reticular activating system and the limbic system. This brain system is known to be involved in emotional activation and may therefore also influence the excitability of the autonomic nervous system, which is also thought to be related to neuroticism.

Although Eysenck's theory has generated a great deal of further research in many related areas, there are a number of obvious criticisms which should be raised. By narrowing personality differences down to three dimensions, the theory is much too narrow and overlooks many interesting aspects of personality. While these dimensions of personality are easy to describe and assess, they trivialize rather the complexity and richness of personality differences. Although it is laudable to relate personality to physiological underpinnings, the evidence for the physiological bases of extroversion and neuroticism is speculative and as yet inconclusive (Powell, 1979). However, there have been some useful studies relating individual differences in various cognitive processes to Eysenck's personality dimensions.

It has not been possible to do more than give an indication of some of the ways personality and behavioural differences have been related to biological factors. There are a number of intrinsic problems for biologically based theories of personality at present. The brain mechanisms mediating emotional and social aspects of behaviour are still very poorly understood and certainly less so than those involved in cognitive processes. While it is difficult enough trying to describe personality, the problems of relating these descriptions to brain mechanisms are effectively beyond the bounds of current knowledge. There is also the danger that attempts to do this may end up by being too reductionist. While it may be useful to say that one person differs from another because of differences in limbic system functioning or in brain amine metabolic rates, we still need to be able to describe these differences in psychological terms if we want to understand how people differ in the way they react. Biological explanations might ultimately help to explain why these differences arise. Psychological descriptions are essential for knowing how these differences manifest themselves in everyday life in general and in response to illness and treatment in particular.

● **7.4. The assessment of personality**

The techniques available for assessing personality are as diverse as the theoretical approaches and in many cases they stem directly from the theories. Measuring personality characteristics involves many problems, some of which are intrinsic to all psychological measurements and some of which are additional to these. One of the most obvious is that it is very difficult to take direct samples of someone's behaviour from which aspects of 'true' personality can be inferred. It might be reasonably argued that one way out of this difficulty would be to obtain an assessment of an individual from a group of close acquaintances who would have a great deal of knowledge to base their comments on. In a sense this is what happens when references are provided for jobs. However, this approach would have all sorts of weaknesses as a formal assessment procedure. Different people's assessments of the same individual might produce quite varied pictures and it would then be necessary to know something about the assessors. Also, there is no such thing as a standard group of acquaintances from whom a representative data base could be obtained. It would be impossible to compare assessments because they would all be made in quite different ways.

This raises a fundamental question. Is it really necessary to be able to make comparisons between personality assessments or is it more important to say something unique about an individual? This is an issue which runs through all psychological assessment and appears to be of particular significance in assessing personality. By and large, psychologists have recommended the use of standardized tests which give everyone the same questions and evaluate their answers in a comparable way. These questionnaires have a great merit in large-scale research projects, where comparisons on many measures might be made. It is probably fair to say that they have a limited usefulness for dealing with individuals since everyone is evaluated on a narrow range of criteria such as introversion–extroversion and neuroticism. One result of this has been the development of tools which provide the opportunity to investigate the individual in more detail without the use of existing classification schemes. In this brief account there will be an attempt to consider both types of approach.

There are many ways of classifying the large number of personality assessments. Five categories of approach are briefly considered here to provide examples of procedures rather than as a definitive account. The five categories are:

- *a.* Projective techniques.
- *b.* Behavioural techniques.
- *c.* The assessment of individual cognitions.
- *d.* Questionnaires.
- *e.* The interview.

a. Projective techniques

These refer to various assessment procedures which are used within the psychoanalytic approach. Typically they involve test items which are in some way ambiguous and which the individual has to interpret or comment on. Since the items are ambiguous or unstructured, it is found that different people give quite different responses, which can be taken to reveal something of their underlying personality. Thus the tests are called projective techniques since it is thought that people will project aspects of their personality onto the ambiguous material in their individual attempts to interpret them.

In many ways the psychoanalytic technique of word association can be thought of as a projective test since the therapist is looking for significant associations to particular words. This may give a clue to underlying conflicts or needs. However, the word association procedure does not normally involve a fixed set of items as would be expected in a specific test. These can be found in the two best known projective tests, namely the *Rorschach Test* and the *Thematic Apperception Test*.

The Rorschach is the oldest of the projective techniques and consists of ten cards each with a different inkblot pattern. Most of these are in black and white but some incorporate red and others contain a variety of colours. All of them have a bilateral symmetry since they were originally derived by vertically folding in half a sheet with wet ink. These ambiguous shapes are presented with the instructions to say what they might represent. The responses are analysed in various ways according to the structure or style of the responses and the reported content (i.e. what is 'seen' in inkblots). There are detailed instructions for evaluating the responses and these are intended to reveal different aspects of personality. Even so, there are enormous problems associated with the interpretation of inkblot responses and whether these really do represent fundamental aspects of the individual. There has been growing criticism of the technique as a formal assessment but some clinicians continue to use it as a way of understanding their patients. For example, it has been argued that it can be useful when more formal questionnaires or interviews are met with resistance and that inkblots may provide an apparently neutral way of eliciting useful clinical information. Even where inkblots are still used, it is probably true to say that they provide a basis for a description of an individual rather than a set of scores which allow formal comparisons between individuals.

The same criticisms can be levelled against the other well-known projective technique, the Thematic Apperception Test (TAT). The TAT consists of a series of pictures of people in various settings, some alone and some together with other people. Each is presented for 5 minutes and the person taking the test is required to say what is going on in each picture and to say what led up to the events in the picture together with what the outcome will be. The descriptions which are offered are assumed to reflect someone's previous experiences as well as their current concerns. Again, there is a system for interpreting performance based on various categories of the response such as the content, length of story, emotional issues and the interpretation of the roles of the people. Similar advantages and disadvantages which were noted for the Rorschach are applicable to the TAT. The test tends to be unreliable and different testers have been found to produce quite diverse interpretations of the same data. For these sorts of reasons, projective techniques are now used much less frequently. Where they are used the emphasis tends to be on the suggestive individual descriptions which can be derived rather than on their usefulness as formal assessments.

b. Behavioural techniques

Behavioural techniques for assessing personality do not generally involve specific tests but comprise a general method for describing salient aspects of behaviour. As was suggested earlier, many behaviourists have argued that there may not be much to be gained from attempting to measure universal personality traits since behaviour is thought to be determined by situations and may vary consistently from situation to situation. A behavioural assessment may be called for to assess problematic behaviour which occurs in certain situations and, as such, it is an attempt to provide a clear description of a set of selected and carefully defined behaviours.

Behavioural assessments constitute a general approach which can be applied to specific types of behaviour, often referred to as target behaviours. In the clinical context these might refer to unpleasant feelings such as anxiety or fear or to overt behaviour such as crying or tantrums in children. These target behaviours are carefully observed and described so that the situations which give rise to them as well as their nature and frequency are clearly understood. There are general guidelines for obtaining behavioural assessments as well as a number of quite detailed procedures for monitoring specific types of behaviour. Common to all of these are the detailed descriptions of the quality and quantity of the behaviour being observed. These descriptions specify the conditions under which the problem behaviours occur and therefore provide the basis for treatment since the latter usually consists of altering environmental factors.

Behavioural assessments are generally used as an adjunct to behaviour therapy since they provide the first step from which a treatment programme can be formulated. The value of behavioural assessments lies in their precision and clarity in describing aspects of behaviour. Thus the effectiveness of any behavioural treatment can be easily evaluated since it becomes a question of observing the extent to which a problem behaviour has changed as a function of a therapeutic intervention. However, it would seem that this precision not only makes for the strength of this approach but may also give rise to some difficulties. There may be important factors which cannot be directly observed and these may typically involve what the person is thinking or feeling at the time. Strict behavioural techniques do not take account of cognitions and feelings since they are dismissed as 'unobservables' and in doing so they may fail to provide an adequate and useful assessment. However, it is important to note that many recent developments in this area have encompassed a broader approach which takes account of a person's thoughts and feelings. In doing this, behavioural assessments may therefore be able to give a more meaningful account of behavioural problems but paradoxically they may lose some of their apparent precision. There is also a danger that complex thought processes cannot be described adequately by behavioural assessments and other techniques for investigating individual cognitions may be more useful. Some alternative approaches are now briefly described.

c. The assessment of individual cognitions

In contrast to behavioural assessments, which attempt to produce an accurate description of a set of behaviours, the cognitive approaches are concerned with how people view their world and with understanding their behaviour as arising from these views. This approach is therefore very similar to some of the cognitive theories of perception which seek to understand perceptions in terms of mental hypotheses which are built up as the result of perceptual experiences. In the same way, cognitive personality theorists have sought to elicit the nature of an individual's hypotheses, views or constructs about the world since these will not only reflect prior experiences but also help to account for behaviour. Two assessment techniques which provide some insight into an individual's cognitions are described here. First there is an account of the *Repertory Grid* technique and then there is a description of the more limited *Locus of Control* assessment procedure.

The Repertory Grid is based on Kelly's Personal Construct Theory and offers a technique for eliciting an individual's constructs. The technique for doing this is fairly simple. First, the individual provides a list of key individuals in his or her life. These will include individuals such as family members and close friends as well as those who fit a certain category (e.g. the most successful person you know, a person you pity, etc.). Once this list of about 15–20 individuals is assembled, groups of three are then successively presented to the individual who is then asked to say in what way two are similar and the third different from the other two. Thus, someone given the triad of mother, father and teacher might say that the father and teacher were critical but the mother was accepting. This process of presenting groups of three continues until a set of ways of classifying (constructs) is derived. Usually about the same number of constructs as individuals are derived but this can vary. From this it can be seen that constructs represent dimensions along which significant people in the individual's life are ordered. Once the constructs are elicited, all the people are then evaluated in terms of those constructs.

The Repertory Grid therefore provides a fairly neat way of looking at unique aspects of the individual through an analysis of his or her ways of construing the world. Using some quite sophisticated analysis techniques it is possible to analyse the responses to find a few basic constructs that are typical of the way a person perceives and classifies others. It is also possible to look at different people's constructs by comparing the number of constructs and the ways in which they are organized.

Repertory Grids are not only used for discovering constructs about key individuals. They can be used for working with individuals with quite specific problems for finding out constructs specific to those problems. They can be used for discovering differences between actual constructs and idealized constructs (i.e. how the person would like to see their situation) and this can provide indicators for treatment and for evaluating treatment progress. Furthermore, it is possible to use grids in marital therapy to look at the quality of a relationship as revealed through the two partners' respective views of the relationship and each other. These are a few examples of applications of this technique. It appears that it can be used in a wide range of clinical and non-clinical contexts where one is interested in finding out how people view events, people or situations.

The Repertory Grid is still a fairly new technique and it is too early to provide a comprehensive evaluation of it. It appears to be a flexible and yet reliable procedure which can provide very interesting and useful information. It has the great advantage of focusing on the individual and can be of particular use in the clinical situation for defining problems and suggesting approaches to treatment.

A quite different approach to understanding personality through an analysis of cognitions or views of the world can be found in attempts to measure locus of control. The original scale to do this was derived by Rotter (1966) and took the form of the I–E control scale. This scale can be used to determine beliefs that individuals hold about the causes of events and the extent to which events in their lives are attributed to themselves (internal control) or to external or chance factors (external control).

For example, someone who obtains a high exam mark might attribute this to a particular ability or to having worked hard (internal control) or to the fact that it was very easy or that the selection of questions just happened to be advantageous (external control). Of course many people would see both possibilities as explanatory in this situation but the strong tendency to opt for one or other explanation is indicative of being a high 'internalizer' or 'externalizer'. Locus of control therefore refers to a bias of one type which influences how individuals perceive their control over the environment in a wide range of situations. Although it is a way of examining a person's cognitions it arises primarily from a behaviourist approach since it refers to the perceived causes of rewards.

The I–E scale comprises a number of sentences which have to be rated as true or false depending on the person's beliefs. From these responses, it is possible to see the extent to which a person can be characterized as having an internal or external locus of control. Although this refers to a relatively limited aspect of behaviour it does appear to be a fairly stable and important characteristic. The way in which people construe causality has been found to have implications in the clinical context, as we saw in Chapter 5.

d. Questionnaires

Questionnaires and rating scales are probably the best known and most widely used techniques for personality assessment. The majority of these procedures are based on trait descriptions of personality and therefore comprise questions or rating procedures which reflect aspects of a particular personality trait. Typically, the questions will refer to behaviour or feelings in real-life situations and the individual will be required to indicate, usually by replying 'true' or 'false', the response which is most characteristic of himself or herself. Each questionnaire generally measures a number of traits and these are scored with reference to the performance of large samples of individuals. In this respect, personality questionnaires work in a similar way to standardized intelligence tests since the scores are primarily evaluated with reference to the performance of others. The scores therefore give an idea of the relative standing of an individual on a particular behavioural trait.

Although questionnaires and rating scales have the advantage that they are standardized and can be used easily for comparing individuals, they do have a number of serious problems. First, responses are always evaluated in terms of pre-existing categories or traits which are thought to be fundamental aspects of personality. This inevitably results in a type of pigeon-holing procedure, and this may not provide the best way of understanding personality. Second, there is no guaranteed way to tell whether the responses on questionnaires are entirely truthful or valid. This may partly be because the questions force a response too strongly in a particular direction. Thus, a response may appear to be global when it may only refer to a range of situations and not to certain specific situations. A problem may also arise because responses might be fabricated to give an idealized picture of an individual. People are not always able to describe their own motives and feelings accurately even if they try to do so. Some questionnaires have built-in checks to determine the consistency of responses to see whether 'faking good' has occurred. The latter might consist of a number of items which refer to rather perfect forms of behaviour and if an individual rates positively on a large number of these, it would suggest that the other responses might be dubious.

One final and potentially serious problem with personality questionnaires is the lack of unambiguous criteria for evaluating test validity. Or to put it more simply, how do we know that tests purporting to measure certain traits are really measuring them? It is not really possible to measure predictive validity in the way described for intelligence testing since it is much more difficult to define real-life behaviour with which trait scores might be correlated. One way out of this problem has been to compare groups of people who have already been classified in a certain way as, for example, by psychiatric diagnosis. It is for this reason that a number of well-known procedures were developed on clinical populations and some of their scales are referred to by rather clinical labels (e.g. neuroticism, paranoia, etc.). The two personality inventories to be described below were both originally developed in this way and this should be borne in mind when considering the information they give.

The *Minnesota Multiphasic Personality Inventory* (MMPI) was developed originally for the differential diagnosis of psychiatric disorders and still has a large number of scales which have a psychiatric label, such as depression and hysteria. A number of less overtly clinical scales are also included in the 13 scales which are derived from the vast number of questions that have to be answered. For each individual, one obtains a personality profile based on the scores on each scale. In addition to this, a number of computer programs have been developed for evaluating MMPI answers and these can elicit and describe more general personality characteristics.

The MMPI has probably been researched more than any other personality inventory and it has also given rise to a number of other more specific inventories based on subsets of MMPI questions. Despite the impressive amount of work carried out with this test, it still has its problems. There are reported problems with its reliability which is perhaps not too surprising in the light of the problems in measuring traits as supposedly invariant aspects of behaviour. Some writers have concluded that the MMPI has been more successfully applied for research purposes and in spawning further inventories than for routine personality assessment.

The same comments about research applicability can also be made about the *Eysenck Personality Inventory*. This is a much briefer inventory of questions producing three separate measures of personality, which Eysenck believes represent the three main differentiators of individual personality. The three dimensions of personality which are revealed are neuroticism, extroversion–introversion and psychoticism, which are described briefly in section 7.3. Again, this inventory has been used in a large number of research studies and has allowed investigators to examine easily the relation between these personality variables and many other aspects of behaviour including cognitive processes, sexual behaviour and sensitivity to drugs. Its ease of administration, scoring and interpretation are appealing characteristics but many critics feel that it provides too minimal a picture of personality. In attempting to tie down personality to scores on three dimensions, it is felt that the resultant picture is too limited and ultimately rather trivial. Against this criticism, supporters of this approach have argued that these three dimensions represent fundamental biological properties but this has yet to be conclusively demonstrated.

e. The interview

The interview can be used to discover aspects of an individual's personality in a variety of contexts. It is probably used most for selection purposes where interviewers are usually faced with the improbable task of deciding whether someone would be suitable for a job or a course on the basis of a fairly short interview. Skilled selection interviewers argue strongly that they can obtain useful information from an interview and that this can be used in a positive or negative way (i.e. in deciding for or against someone). Controlled studies of selection interviewing have demonstrated that there can be large differences between different interviewers' rating of candidates and that many variables can affect the final outcome. Despite all the evidence to the contrary, the interview remains as popular as ever and probably serves as a reminder that we all feel we are intrinsically good judges of personality.

In the clinical context, the interview probably still represents the most frequently used and most influential source of evidence for those who deal with people's personal problems. As we see in Chapter 10, skilled interviewing consists as much of providing an opportunity for the patient to discuss problems as of asking structured questions. Moreover, the skilled interviewer will be able to pick up useful information from the way things are said and from other non-verbal cues. Good clinical interviewing develops partly from an understanding of the nature of the problems being dealt with but ultimately often owes more to the interviewer's sensitivity and empathy.

Unfortunately, as we also see in later chapters, communication in the clinical setting can often be quite flawed and gross misinterpretations can occur. There is not a particularly high inter-rater reliability between psychiatrists in their interview assessments of personality and personal problems. It would appear that many biases and preconceptions can influence the outcome of an interview. Patients may also be unwilling to discuss personal details with an interviewer whom they perceive unfavourably or indifferently. For this reason, it is interesting to note that a number of investigators have reported that patients have preferred giving details of psychological problems to a computer-based medical interviewing system rather than in a face-to-face interview. Despite all these problems the interview continues to be used as an assessment procedure and it is hoped that with improved training in interviewing skills many of the imperfections can be overcome.

● 7.5. Personality differences: some concluding remarks

For many readers the question of why people behave and react differently may stand out as one of the most interesting and potentially useful areas of psychology. Everyone would like to know more about why people react to a problem in a particular way and to be able to predict how they will be able to cope with future events. Given this basic interest and applicability, it may come as something of a disappointment to find that there are so many approaches and it is not clear which is best. One can sympathize with the critic who maintained that there are more theories than firm conclusions in this area. Many psychologists do opt for one of the approaches outlined earlier and base their work with patients primarily on specific lines. However, in attempting a brief review of this type, it should become clear that no single approach emerges as the ideal. There are strengths and weaknesses in each although some are clearly weaker and less useful than others. Also, in dealing with many psychological problems, the commitment and enthusiasm of the therapist may be as important as the methodology adopted, as is discussed in Chapter 14.

Given that there is a considerable diversity of approaches, it is worth making some concluding remarks to round off this discussion. First, it is apparent that theories and tests of personality are beset by many of the conflicts of interest that are found in approaches to intelligence. Should the emphasis be on 'normative' approaches which provide a system for classifying and comparing individuals? Or, should personality theories be concerned with ways of understanding the world of the individual without necessarily wishing to say anything about them in relation to others? At least part of the answer to this question depends on what one wants to achieve with a theory of personality. If one's needs are for a simple classification scheme, it becomes obvious that only certain aspects of individual behaviour can be described and compared. Nevertheless these restricted comparisons can be very useful for research purposes where it is necessary to have objective and comparable data on each individual. In the clinical context the emphasis should be on the indiviudal in order to provide the most useful account of problems and indications for treatment.

This still leaves the question which was hinted at earlier concerning the relative value of different personality theories. A demanding and possibly exasperated reader might still be wanting to know which theory is best and does it really matter anyway? Taking these two issues in reverse order, the answer to the second point is that it can matter in practical terms which theoretical approach is adopted.

The theoretical stance of a therapist can radically influence the shape and form of a treatment schedule. For some problems there is evidence that a range of treatments can be effective in quite different ways, but there are indications that some approaches are more successful or more efficient in dealing with specified problems. This issue is returned to in Chapter 14 on psychological approaches to treatment.

The above discussion on the relation between theory and application hints at the answer to the question of which theory is best. It should be obvious by now that there is no complete theory of personality and perhaps there never will be. The work to date has at least provided us with a number of distinct insights into different aspects of personality and some of these can be quite usefully combined or interwoven. It would be difficult to deny the importance of early development and social attachments, the influence of learning and interactions with the environment and the role of individual interpretations of the self and the world. These are not necessarily mutually exclusive approaches even though they are often presented as such. So, the answer as to which theory is best would appear to be all of them and none of them, since they all appear to contribute to and broaden our understanding of personality differences but none is totally acceptable on its own. Finally, it ought to be said that the very diversity of these theories is a tribute to the richness and complexity of human personality.

- **Recommended reading**

Engler B. (1979) *Personality Theories: An Introduction.* Boston, Houghton Mifflin.
Maddi S. R. (1976) *Personality Theories: A Comparative Analysis*, 3rd ed. Homewood, Dorsey Press.

8

Child development

Most specialist areas in medicine either are concerned with specific types of problem (e.g. neurology, dermatology, etc.) or are defined by particular skills (e.g. surgery, pathology, etc.). In contrast, two specialties are defined primarily by the age range of the patients who are dealt with. These are the specialties of paediatrics and geriatrics which are concerned with the medical needs of the young and the old respectively. They have developed as separate disciplines following on the recognition that the changes associated with child development and with the ageing process need a particular understanding and expertise. Many of the medical problems found in these two groups can be quite similar to those found in other age groups but separate skills may be necessary in caring for children or old people. However, these two periods of life can give rise to some quite specific problems and there will be some mention of the psychological problems which fall into this category. This chapter is taken up with a consideration of the characteristic psychological changes which accompany child development and the following chapter is concerned with the ageing process.

Many accounts of child development understandably begin with the newborn baby and describe the sequence of changes through to adolescence and early adulthood. This convention is adopted in the section outlining developmental changes. One problem with this type of approach is that it can present a somewhat oversimplified picture of development as an invariant and well-defined sequence which every child follows in a similar fashion. In reality there are many diverse factors which can influence the process of development at any stage from conception through to adolescence. Thus there follows an account of some of the factors which can affect development, some of which can have lasting effects on the child and some of which are of direct clinical significance. Following this there is an outline of some of the main changes which take place during development. Finally, there is an introduction to some of the psychological problems associated with the developmental process.

● **8.1. Factors influencing child development**

The factors influencing development considered here are:

a. Genetic influences.

    b. Prenatal influences.
    c. Neonatal influences: birth complications.
    d. Nutrition.
    e. Environmental chemicals.
    f. Physical handicaps and brain injury.
    g. The early environment.

a. Genetic influences

The whole process of normal brain formation and development is under the control of genetic mechanisms. However, the expression of an organism's genetic endowment will depend on many environmental constraints, as we have seen in earlier chapters and also discuss below. Once a child is born, the effects of inheritance and experience become increasingly difficult to untangle and so an account of genetic or environmental influences must be attempted with considerable caution.

Physical characteristics have a clear genetic basis and some of these may directly or indirectly affect behaviour. As we see later, parental reactions appear to differ in response to male and female babies and so this is one broad way in which an inherited factor can indirectly affect later behaviour. Such factors as height and rate of maturation can also indirectly affect aspects of behaviour on account of the differing patterns of social reactions to people of different heights or to early or late developers in adolescence. Social evaluations of various physical attributes can therefore produce effects at a behavioural level. In contrast, there is relatively little firm evidence to show that specific types of behaviour or ability are under direct genetic control, except in certain extreme circumstances. There are some diseases which are genetically transmitted and which produce well-defined behavioural changes. For example one of these, Huntington's chorea, is a degenerative disease of the central nervous system which produces progressive mental deterioration in adulthood. This disease depends on the presence of a single dominant gene.

It is much more difficult to demonstrate that an individual's genetic endowment directly determines the sorts of personality differences described in the previous chapter. One strategy for doing this has been to compare selectively identical and non-identical twins on personality tests. Another method is to compare adopted children with their biological and adoptive parents. In either case there are still many methodological problems, as we saw in the discussion of genetic and environmental influences on intelligence in Chapter 6. There it was concluded that intelligence differences depend on a complex gene–environment interaction which may be difficult or even futile to untangle. There is evidence that young babies do show consistent differences in their general responsiveness and level of activity. Although intra-uterine and early environmental factors can play a role here, as we see shortly, many researchers believe that these differences are at least partly inherited. Such findings have led to the speculation that some very general personality dimensions such as introversion–extroversion may have a genetic basis. However, it is difficult to see how individual cognitions about the world could do anything but develop from actual experiences.

While there are many problems in directly assigning genetic influences to specific types of behaviour, some important clinical links have been found. Although the majority of mentally handicapped children are probably not the victims of their inheritance, some with severe mental handicap have been found to have a chromosomal defect. Down's syndrome (mongolism) is the best known example of this since it appears to be the result of an extra chromosome in one of the 23 pairs. Most of these children function at a very low level of intelligence. Another form of mental retardation which is known to be inherited is phenylketonuria, in which sufferers are unable to convert a chemical found in many foods to a harmless form. The resultant toxins accumulate and damage nerve cells, giving rise to mental handicap. However, unlike Huntington's chorea and Down's syndrome, there is a good preventive treatment which consists of strict dietary control. If this problem is detected early enough, the inherited disorder can be minimized by environmental control.

b. Prenatal influences

These refer to a wide range of factors which can affect fetal development. These include the mother's age, diet and state of mental and physical health as well as such external factors as drugs and environmental toxins.

There is some evidence that women younger than 20 or older than 35 have a slightly greater probability of giving birth to children with physical defects. The probability of having a mentally retarded child also increases slightly in older women. This group may also be likely to experience difficult pregnancies and labour, both of which may be associated with psychological and physical problems.

Maternal diet can also determine the physical quality of the pregnancy since mothers with poor diets are found to have a greater incidence of toxaemia, threatened and actual miscarriages and premature babies. Also their babies are found to be less healthy after birth. The effects of inadequate maternal diet on the child's psychological development are more difficult to establish. There may be some direct adverse effects on brain development but there are also likely to be indirect psychological effects associated with some of the physical problems. However, it is important to remember that mothers with inadequate diets may also be living in poor environments and these environmental disadvantages are also likely to have their effects on mental development.

Although there are no direct connections between the nervous systems of the mother and the fetus, it is still possible for the mother's psychological state to affect the fetus. The mother's emotional responses will result in the release of hormones and other chemicals into the bloodstream as we saw in Chapter 5. These substances can diffuse into the bloodstream of the fetus and thereby affect its nervous system. In addition it is possible that these substances can alter placental blood flow and indirectly affect fetal nutrition. It has been found that when mothers are emotionally upset there are marked increases in the number of bodily movements made by the fetus. Again it is difficult to say whether maternal anxiety or stress is directly associated with problems in psychological development, particularly as mothers who are anxious during pregnancy are also likely to be so afterwards.

Physical illness in the expectant mother can have considerable effects on the physical and psychological status of the child to be. The barrier between the bloodstream of the mother and the fetus is only partially effective at blocking viruses and so it is possible for a mother's illness to affect the fetus. Babies can actually be born with certain diseases but maternal infections can also have strong effects on the neurological development of the fetus. The most common example is that of German measles (rubella) which is particularly dangerous during the first three months of pregnancy. Between 10 and 15 per cent of these mothers have been found to give birth to children with various sensory and neurological disorders. The commonest defects are deafness, cataracts of the eyes and certain forms of mental handicap.

Finally, an increasingly recognized source of physical and psychological problems in childhood are the various drugs which are medically prescribed or self-administered during pregnancy. The gross anatomical defects associated with thalidomide in pregnancy are now well known and have ensured a greater awareness of the potential problems of drugs in pregnancy. There is also a range of drugs which appears to give rise to behavioural deficits in newborn animals and may have similar effects in humans. Indeed a separate discipline, behavioural teratology, has developed and is concerned with the study of such effects (Barlow and Sullivan, 1976). Cigarette smoking by mothers during pregnancy is associated with low birth weight babies and with later learning problems. Heavy drinking by expectant mothers has also been found to cause such problems as premature births, sensory defects and disturbances in early behaviour and sleep patterns. These teratogenic effects are variable and one factor which might explain this variability is the time at which exposure or maximum exposure to a drug occurs during the pregnancy. Embryological research on the fetus has shown that different brain areas are formed at different stages during pregnancy and appear to be particularly vulnerable at these times.

c. Neonatal influences: birth complications

Following on from the last section discussing drug effects during pregnancy, it has also been found that drugs given to minimize pain during delivery can affect the behaviour of the newborn. Sedatives and analgesics given during labour have been found to reduce motor activity and suckling in the newborn for up to 1 week following birth and this in turn can affect the quality of bonding between mother and baby.

Complications during the process of delivery can affect the physical and psychological wellbeing of the baby. With certain complications the supply of oxygen to the baby's brain can be seriously reduced or even temporarily cut off. This presumably results in degeneration of brain cells and, in behavioural terms, has been found to result in disorders of motor coordination and attention. It has even been claimed that neonatal anoxia can have a selective adverse effect on the hippocampus and therefore give rise to disorders of selective attention in the child. Some researchers have claimed that this can provide a basis for later vulnerability to schizophrenia but the evidence for this is questionable.

In recent years there have been attempts to make the experience of birth a more personal and meaningful one for those involved. Up to fairly recently it has generally been assumed that increased technical innovation and use of analgesics in obstetrics must be beneficial. However, many obstetric departments are recognizing the value of focusing on psychosocial conditions surrounding the birth. In these departments there is a greater emphasis on 'natural childbirth', which means that there is minimal medical intervention and maximal involvement of both the parents. It is obviously difficult to carry out random-controlled trials to test the efficacy of this approach but there are several indications that it makes the birth a much less threatening and more enjoyable experience for the mother and also perhaps for the baby. There may also be a negative advantage in that the absence of analgesic medication can make for greater responsiveness in the neonate and may result in a more satisfactory early bond between mother and baby.

d. Nutrition

The nutrition of the newborn can have serious biological and psychological consequences. Malnutrition appears to have its greatest effects during the latter stages of pregnancy and the first few months of life when a great deal of brain development occurs (Dobbing and Smart, 1974). Poor nutrition at these times appears to affect myelinization, dendritic growth and nerve cell formation. This may be a reason for the reported reductions in IQ scores found in children with poor early nutrition. However, as was pointed out earlier, poor nutrition is very often associated with an impoverished psychosocial environment and it is difficult to disentangle these two causes.

e. Environmental chemicals

Some of the chemical products of modern industry also appear to have a potentially harmful effect on the development of brain mechanisms. These products include pesticides, herbicides, fungicides and a whole range of industrial pollutants. These can be ingested by the mother during pregnancy and may then affect the fetus. One of the best known examples of this was in the Minamata Bay area in Japan in the early 1960s, when effluents containing mercury were discharged into the sea and cumulated as methyl-mercury in the fish. A great deal of fish is eaten in the area and the result was that a large number of adults developed degenerative neurological disorders and 6 per cent of all the babies exposed prenatally were found to have brain damage. Another potentially harmful substance is lead which was formerly used in paint and can be ingested by children as the result of chewing old furniture. There is evidence of serious damage to the central nervous system in children who have taken in a great deal of lead paint in this way. It is also claimed that retarded intellectual and motor development is found in children who live near lead smelting works and busy motorway systems. With the latter the lead from the petrol is discharged into the atmosphere and higher blood levels are found in these children.

f. Physical handicaps and brain injury

As we see in Chapter 12, both congenital and incurred physical handicaps in children can have lasting influences on psychological development. These effects may be direct and be reflected in lost or altered behavioural functions, which in turn can affect other aspects of behaviour. For example, with congenital deafness there is a loss of auditory input which gives rise to very serious limitations in language development. Moreover, a restricted language capacity inevitably affects a person's social and vocational possibilities later in life.

The effects of a physical handicap can also have lasting indirect effects on psychological development by giving rise to adverse patterns of social reaction. These may first be seen in the parents in their reactions to dealing with the reality and the complications of the handicap. Later they may arise from the reactions of peers and others who may behave differently and even unpleasantly. Finally, it should not be forgotten that, for many children with congenital handicaps, it may be necessary for the child to have long stays in hospital or to undergo unpleasant treatment. This may therefore involve separation from the home during the early years and, as we see later, this can have lasting social and emotional consequences.

The effects of congenital or childhood brain injury are variable and depend on the extent, localization and timing of the damage. In the past, the general term 'cerebral palsy' was given to the behavioural consequences of brain injury in children. However, it is now recognized that damage to different regions may give rise to different behavioural deficits as was indicated in Chapter 3 and that with early damage, it is possible for compensatory changes to occur. It is also important to point out that some forms of brain damage, such as those arising from obstetric and neonatal complications, are found more commonly in children from socioeconomically disadvantaged families for a variety of reasons. In these cases it may be difficult to disentangle the organic from the environmental causes of later behavioural deficits or problems. Even so it does appear that brain injury in children increases the chance of psychological problems. In a well-organized study it was found that in the region of 50 per cent of children with brain damage or epilepsy were found to have a psychiatric disorder as compared with under 10 per cent in a non brain-damaged group (Rutter et al., 1970).

In broad terms, it seems that the young developing brain is more vulnerable to generalized damage. Thus the neurological and cognitive deficits following encephalitis or meningitis are more likely to be long lasting when these illnesses occur during the first 2 years. Also malnutrition appears to exert its greatest adverse effects on brain functions early on, as was discussed above. In contrast, the effects of localized brain damage on more specific behavioural functions appear to be more serious in later childhood.

The impact of localized damage can be minimized in the young brain because there appears to be sufficient plasticity in the first few years to compensate. Once cognitive functions have been well localized there is an increasing likelihood of a permanent impairment.

g. The early environment

The early environment in which the young child develops can have many important long-term influences. Some writers on development have argued that these early influences can be very pervasive in that they provide the basis for later growth. Thus an adverse early environment is assumed to make for later difficulties whereas a beneficial environment can have a protective effect against adversity later in development. There is evidence both for and against the primacy of the early environment in determining later behaviour and there is an attempt to evaluate the evidence in section 8.2.

i. Critical periods

One of the strongest arguments for the importance of the early environment arises from observations of animal behaviour and involves the notion of 'critical periods' in development. Observers of animal behaviour have noticed that there are defined periods when various species of animals have to receive appropriate stimulation in order for certain behaviours to develop normally. Failure or distortions in environmental stimulation at those times give rise to omissions or peculiarities in later behaviour. These critical periods have been observed for a variety of behaviours in a range of species. An example of this was presented in Chapter 2 in the discussion of perceptual learning, where the dependence on environmental stimulation of feature-analysing neurons in the visual cortex of the cat was described. It has been found that these neurons are particularly sensitive to environmental inputs during a very well-defined period in the first few months of the kitten's life.

There has been considerable debate as to whether there are equivalent critical or sensitive periods in early human development. The evidence to date suggests that there are early sensitive periods but that the effects are not so dramatic as those found in the animal world. This presumably reflects the greater neocortical development and the greater scope for adaptation and learning. However, it is instructive to look at some examples which involve a range of human behaviour from perception through to social development.

ii. Early environment and vision
There are claims that there is the equivalent of a critical period in early visual development. Some weak evidence for this comes from observations of hospitalized infants who spent some time in white-sided cots. These infants were found to be retarded in their perceptual development and it was felt that a lack of patterned visual input during the early period was the reason for this. Eventually these babies appeared to make up this lost ground after returning to a normal visual environment.

Much more dramatic evidence comes from people who are born with congenital cataracts in both eyes and do not have these removed until adulthood. Nearly all the studies of these people have found that they do not develop usable visual capacities following the surgical removal of the cataracts. Hence the conclusions of one study that 'the visual cortex of HD's [the patient's] brain, having been deprived of adequate stimulation at a critical period in early childhood, had become by the time of the operation virtually useless' (Acroyd et al., 1974). These authors also speculated on the basis of their results that the critical period for the development of cortical feature analysers in humans might be from about 2 months to 3 years. These are very approximate suggestions, but it is clear from the study of such patients that a lack of patterned visual input during the first few years of life inevitably means that later attempts to make use of a surgically corrected visual apparatus will be very unlikely to be successful.

Related findings can also be found in the work on the treatment of congenital squint. Here the two retinae are not aligned and the result is that cortical neurons do not receive binocular inputs. As a consequence there is a failure in the development of functional binocular vision, particularly stereopsis. It is generally found that if children with a squint are treated before they are 5, binocular visual development is possible but after this age it becomes most unlikely. These findings suggest a longer sensitive period for the cortical organization of binocular vision but again they do show that such a period appears to exist for this aspect of vision.

iii. Early environment and language
Similar claims for the importance of appropriate early environmental stimulation have also been made in relation to language development. These claims are based on a range of evidence including studies of the congenially deaf, observations of the

effects of brain injury in childhood, inferences from the descriptions of so-called 'wolf children' and psycholinguistic studies of children exposed to bilingual environments. The evidence on the limited language development in the congenitally deaf is discussed in Chapter 12 and this shows that a lack of spoken language input can have devastating effects on later language ability. Moreover, language development will be enhanced if deafness can be detected very early on and if specific intervention can be carried out to give compensatory language and communication experience. The evidence on recovery from brain injury was mentioned above and showed that young children can recover language skills whereas adults are much less able to do so. Some children have even acquired language ability following removal of the left hemisphere. The plasticity in language development is thought to coincide with the critical period and has been related to the lateralization of language functions in the brain.

There are wide variations in the estimates of the duration of the critical period for language and these range from the first two years to the whole period up to puberty. Although these estimates vary, there is a reasonably impressive body of converging evidence that there is an optimal period for language acquisition. Learning a second language during this time appears to be relatively effortless when compared with the struggle many people have later on. Perhaps the most convincing evidence comes from the rather dramatic examples of otherwise 'normal' children who have been brought up without exposure to language. Some of these so called 'wolf children' have been brought up in very strange surroundings but many of the reports are rather old now. However, one study reported the progress of a young girl brought up in the USA in a most bizarre family and yet totally isolated from them in a separate room until the age of 13, when she came to the attention of the welfare department. At that time she had no conventional language available and, even after intensive therapy, she developed only a limited ability to produce and understand speech. The research workers involved concluded that her language abilities were probably mediated by the right hemisphere because they were acquired outside the normal critical period for language development. Thus it was postulated that 'after the critical period, the left hemisphere may no longer be able to function in language acquisition, leaving the right hemisphere to assume control' (Curtiss, 1977).

iv. The early social environment

Some of the most debated and interesting work on these lines has been in relation to early social behaviour and the subsequent effects of this. This debate has stemmed primarily from the work of Bowlby (1951) and his ideas about the effects of maternal deprivation on young children's behaviour and development. In an influential review of the effects of early social and emotional environment, Bowlby concluded that a warm continuous relationship with a mother figure was vital for later personality development. He concluded that the failure to establish such a close relationship would result in, what he called, an affectionless personality. Thus the quality of the first relationship between mother and child was held to determine the quality of all later ones and therefore constituted a critical period in social development. These conclusions have forced clinicians and psychologists to examine the effects of different types of infant care and of early separations on later behaviour.

It now seems that Bowlby's original ideas about the effects of maternal deprivation were rather overstated and oversimplified (Rutter, 1972). A less dramatic and more complicated picture has emerged from recent research but this still highlights the lasting importance of the quality of the infant's early social interactions. As we see below early social development goes through a number of stages and the effects of disruptions can be quite different at different times.

Whereas Bowlby argues that babies innately attach themselves to a single figure, it now appears that different attachments can be made.

Moreover, the psychological effects of day-care centres or institutions are not necessarily adverse. In institutions where there are good material provisions, reasonable staffing levels and sustained contacts between staff and children, relatively few emotional and social problems are seen. However, if young children are exposed to many caretakers this can create an unpredictable environment and may mean that the individual child's needs are never really met. In general terms, the longer the deprivation of an attachment figure, the harder it becomes later to develop attachment to an individual. If children spend long periods of time in impersonal, cold environments without sustained contact with one or a small number of individuals, then forming attachments may become virtually impossible.

There are still many unanswered questions concerning the long-term effects of early social interactions. In particular there is a need to unravel the factors associated with attachment and the consequences of failing to form sustained attachments. Another point worth making at this stage is that many studies of environmental influences implicitly regard the infant or young child as a passive recipient of external influences. It is now clear that the early behaviour of the child can be instrumental in determining some of these environmental influences. For example, very active children may demand and seek out more stimulation and some caretakers or parents may respond to this appropriately whereas others may find it irritating and ultimately stressful. It is important to be aware of the fact that infants do differ in their early behaviour and what may be most important is the interaction between this behaviour and the environmental response to it. Another complicating factor is that it is not entirely clear to what extent later social learning can override adverse early experiences. For the present it is possible to conclude that early experiences can have important and sometimes critical consequences for later social behaviour.

A number of common themes can be detected in the rather diverse examples given here to illustrate the importance of the early environment. While it does not appear that there are such specific critical periods as are found in many animal species, some behavioural processes can be strongly influenced by environmental variables. In the extreme, a sustained early environmental distortion can have a permanent influence on later social and cognitive development.

Such extreme effects are rare and for many children brought up in adverse conditions it is still possible to reverse some of the effects. In the chapter on 'Intelligence' there was a review of the success of some compensatory educational programmes in reversing the cognitive retardation that can be found in young children brought up in very restricted socioeconomic conditions. There it was shown that if the intervention is early and sustained enough, compensatory programmes can be effective. Even so, it is clear that it becomes more and more difficult to reverse intellectual and personality distortions with increased age and this underlines the contribution of the early environment to later behaviour.

● **8.2. An outline of child development**

There are many excellent accounts of the various psychological changes accompanying development and some of these are given in the suggestions for further reading. With this in mind, the present account of developmental changes does not attempt to give a comprehensive coverage of all the major changes but is more concerned with presenting an outline. Following the convention adopted by many developmental texts, there is a description of newborn behaviour followed by separate accounts of motor, perceptual, cognitive and social development in children. Finally, a brief account of adolescence is included.

a. The newborn

Some readers may be surprised to learn that the newborn baby merits separate consideration since they may believe that babies are pretty well incapable at birth. Certainly psychologists have held similar views in the past and have accepted that all behaviour is acquired through experience. More recently this picture of the newborn has undergone some radical changes since it can now be seen that many important capacities are present at a very early stage. One of the great difficulties in studying psychological processes in babies is that they cannot tell you what they are doing or thinking. As a result, psychologists have derived many ingenious techniques for investigating perception, memory, learning and social behaviour in babies. Some of these rely on careful observation and make use of detailed filmed or videotaped analyses of segments of behaviour. Other techniques involve the use of more specific interventions such as simple conditioning or learning procedures to provide information about underlying cognitive mechanisms. The evidence from recent studies now shows newborn behaviour to be much more complex and purposeful than was previously thought.

Some very simple experiments have elegantly demonstrated that newborns have considerable *learning ability* from the outset. After only a few hours of life babies are able to discriminate between different sounds and make specific responses (e.g. head turning to the left or right) to obtain rewards. For example, within a few trials, babies can learn that they have to turn their heads to the right after a tone stimulus and to the left after a buzzer stimulus to obtain the reward of a sweet-tasting solution in the mouth. Morover if the situation is then reversed (i.e. tone = left head turn; buzzer = right), babies can relearn the appropriate response within a few trials.

The *perceptual abilities* of the newborn also appear to be more elaborate than would be imagined from casual observation. From birth babies can turn their eyes appropriately towards a sound source presented to the left or right of them. This finding shows that there is a complex interaction between different perceptual systems and this appears to be present from birth. Information can be processed in one modality and responded to in another.

Within a few days of life and possibly from birth, it appears that babies can locate objects visually and attempt to avoid an object that appears to be approaching them. If newborn babies are supported, allowing the arms and hands to move, then they can make reaching movements for objects with their hands. These early reaching movements are slow and crude in comparison with later abilities but they appear to be present within the first days rather than months, as was previously thought.

It is now thought that some *social behaviour* is also present in the earliest days of babyhood. There is evidence that babies, less than 1 week old, will imitate simple facial gestures shown by other people. If simple gestures such as sticking out the tongue or opening and closing the mouth are shown to babies of this age, then these are sometimes copied by the baby. Clearly this requires quite complex perceptual and motor capabilities as well as indicating a degree of social interaction. On the basis of this sort of evidence Bower (1977) contends that 'the newborn baby imitates facial gestures of the adults around him for no reward other than the pleasure of interacting with them'.

There is also evidence that babies make body movements which are coordinated with the speech patterns of adults who talk to them. These movements may be the precursors of the various non-verbal concomitants of spoken communication which are observed later in life. It has even been claimed that various prenatal disturbances can reduce or abolish these interactional movements. When this happens it has been found that mothers feel their babies are not responsive and may communicate less with them as a result.

Although there is a growing body of evidence to indicate that the newborn baby is far more competent than psychologists have previously imagined, it is clear that their behavioural repertoire is still extremely limited. The acquisition of a whole range of skills takes place during infancy and childhood as can be seen in the following sections.

b. Motor development

This is the most easily observed and described process taking place in infancy and early childhood. Although the newborn does not have an extensive range of motor behaviours, these emerge rapidly as can be seen in *Fig.* 12, which shows a typical schedule of these changes leading up to walking. These changes occur at a regular rate and in a predictable order. The exact timing of particular changes is subject to variation between babies as is indicated by the bars in *Fig.* 12. However, the regularity and sequence of motor changes provide the basis for many of the tests used by paediatricians to assess normal development in infancy.

The regularity and self-contained nature of early motor development has prompted the conclusion that it must be a genetically preprogrammed sequence. There is evidence for this from a range of sources but it is still possible for specific environmental factors to alter the rate with which the changes take place. For example, babies born with Down's syndrome, which is a genetic deficit caused by the presence of an extra chromosome, typically show slowed motor development. Even with these babies it is still possible to use specific intervention programmes to give very large amounts of practice on sensory-motor tasks in order to accelerate their motor development to almost normal levels. In cases of babies

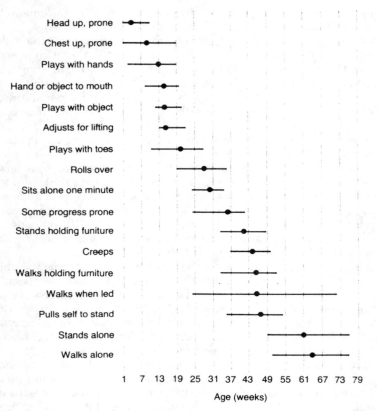

Fig. 12. An outline of the sequence of motor development. (From *A Primer of Infant Development* by T. G. R. Bower. W. H. Freeman. Copyright © 1977.)

with congenital blindness, some aspects of motor development take place fairly normally but behaviours involving reaching and moving independently are critically affected. Again the provision of specific intervention can help blind babies to develop reaching responses towards a sound source and to walk independently. These two clinical examples therefore demonstrate the value of early diagnosis and intervention. More generally they indicate the importance of the environment in determining the outcome of something as apparently preprogrammed as motor development.

Motor development is effectively completed in infancy. The changes in motor ability which follow walking tend to be refinements of existing abilities rather than complete new skills. Walking gradually becomes more competent and running becomes fluent and controlled. Eye–hand coordination becomes much more precise and elaborate with increasing experience. Also the coordination of the two hands in bimanual tasks becomes more skilled.

The dominance of one hand tends to emerge at a fairly early age and appears to be linked to hemisphere dominance for language processing, but not exclusively. It is known that the left hemisphere controls the right hand and that the right hemisphere controls the left hand. Nearly all right-handed people appear to be strongly left-hemisphere dominant for language processing and the majority of left-handers are also left-hemisphere language dominant. However, there is a small group of left-handers with right-hemisphere language dominance and a number with bilateral cortical representation of language. Some children with specific motor retardation, who are found to be particularly clumsy, may fail to show a clear manual dominance and also demonstrate much poorer coordination between the hands.

c. Perceptual development

In many ways this is bound up with various aspects of motor development. Indeed the theories of Jean Piaget, which are outlined below, contain the proposition that perceptual development in infancy is based on early motor development. The evidence which is available to date suggests that Piaget's views on this issue are questionable since there are now many studies showing that young babies are able to process directly many aspects of their visual environments.

Given the difficulties in discovering what babies are experiencing perceptually, psychologists have resorted to a range of techniques for investigating the ways in which babies look at their environments. Studies of the eye movements of infants have shown that they fixate specific features from birth and are attracted to areas of greatest contrast or discontinuity in a visual stimulus. With increasing age, scanning becomes broader and a progressively larger amount of information is sought. Even in very young babies, perception does not appear to be a passive process since their eye movements indicate that they are seeking out specific types of information. The selectivity and adaptability of eye movements in perception according to the demands of the situation were outlined in Chapter 2. This is something which clearly comes with age as children develop their knowledge of the environment. This can be seen in a study comparing the eye movement patterns of 6-year-olds and adults (Mackworth and Bruner, 1970). Compared with the adults in that study, the children tended to cover less of the object and to fixate on details. Perhaps the most important difference was found with the type of information attended to since children tend to look at less informative parts of a picture. Adults carried out broader initial scans and were able to fixate more on informative aspects.

The eye movement studies can give valuable insights into some aspects of perceptual development since they provide an indication of the knowledge which the perceiver has about objects in the environment. A similar advantage which accrues from greater experience can be seen in the developmental changes in selective attention. In Chapter 2 it was shown that adults are able to attend selectively to specific perceptual inputs and automatically to switch attention if necessary.

An important function of experience is to determine which messages merit sustained attention and which can be safely ignored. It appears that between the ages of 5 and 7 years there is a marked improvement in selective attention. At this time children become much more efficient at selectively attending to one particular message and correspondingly are less distracted by competing messages. This change in attentional capacity is thought to be mediated by the frontal lobes (Mackworth, 1976).

Another technique used for studying infant perception has been to present a number of stimuli concurrently and to see whether particular stimuli are systematically preferred. It has been found that from the earliest days there is a preference for novel and moderately complex patterned stimuli rather than for homogeneous ones. Earlier studies indicated that there was a strong preference for looking at faces from birth but this preference does not seem to appear until about the fourth or fifth month. At this age babies are able to discriminate and identify the human face and can distinguish between different people in their environment on the basis of facial information. With increasing age children also become more efficient at discriminating between different visual patterns and reach something approaching adult proficiency by about 8 or 9 years.

Recent research has also produced some surprising evidence about the development of depth perception. Formerly psychologists tended to argue that newborn babies were not able to appreciate the spatial properties of their environment until they were able to move about and translate motor information into perceptual knowledge. It now appears that this is not entirely true since young babies do appear to be able to utilize cues about the distance of objects on the basis of visual information only. Thus they are able to respond appropriately to objects that appear to be approaching them and to reach out for the nearer of two objects within the first few weeks of life. It would appear that there is sufficient information available in the retinal image to supply direct information about the relative distance of objects. Experience increases the knowledge about the relative sizes of different stimuli and increased mobility helps to give a better appreciation of the spatial characteristics of the environment.

As we observed earlier, the newborn child does have a reasonable set of perceptual capacities. Some structural changes take place within the first few months and these radically improve visual acuity and the size of the visual field. The majority of perceptual development seems to consist of increased selectivity and organization as a function of the growth of knowledge about the perceptual environment.

d. Cognitive and language development

From the previous description of perceptual development it is clear that a great deal of this is bound up with changes in cognitive functioning. For example, changes in selective attention and eye movement patterns are associated with the development of the child's knowledge and expectations. In this section there will be an outline of changes in the child's modes of thinking followed by a brief account of language development. Finally, there will be some concluding remarks about the relationship between language and thought.

i. The development of thinking

The cognitive capability of the child changes radically from birth through to adolescence. Psychologists have found it convenient to think of this overall process as consisting of a number of different stages. The person who has done more than anyone not only to engender this view of stages of cognitive development but also to influence our ideas about children's thinking is the Swiss scientist, Piaget. On the basis of some very detailed observations, mainly on his own children, he has identified several periods, subperiods and stages in the cognitive growth of the child. In addition to the classification of stages of development, there are four key concepts in Piaget's theory and these help describe the way children process information and deal with the world. The four concepts are: schemata, assimilation, accommodation and equilibrium.

The *schemata* are the inferred cognitive structures or internal processes that the child uses in conceptualizing experiences. Younger children are thought to have fewer schemata with rather poorly defined boundaries (e.g. if the young child has learned to call one man 'daddy', he or she may well categorize any other man as 'daddy'). Experience results in the child's schemata becoming more numerous and precise. These changes in the child's knowledge structure are mediated by the two processes of *assimilation* and *accommodation*. Assimilation describes the way in which the child deals with new information, using existing schemata (e.g. a new male visitor is referred to as 'daddy'). Accommodation occurs when an existing schema is modified to incorporate new information or when a new schema is created for this purpose (e.g. a new category or schema of 'non-daddy men' is created). According to Piaget, *equilibrium* is said to exist when these two processes are in a state of relative balance. Imbalance results in cognitive processing or reorganization failing to return to a state of equilibrium. Equilibrium therefore corresponds to a state of mental homeostasis which the individual tries to maintain

Recent work since Piaget has focused more on the actual processes used by children in forming concepts and solving problems. Some of this evidence has called into question certain assumptions arising from Piaget's classification of stages of cognitive development. Before mentioning these, a brief outline of these stages is now presented.

Piaget sees children's thinking as passing through four broad stages:

1. Sensorimotor stage

This stage lasts for about the first 2 years of life and consists of the infant constructing sensorimotor schemata based on his or her interactions with the environment. These schemata are based on the infant's processing of the relationships between sensory information and actions. At the outset, the baby's actions primarily consist of reflexes and there is no awareness of objects as distinct from the actions they elicit. Development during this period consists of the creation of action patterns which take into account progressively more properties of external objects. Thus the prime achievement of this period is what Piaget calls 'object permanence'. This means that the infant can now think of things as being permanent and continuing to exist when out of sight. In terms of human thinking ability, this is an important level to reach because it means that there is an internal representation of the world available to the child. As we shall see in the section on problem-solving in Chapter 11, an internal representation is a vital first stage in problem-solving since it means that the person can think about objects without having to see them directly.

2. Pre-operational thought

This is the description applied to Piaget's next stage which runs from about 2 to 7 years. During this time the child begins to use an internal representation of his or her external world. This newly acquired mode of thinking allows the child to predict outcomes of behaviour and events. The rapid development of language at this time appears to facilitate these changes, as we see in section iii below.

Although pre-operational thought is an embryonic form of adult thought, it is still restricted in a number of characteristic ways. Thinking at this age tends to be egocentric and cannot generally encompass another person's point of view. It also tends to be rather single-tracked and inflexible. One of the most characteristic aspects of the pre-operational stage is that thought processes appear to be irreversible. Although the child can imagine the outcome of a sequence of thoughts, he or she cannot return to the original state. The most famous examples of this are the so-called conservation problems, in which transformed amounts of liquids or solids are no longer perceived as being the same in volume or area as the original. For example, if the same amount of water is poured into two identical glass beakers, the child can agree that there are equal amounts of water in each. However, if the water from one of these is poured into another beaker of a different shape (e.g. taller and narrower), the pre-operational child will maintain that the amount of water has changed (e.g. more in the tall beaker). The child is said to lack the concept of conservation, which would allow him or her to realize that numbers, areas, volumes and weights remain the same despite changes in position or shape.

3. Concrete operations
This is the name given to the stage of thinking from about 7 to 11 years. By this age children generally do not have trouble with conservation problems and are able to apply logical reasoning to concrete objects and problems. The child can now think about something from another person's point of view and to consider more than one characteristic of a situation. The child begins to learn the rules about such concepts as number and space but thinking tends to be rooted to concrete objects and events, lacking any true ability for abstract thought.

4. Formal operations
Formal operations is the name given to the last stage in the transition to full adult thinking ability. It begins at about 11 years and is characterized by the emergence of abstract reasoning skills. The child's logical abilities can now be applied to deal with such abstractions as possible and probable outcomes of situations. Whereas children in the previous stage tended to deal primarily with the present, with the here and now, they can now concern themselves with the hypothetical and the future. Older children also become capable of thinking about their own thinking processes and can therefore reflect on how they solved a particular problem. This so-called 'metacognitive' ability means that the older child can monitor and introspect on his or her thinking in order to be able to describe these thinking processes to others.

These four stages of cognitive development described by Piaget are summarized in *Table* 1. Although this description has provided a very powerful influence on nearly all research concerned with understanding children's thinking, it is not without its problems. A few criticisms are now considered.

ii. Problems with Piaget's theory
Since the time when Piaget's theory was formulated, the detailed study of infant perception has developed enormously and the evidence from this casts serious doubts on some of Piaget's interpretations of his data. A central tenet of Piaget's theory of perceptual and cognitive development is that this originates in the infant's early action schemes. For Piaget the young child does not directly perceive the world but becomes aware of it through his or her own actions and interactions with the environment. Thus perceptual knowledge is thought to be empirically gained through behaviour. However, the work of Bower (1977) and others has convincingly demonstrated that very young babies do appear to be able

Table 1. An outline of Piaget's stages of cognitive development

Approximate age	Description
0–2 years	*Sensorimotor Stage*. From initial reflexes to object permanence through the development of sensorimotor schemata
2–7 years	*Pre-operational Thought*. Language development starts; internal representations of concrete objects and situations. Thoughts are egocentric and irreversible (i.e. conservation not possible)
7–11 years	*Concrete Operations*. Logical thinking starts but only with concrete situations. Concepts of conservation and reversibility are developed
11–15 years	*Formal Operations*. Development of logical abstract thinking, capable of testing hypotheses and considering possibilities

to derive usable perceptual information directly through their sensory systems (*see* Butterworth, 1978, for a detailed account of this point). Moreover, it has been found that in thalidomide babies, born without hands or limbs, object permanence develops quite normally.

Another crucial point that is emerging from more recent research is that Piaget's theory tends to overestimate the limitations of the thinking abilities of younger children. For example, there is now considerable evidence to show that not all pre-school thinking is egocentric. It would appear that Piaget's conclusions may have stemmed from some of the limitations of the experimental situations he used as well as on some questionable interpretations of his findings (*see*, for example, Gelman, 1979). By implication, Piaget's theory also assumes that adult thinking is logical and coherent since cognitive development is seen as a series of progressions towards this, starting from innate reflex behaviour. Again a great deal of fairly recent research has shown that adult thinking can often be illogical and biased in all sorts of ways. To put it more simply, it would now appear that young children are not as dumb and adults are not as smart as would be predicted from Piaget's theory. A related point is that cognitive development does not appear to be as tightly 'stage-bound' as implied by the theory.

Despite these criticisms, some of which may be inevitable in view of the rapidly increasing knowledge in this area, Piaget's work and theory have had a monumental influence on current ideas about children's mental processes. Instead of thinking of children as incomplete adults who passively acquire knowledge, we can now see that young children use characteristic and complex mental processes for making sense of the world. While these processes certainly change through the course of development, it is a mistake to underestimate the cognitive capacities of the child.

iii. Language development
Language development provides a very clear example of the rapid changes in cognitive abilities that take place in childhood. The newborn shows a remarkable ability to distinguish among speech sounds. Certainly young babies are responsive

to language from a very early age and, as we saw earlier, show coordinated body movements in response to the patterns of speech presented to them. Moreover, well before the time that babies begin to utter their first words, it is clear that they are able to understand quite a range of words. Speech production consistently lags behind the capacity for recognizing and responding to speech.

Speech production can be traced through a number of distinct stages from the earliest months. After a few months the infant begins to babble and the sounds which are produced are the first combinations of vowels and consonants. A very wide range of sounds is produced in this early babbling but in the latter half of the first year this range narrows as the infant begins to produce the speech sounds of his or her own environment. Early babbling appears to be preprogrammed since it is produced by congenitally deaf children, who have no experience of hearing the spoken language of others or their own vocal output. However, they do not progress to the second stage of more restricted and environmentally determined vocalization, which precedes the emergence of the first words at about 1 year. After this the infant's vocabulary develops slowly at first until the latter part of the second year when it begins to accelerate. By the age of 5 a child can use over 2000 words and can understand far more.

A related aspect of language development is the development of sentence length. At about 18 months sentences usually consist of one or two words but from then on there is a steady increase in sentence length and complexity. The adult level of sentence length is usually given as six or seven words and this is generally achieved by the age of 7 or 8 years. This increase in sentence length reflects important changes in the development of grammatical ability. It is not enough for children to know what each word means, they must possess the rules to be able to combine them into sentences.

Within the first few years the child not only accumulates a large vocabulary but also learns the rules for producing grammatically correct utterances. The way in which this comes about has been the subject of much debate. Behaviourists, notably Skinner, have claimed that language competence is largely learned by exposure to adult language. Although environmental determinants are important for learning specific words and for aspects of pronunciation, there is no good evidence to show that parental rewards and punishments significantly affect grammatical development. Cognitive and linguistic theorists, following the work of Chomsky, have argued that there are inborn capacities that make it almost inevitable that the child will acquire language, just as there are innate mechanisms which provide the basis for appropriate perceptual processing. Experience is essential but what is critical is the nature of the internal structures which make use of this experience.

Recently there have been many experiments showing that young children acquire general sets of rules for generating grammatical utterances. The child's grammatical competence appears to be closely linked with the development of cognitive and intellectual capacities. As these capacities increase, on the lines described earlier, the child can learn and use more complex grammatical rules. In other words it is important to think of the child's language capability as somehow reflecting his or her ability to make sense of and conceptualize the environment. As the latter becomes more competent and flexible, so does the language system necessary for providing an adequate account of the developing thoughts and ideas.

iv. *Language and thought*

Language and thought are therefore tied together in an important way in the process of development. There are some very divergent views as to the nature of the relationship between language and thought. Some writers have claimed that language determines thinking and have cited various cultural differences in language and thought as examples of this. On the same lines, it has been argued that thought is no more than internalized language. Contrasting with this view is the notion that thought develops prior to language and is necessary for language development.

There is evidence for and against these two conflicting views. Studies of the thinking abilities of congenitally deaf people are often cited against the idea that language determines thought. As we see in Chapter 11, formal language development is relatively limited in the congenitally deaf yet there is abundant evidence that many of their problem-solving abilities show the same range of competence as their hearing counterparts. Similarly, brain damage which produces marked language dysfunction does not necessarily disrupt all cognitive processing. However, there are clearly some tasks on which verbal ability seems to be associated with good performance and where the congenitally deaf may not do so well.

There is now less preoccupation with whether language determines thought or vice versa. Psychologists appear to accept an interactionist viewpoint and seem more concerned to understand the nature of the interaction between these two processes. This is seen very clearly in developmental studies where it is possible to relate changes in cognitive ability to aspects of language development. Even here opinions are divided. Piaget has suggested that language development follows cognitive development while others, such as Vygotsky (1962), suggest that thought and language have independent origins and become interdependent during development. At present we can say that language and thought are related but we are still a long way from understanding all the complexities of this relationship.

e. Social development

i. *Early social attachments*

As we saw earlier when considering the newborn, there is now abundant evidence to indicate that elements of social behaviour can be found in very young infants. The earliest social behaviours of the newborn appear to be quite non-specific since they are not directed to specific individuals. During the first few months they become more specific and social interactions with parents or caretakers lead to the formation of attachments. The infant directs most of his or her attention and behaviour towards these individuals, feels discomfort when they are not around and is calmed by their presence. At about the age of 8 months infants begin to show a definite fear of strangers and, not long after this, they will show fear of separation from their caretakers. Actual separation usually results in distress for the baby, who will cry and scream or sometimes become withdrawn and still. The occurrence of these two behaviours, stranger fear and separation anxiety, are taken to indicate that the infant has formed a social attachment to one or sometimes two specific individuals.

In the next few years babies tend to form more attachments and the departure of any one of these people may give rise to separation anxiety. This anxiety remains high for a few years after infancy and seems to decline quite sharply by about 4 or 5 years of age. This is consistent with the studies of children in hospital, which are described in Chapter 12 and which show that after this age there is much less likelihood of distress on entering hospital.

As we saw earlier in this chapter, there can be a number of quite adverse consequences of the failure to establish close early social attachments. Infants who are raised in institutions or in environments where there is little or no interaction with adults, are likely to become very passive and withdrawn. It would seem that the longer this state of affairs continues, the less likely it becomes that the child will be able to develop an attachment to an individual.

It has been found that the formation of early attachments is associated with a better social adjustment later in childhood. A strong early bond seems to provide a good basis for engendering trust and friendship with peers. Occasionally too close an early attachment can result in problems in social development. Some children develop an overdependent and anxious relationship with their parents and this may prevent them from becoming independent as they get older. A high incidence of children with school phobia or agoraphobia (fear of going out) has been found in family situations where there is a distortion in the normal pattern of parent–child attachment. Parents may keep their children at home for company or because they fear that something bad may happen to the child if he or she is at school. Alternatively, children may be afraid to leave the home for various reasons.

A problem with these children is that they are failing to make the transition in their social needs from parental dependence to friendship with peers. This transition is a necessary part of social development which allows the child to move from the home environment to the outside world of playgroups and schools. During the pre-school years many new behaviours and attitudes develop as children increasingly interact with their social environment, as part of a general process which is usually referred to as 'socialization'. Parents and other social agents attempt to teach children to control and modulate their behaviour in accordance with prevailing cultural expectations about appropriate behaviour.

ii. Sex role behaviour

A great deal of socialization appears to be mediated by the process of identification, which describes the way the child takes on the patterns of behaviour and the social values of influential adults, usually the parents. One area of behaviour where this is clearly seen is in the development of sex roles, that is in the different types of behaviour considered appropriate for one's sex. For example, in Western societies, females are encouraged to inhibit aggression and to be passive whereas males are encouraged to be assertive, aggressive and control their emotions. Similarly, little girls are supposed to play with a certain range of toys and little boys with an entirely different range of toys. A great deal of research has attempted to discover the origins of these sex roles, particularly in determining the extent to which they are innate and based on hormonal differences or acquired and based on different patterns of parental behaviour towards boys and girls. Undeniably biological factors must be important since these will determine the physical characteristics associated with masculinity or femininity. However, there is a large body of evidence showing that sex role behavioural stereotypes (i.e. 'typical' behaviours associated with boys or girls) are learned early in life, particularly during the pre-school years. During this time sex typing figures prominently in the socialization of the child and most parents pay attention to the sex appropriateness of their child's behaviour. There are a small number of dramatic examples where, for various reasons, children are brought up in a way generally considered inappropriate for their biological sex (i.e. 'biological' boys are brought up as little girls and vice versa). In these cases social influences appear to dominate later sex roles. Thus genetically male children, who are brought up as girls, show the range of behaviour generally considered to be associated with the female sex role (Money and Ehrhardt, 1972).

From these studies it would seem that by the age of about 3 or 4, children have learned many of the skills associated with being a boy or a girl. Since the parents are the prime influences during this period, this would appear to locate the determinants of sex role typing. Parents appear to react differently to boy and girl babies from the outset and young children will therefore pick up clues as to 'sex-appropriate' behaviour from the attitudes of their parents.

iii. Parental influences and the home environment

The development of moral constraints on behaviour seems to develop in part through identification with parents. Children of warm and accepting parents tend to identify more strongly and seem to develop a stronger sense of guilt associated with misbehaviour. These children are also more likely to exhibit altruistic behaviour, such as sharing, in their dealings with their peers. Broad characteristics of home environment, particularly those involved in the general nature of parental discipline, appear to affect other aspects of personality and social development. Such positive factors as competence, maturity, friendliness and self-reliance are fostered by emotionally warm home environments, in which independent actions and responsible behaviour are rewarded and encouraged. An appropriate degree of parental control seems important here since the children of warm but indulgent parents and children of firm but rather cold parents do not appear to be so well adjusted (Baumrind, 1971). Clearly these sorts of findings represent fairly broad generalizations and it should be stressed that patterns of social adjustment will ultimately depend on many factors.

This account of social development has been inevitably sketchy and selective. The interested reader is recommended to read one of the textbooks on child development for a more comprehensive account. Social and personality development must also be seen in conjunction with cognitive development. Both cognitive and social development can be considered to be completed when the individual's thinking and social functioning have attained a state of relative autonomy. For cognition, this entails attaining the capacity for critical abstract thought and for reflecting on one's own thinking ability. For social development, there is clearly not a single endpoint but attaining an awareness of one's relations with one's peers and of the nature of the social world is a reasonable expectation. The final stages of childhood and the transition to adulthood seem to be an important time in establishing these aspects of social development and a separate consideration of adolescence now follows.

f. Adolescence

Adolescence marks the final stage of child development since it is usually defined as the period between the end of childhood and beginning of adulthood. It is generally taken to begin with the onset of puberty and with the characteristic physical changes which take place in girls and boys at this time. The period of time which is spent in adolescence is in some senses rather arbitrary since there is no obvious landmark for the beginning of adulthood. Also there is a considerable variation between individuals as to the age of onset of puberty. Puberty generally begins about 2 years earlier in girls and lasts for a slightly shorter time. It has been suggested that the variation in the onset of puberty can have psychological repercussions. Some studies have shown that early maturing boys tend to be more relaxed, more good natured and generally more confident whereas later maturers have been found to feel less confident and more anxious. It is not clear how lasting these effects are but one study has shown that they can continue into the early thirties. The equivalent evidence on girls is far less consistent.

There are important changes in the social environment of young people entering or about to enter adolescence. In Britain there is the change from primary to secondary education and the transition from being the oldest group in one type of educational setting to being the youngest in a quite different social structure. The secondary school system is much more obviously geared to exams and to selection for higher education. For those who leave secondary education there can be the advantages of relative financial independence but for an increasing number there are the frustrations and stultifying effects of periods of unemployment. For many young people in industrialized societies, adolescence can represent something of a no-man's-land between the dependence of childhood and the independence of adult life. Although physical and cognitive development may be relatively complete there is still usually a financial, social and often psychological dependence on other adults.

When considered in these terms, it is perhaps not surprising to find that writers on adolescence tend to see it very much as a time when individuals begin to establish a personal identity. This process does not start magically at puberty because self-knowledge accumulates all through childhood. However, the cognitive and physical changes in adolescence appear to give rise to a different sort of self-awareness. This may be hardly noticeable in some young people or may give rise to a transient shyness or awkwardness in others. For children with physical handicaps, adolescence can be a time of considerable emotional distress when the impact of their disadvantages and differences from others is fully realized.

Although there is evidence that adolescents are able to adopt a more critical viewpoint, there appears to be relatively little empirical support for the idea that adolescence is a time of universal rebellion against all adult values. Adolescents are better equipped than their younger counterparts to evaluate generally accepted patterns of behaviour and a small number may actively strive not to conform. There is a growing influence from peers during later childhood and this increases considerably during adolescence. Correspondingly adolescents become less likely to accept authority control but this does not necessarily involve alienation from parents but appears to represent the evolution of a different sort of parental relationship. Increasing independence and self-sufficiency generally take place without any loss of family ties and most adolescents still appear to trust their parents and share many of their values.

There is also relatively little support for the contention that adolescence is a time of universal psychological distress. During the early part of this century adolescence was seen as a time of great mental turmoil and a struggle to gain control over newly developed sexual capabilities and drives. This view seems to be something of a relic from prevailing Victorian ideas about sexuality and may have had something to do with the liberal use of cold showers in British public schools! More recently researchers have shown that adolescence, particularly in other cultures, is not necessarily a time of inner turmoil and it may be just as important to relate any psychological changes to the broader social context. Surveys have shown that most adolescents do not show marked emotional disturbances. However, many do appear to react strongly to certain issues, particularly those concerned with decisions about their own behaviour, and a tendency towards moodiness is relatively common at this time. One recent British study of 14–15-year-olds showed that just under half of these reported feeling very miserable at times or that they wanted to get away from everyone (Rutter et al., 1976). Oversensitivity to criticism and feelings of misery are therefore relatively common and may appear to be disproportionally upsetting at the time but they rarely last for appreciable lengths of time. Moreover, just over half the group of adolescents in the recent British study did not report any of these negative feelings. Establishing true independence from parents is seldom a straightforward process in Western-type cultures. There are likely to be strong motives for independence as well as a need for continued dependence and this can result in conflict and uncertainty.

In summary, then, adolescence is a time of great biological, psychological and social change. In the few years between childhood and adulthood, adolescents must gradually establish a personal identity, adjust to major biological changes and develop workable relationships with their peers while achieving independence from their families.

● **8.3. Problems in psychological development**

The existence of the separate medical disciplines of paediatrics and child psychiatry is a sufficient indication that there are clinical problems which are specific to childhood. Since it is not intended to provide a comprehensive account of all of these, the present section will briefly describe the range of psychological problems which are found and focus on two particular ones.

There are five broad groups of psychological problems which are found in childhood:

  a. Conduct disorders.
  b. Emotional disorders.
  c. Autism.

    d. Specific delays in cognitive development.
    e. Mental handicap.

a. Conduct disorders

The so-called conduct disorders are characterized by aggressive and socially disapproved behaviour. They are the commonest group of psychological problems found in older children and in adolescents. The causes are not well defined but most of the evidence points to the importance of certain adverse environmental factors. The vast majority of these children do not show evidence of brain damage or mental handicap.

b. Emotional disorders

The emotional disorders found in children are not dissimilar to those found in adults. Thus they are characterized by such feelings and behaviours as anxiety, fearfulness, unhappiness and social withdrawal. There is inevitably a range of fears and worries found in all children, particularly in response to strange or stressful situations. An example of this are the reactions of children in hospital as is discussed in Chapter 12. Many behaviours such as bed-wetting and nail-biting, which are found in children with emotional problems, are also found in children without psychological difficulties. The diagnosis of emotional disorder is therefore made when a pattern of 'neurotic' symptoms is found consistently and causes problems for the child. In a recent British study the rate of such problems in the region of 2·5 per cent was found in 10 and 11 year-old children, about half the rate for conduct disorders. Although some emotional disorders persist into adulthood, most emotionally disturbed children go on to become 'normal' adults without obvious neuroses (*see* Hersov, 1976, for a more detailed account).

c. Autism

Autism is a marked disorder of development which usually begins in the second or third year of childhood and has profound effects on social and cognitive adaption. According to Rutter (1976) there are three broad groups of symptoms which are found in autistic children:
    i. A profound and general failure in developing social relationships.
    ii. Language retardation involving impaired understanding and production as well as some rather strange language habits, such as the tendency to repeat or echo the speech of others.
    iii. Various ritualistic or compulsive behaviours, which are mainly manifested in stereotyped behaviours or routines and a preoccupation with order in the environment.

The impaired social development found in autistic children has a number of characteristic features. There tends to be a lack of attachment or emotional bonding to specific individuals. The quality of social interaction also appears to be quite different since autistic children do not show an appropriate use of eye contact. Later on autistic children tend not to make friends and not to play with other children.

There are significant delays in the acquisition of speech as well as the development of some characteristic oddities in language behaviour. The language disorders in autism are sometimes confused with deafness or with specific developmental disorders but they do have distinguishing characteristics.

There is a wide range of explanations for autism and these range from the environmental to the biological. The earliest explanations of autism tended to be environmental and based on an abnormal pattern of parent–child interaction. It was claimed that autistic children were more commonly found in emotionally cold, obsessive families but the evidence for these assertions is inconsistent and the role of the family in the aetiology is uncertain. More recent explanations have focused on the cognitive deficits. One consistent finding that overrides some of the earlier ideas is that about three-quarters of all autistic children are found to have an IQ in the mentally handicapped range. Unlike the mentally handicapped they often show a marked variability in their cognitive abilities with a particular deficit in linguistic and coding skills. Not surprisingly the autistic children with the lowest IQs tend to be the most disturbed and show the poorest prognosis. Because of this association with specific and general cognitive disabilities, there has been an increasing tendency to impute a biological cause. Organic brain dysfunction has been suggested since there is an association with later epilepsy and some evidence of EEG abnormalities. Currently, biological explanations do appear more plausible but as yet there is no clear indication as to which brain areas are involved and which would produce the characteristic collection of behaviours found in autism. Even if a firm biological basis is found, it is obvious that a complete understanding of autism will also have to involve an appreciation of interactive environmental factors.

Psychological approaches to treatment have undergone a change along with the change of thinking concerning aetiology. Earlier treatments tended to be based on psychotherapy (*see* Chapter 14, p. 238) but it is now acknowledged that these were fairly ineffective since autism does not appear to be a withdrawal into a psychotic-like state. There is now more emphasis on the language deficit and on other developmental disorders. Specific behaviour modification programmes are often used to bring improvements in linguistic and social functioning. These have been found to be of help although it is always necessary to provide supportive help for the parents since the presence of an autistic child can cause a great deal of stress within the family.

d. Specific delays in cognitive development

There are a number of specific delays in development which have been observed and constitute problems meriting psychological intervention. These problems include delays in reading, arithmetic skills, speech and in motor development. Sometimes these occur in isolation as a specific problem and sometimes they are more widespread manifestations of general learning difficulties. Since lack of space prevents discussion of all these problems, the example of reading retardation is pursued here. Although there are some specific factors associated with reading difficulties, some of the more general points which are made are also applicable to other cognitive developmental problems.

i. Reading and reading problems

Reading retardation refers to a specific developmental delay or deficit in acquiring the skills involved in reading. It is sometimes referred to as dyslexia, which can give the impression that it is a well-defined single problem but this is rather misleading. Reading is a complex skill and in many ways represents one of the first formal and specific cognitive challenges to the growing child. Spoken language skills appear to be acquired fairly effortlessly by the vast majority of children but reading requires a fair amount of formal learning, usually within the school.

The psychological processes underlying reading are still not fully understood although experimental psychology has made some interesting recent contributions to understanding how single words are processed (Coltheart, 1978). There appear to be a number of processes which lie between the visual analysis of the squiggles representing written words and the final acquisition of meaning. The first stages must involve detailed perceptual processing on the lines outlined in Chapter 2. However, an accurate perceptual representation is not sufficient to extract meaning from written words. Further processing must therefore be carried out and this probably involves the conversion of a visual into an auditory representation as a basis for discovering what the word is. Studies of skilled readers who have sustained localized brain damage have shown that there can be quite specific disorders of different processes involved in reading. There may be problems in initial perceptual analysis or problems in extracting meaning from a perceptual representation.

Reading retardation in children can take a number of forms and may involve quite specific deficits, more general learning difficulties or even motivational and attentional problems. The more general learning problems are often indicative of restricted cognitive abilities together with adverse environmental factors. Motivational problems may also stem from adverse causes and may be found with other emotional or behavioural problems. However, the category of specific reading retardation is usually reserved for children without other obvious learning and motivational problems. Even this category does not appear to be a unitary one since the causes and manifestations of specific reading difficulties now appear to be quite diverse. Some of these children do appear to have a specific problem with visual processing although these are probably not a very large group. They may have problems in letter identification and written word discrimination. Some researchers have claimed that this group can be identified on the basis of abnormal eye movement patterns but it is not clear whether these are a cause or a symptom of the problem.

More commonly children with specific reading difficulties are found to have problems in integrating visual and auditory information and in perceiving temporally or spatially ordered sequences. Difficulties in spatial sequences include letter reversals and left–right confusions, including the tendency to equate mirror-imaged shapes or letters (e.g. b and d). It has been argued that these sequencing problems reflect localized cortical damage or distortions in the interactions between the two cerebral hemispheres, possibly involving a failure of one hemisphere to dominate for language processing. Although this is an attractive proposition which describes the difficulties experienced by some children, it does not appear to explain all the problems.

ii. The causes of reading retardation

The finding that some children with specific reading retardation do have fairly well-defined difficulties has given rise to the tendency to think of these specific deficits as having a strict biological basis. Certainly children with specific and diffuse neurological damage do show a relatively high rate of reading problems. Moreover, reading problems together with such factors as mixed handedness and clumsiness have been found to run in some families, which has prompted genetic explanations. On the other hand, there is a distinct absence of biological factors in some children and it is apparent that various environmental factors can be causal. However, even with a biological basis, environmental influences must not be overlooked or underemphasized. Thus Rutter and Yule (1976) have observed that 'children with a biological impairment tend to be more vulnerable to environmental adversities, and reading difficulties are often the outcome of an interaction between constitutional deficits and environmental hazards'.

iii. Psychological intervention
In view of the general and specific factors associated with reading difficulties in children, the psychologist has a varied but important contribution to make in helping these children. First, a good assessment is of prime importance. This should not only involve the use of standardized intelligence tests to assess general level of functioning but may also incorporate more specific tests to determine whether there are particular processes or skills which are impaired. In addition to this it may be useful to establish whether there are motivational or related factors involved and this can be done by careful observation during testing or even with certain selected tests.

Once the reasons for the reading difficulty have been established on the basis of a detailed psychological assessment, it is then possible to establish a remedial programme. There is a range of remedial techniques available but none of these has been found to guarantee success. The use of very specific training schemes based on well-defined deficits can sometimes lead to striking improvements but the overall picture is still fairly bleak. The reasons for this stem from a combination of the poor understanding of the exact nature of the reading process, the restricted success of remedial techniques and the limited facilities available for helping children with any learning problems.

iv. Related problems
Reading and the other skills which can cause problems for children are complex processes which need to be understood in their own right. The exact nature of a learning problem must be clearly established but there is a danger in isolating a learning problem and overlooking some of the related problems which may also need considerable attention. Children may become frustrated and stressed by years of failure in reading, particularly when they have seen their peers make advances with relatively little difficulty. The child's negative attitudes and feelings may be a critical factor and constitute an important first stage to be considered in planning help. It is also possible that there may be wider effects of the problem within the family. The presence of a child with a learning problem within an otherwise 'normal' family can give rise to various stresses in the home environment and it may be necessary to deal with these as an adjunct to successful treatment.

These last two points are important since they provide insights into the nature of many psychological problems and not only those found in children. Psychological problems can often stem from a complex of inter-related factors and careful analysis will be needed to establish the bases of a specific problem. Moreover, these problems inevitably have secondary consequences for the individual within the wider social environment. The secondary complications sometimes disappear following the successful resolution of the primary problem but it may often be necessary to deal with these before or along with the specific difficulty.

- ## Recommended reading

Bee H. L. and Mitchell S. K. (1985) *The Developing Person*, 2nd ed. San Francisco, Harper & Row.

Bower T. G. R. (1979) *Human Development*. San Francisco, Freeman.

Rutter M. and Hersov L. (ed.) (1976) *Child Psychiatry: Modern Approaches*. Oxford, Blackwell.

9

Ageing

The process of ageing is not a unitary biological concept with a defined starting point. At this time of life, a complex interplay of biological, psychological and social factors will determine how much any one individual will change and adapt. Thus this chapter is concerned with a range of factors and the way in which they can interact.

• 9.1. The nature of ageing

One striking change in the social demography of industrialized societies has been the relative increase in the number of the elderly. Improvements in medical facilities, social services provisions, housing and nutrition are among the many factors that have increased the numbers of people living into old age. Even in the past 30 years, the ranks of the elderly have grown quite rapidly. In Great Britain, for example, the number of people over 65 years in 1981 was 8·5 million as compared with 5·5 million in 1951. The increase in the proportion of older people in society can be clearly seen in *Fig.* 13.

A separate analysis of the proportions of older men and women is also revealing since the number of older women has increased much more rapidly. This is partly a reflection of the fact that post-war advances in medicine have had relatively little success in dealing with the illnesses which are most likely to kill older men. These diseases are lung cancer, heart attacks, strokes and other circulatory diseases. Thus the life expectancy of a 70-year-old man has increased by 0·6 years since 1951, compared with an increase of almost 2 years for 70-year-old women. Moreover, women tend to outlive men and so the net result is that women constitute over two-thirds of the elderly population and of these, some 40 per cent are widowed. We return to some of these issues in the sections which follow, particularly in considering social and clinical aspects of ageing. For the present these figures are sufficient to indicate some of the more general characteristics of the population which are dealt with in this chapter.

One point which has been deliberately overlooked so far is that of defining ageing. From the foregoing discussion it might be naively assumed that ageing starts at 65 years but this is not a tenable notion at all. This figure is taken because

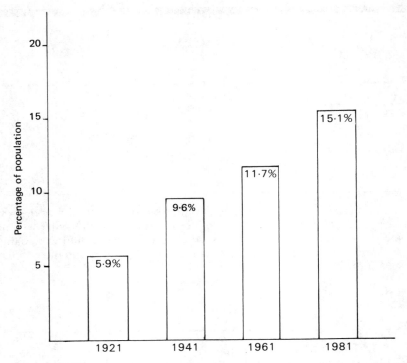

Fig. 13. The proportion of people over 65 years in Great Britain from 1921 to 1981. (Central Statistical Office, 1986.)

it represents the usual retirement age for men and therefore offers a specific cut-off point. However, this cut-off point is not defined by any psychological or biological criteria, as we see later. Many people function efficiently and productively long after this age whereas others may show quite marked declines in ability and health well before they reach 65. Indeed some writers feel that ageing as a chronological concept is totally unacceptable and that functional age is a much more meaningful one. While chronological age is used as a fairly good actuarial predictor of morbidity it is a fairly poor predictor of psychological and social competence. Thus the concept of functional age is an attempt to provide an indicator of age based on performance capacity and is being increasingly used in industrial research with the elderly, particularly in relation to the assessment of job skills.

Ageing is generally taken to refer to a degenerative process associated with a decrease in efficiency and viability and a corresponding increase in vulnerability. A whole range of biological indices has been shown to change in the elderly. In the central nervous system, there are decreases in brain weight and the probable losses of brain cells. The weight of the male brain drops from about 1400 g at 30 years by approximately 5 per cent at 70 years, 10 per cent at 80 years and 20 per cent at 90 years. However, there is no solid evidence for the much quoted statement that 100 000 neurons die during each day of adult life. Added to this are the appearances of various abnormalities, such as tangles and plaques, in certain brain regions and these have been partly correlated with decreases in mental efficiency. Sensory functions are likely to decline in that visual acuity is reduced and hearing declines. There is a loss of body strength and reduced speed of movement. Various physiological processes such as blood pressure and respiration also show adverse changes. This is a selective list but it serves to illustrate some of the biological changes associated with ageing. There is an unfortunate tendency to think of such changes as abnormal but given that they are pretty well universal and inevitable they are no more abnormal than the changes that accompany normal development in children.

As is seen later, the actual chronology of these changes is very variable from individual to individual. There is no fixed age when these changes begin nor is there a fixed time schedule during which they occur. Moreover, the impact of these changes on the individual is not specific. The psychological changes that are described below can partly be seen as functional correlates of the changes in biological status but the correlation between biological and psychological parameters is not a simple linear one. It is shown that social factors exert a very important influence on the ageing process and a separate consideration of these is also presented.

- ## 9.2. Studies of ageing: some cautionary remarks

a. Methods of studying age-related changes

At first glance one might imagine that it would be very straightforward to study age-related changes in behaviour. Take samples of people in various age bands, compare their performance or responses on some psychological measure and this should indicate how that particular function changes with age. Indeed this sort of approach, which is described as a cross-sectional study, is often employed in studies of ageing. While cross-sectional studies may be quite valid for comparing physiological processes or even some basic psychological functions, such as the speed of responding, there are problems in extending this approach to higher psychological functions. The main reason for this is that cross-sectional studies are doing more than comparing people of different ages, they are comparing generations with quite differing patterns of experience.

The logical alternative to the cross-sectional study is a longitudinal approach, in which a cohort of individuals is investigated at various intervals over a long period of time. This obviously avoids the generation difference problem in that changes in the same group are monitored and documented but has the great disadvantage of being very time consuming. Some longitudinal studies have been completed and on the whole these have yielded less dramatic age-related changes than cross-sectional studies. This is an important point to keep in mind when looking at studies of ageing and serves to illustrate the importance of the social context in determining individual differences.

An alternative to longitudinal studies makes use of a 'time-lag' methodology. This approach involves the use of comparisons between groups of individuals of the same age at different times. Thus the performance of a group of 80-year-olds tested in 1980 might be compared with groups of 80-year-olds tested in 1960 and 1940. Time-lag studies of this sort are a relatively recent development in this field and allow generation differences to be observed. The relatively few studies employing this approach have indicated that generation differences can be quite considerable on a range of psychological indices.

b. Individual differences in ageing

At any age there is a range of individual differences in psychological functions, as was discussed in Chapters 6 and 7. This variability actually increases with age as can be seen in *Fig.* 14. This shows the performance on a non-verbal intelligence test and gives the average level for each age group together with the scores obtained by individual subjects. While it is possible to make a general statement about the decline in performance on this task, it is clear that this varies enormously from individual to individual. Some 70-year-olds are performing at the level expected for a 30- or 40-year-old. It might even be argued that the mean decline in performance with age is primarily due to something like a third of the older group who perform very poorly and pull down the overall level. Thus to say that chronological age predicts level of functioning is a misleading oversimplification based only on the comparison of average scores. There is an enormous range and overlap between the ages.

c. The complexity of behaviour

A final cautionary point, which can be applied to many psychological studies but appears to be particularly relevant here, is that such studies inevitably segment psychological functions. Segmentation here refers to the tendency to isolate one particular aspect of behaviour such as memory, problem-solving or impulsiveness, and to compare age groups on a selected task. However, it must be obvious in real life that functions cannot be segmented in this way. Any behaviour depends on the interplay of a range of factors and isolating certain components may lead to incorrect or oversimplified conclusions being drawn. For example, if it was found independently that older people became more rigid and also were able to remember less, it may well be that these two changes are directly related. In this instance it might be that a reduction in memory capacity would lead to a decrease in flexibility because less information could be handled. This is only an example and may not be entirely correct but it serves to make the general point that segmenting functions to allow their investigation is a matter of convenience rather than an acknowledgement that behavioural functions are separate and separable.

When considering the evidence which follows, all these cautionary points should be kept firmly in mind so that ageing stereotypes should not be allowed to form. Most of the conclusions to be outlined are based on average scores from cross-sectional studies and should be treated with the appropriate caution.

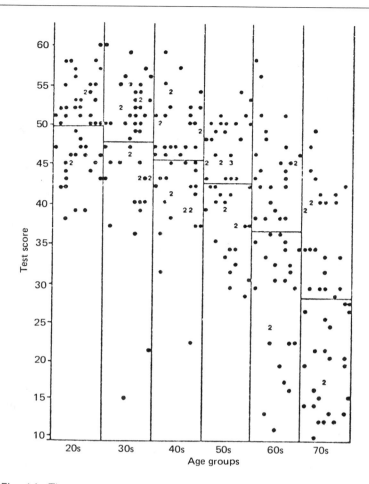

Fig. 14. The scores on a non-verbal intelligence test (Progressive Matrices) obtained by individuals in six age groups (average scores for each age group are indicated by horizontal lines). (From Heron and Chown, 1967.)

● 9.3. Psychological changes

Studies of age-related changes in psychological functions vary enormously in their scope and methodology. Many have sought to measure fairly global changes in intelligence although current approaches are much more concerned with investigating cognitive processes in detail, using experimental techniques. Therefore in this section there will be a brief outline of some of the more general studies followed by an account of the findings from the more detailed studies.

a. Changes in intelligence

Ageing appears to have a twofold effect on global measures of intelligence in that verbal or 'crystallized' intelligence tends to show little or no decrement whereas non-verbal or 'fluid' abilities show a variety of decrements. Tests which are meant to provide measures of non-verbal intelligence, such as Raven's Matrices, tend to show something of a positively accelerated decline with age. This can be seen in *Fig*. 14, in which the average non-verbal intelligence scores can be seen to decline in an exponential fashion with age. In contrast, stored experiences, vocabulary and many other verbal skills remain almost at the same level and may even improve slightly.

In Chapter 6 it was maintained that the concept of intelligence was a somewhat deceptive and meaningless one. Thus when it is reported that non-verbal ability declines with age this does not tell you very much except that older people score less highly on certain intelligence tests. This still leaves the question as to why they should obtain lower scores and this is where the more experimental studies can provide some insights. The most general finding from the experimental studies of ageing is that of a slowing in performance. Older people are found to be slower on many kinds of tasks from simple reaction time through to more complex measures of information processing.

b. Slowing in performance

Simple reaction time is the time taken to respond by pressing a key to the onset of a single stimulus such as a light or sound and can be partitioned into movement time and reaction time. Where this is done, then it is found that both are slower in the aged but that the reaction time contributes most to the overall slowing (Spirduso, 1975). The slowing in movement time has been attributed to slower peripheral nerve conduction velocity, loss of muscle fibre mass and to other changes in peripheral mechanisms in the central nervous sytem. The slowed reaction time may partly reflect raised sensory thresholds and slowed conduction time of brain neurons but the major part would seem to be due to central processing factors. In particular diffuse cerebral atrophy and the hypofunction of the dopaminergic system would seem to play an important role in contributing to slower cognitive performance (McGeer et al., 1977).

This slowing in information processing provides one clear reason for the decline in non-verbal ability since the majority of non-verbal tests are timed and some even have time bonuses for faster performance. This still leaves the question of whether there are any qualitative changes in cognitive functioning with age, over and above this slowing. The answer seems to be that there are other changes, particularly in memory and problem-solving.

c. Memory

Certain aspects of memory become worse as people get older. Visual memory appears to decline more markedly than auditory memory and memory performance in the old shows a larger deficit on tasks which are paced rather than on tasks where individuals are allowed to work at their own pace. The latter is also taken to be a function of the slowing described above since it appears to be a reflection of slower processing. Consistent with this notion is the finding that if the elderly are allowed to work at their own pace, they take longer than young people to learn a task but can do as well on a recall test (Adamowicz, 1976). Slowing in memory performance with age is also seen in the longer time taken to access information in short- and long-term memory. Recall performance generally declines more than recognition which also suggests that the memory problem in the aged is not necessarily a storage failure but due to poor retrieval.

d. Problem-solving ability

Studies of problem-solving in the elderly show that they tend to be slower and poorer. This appears to be a function both of the difficulty in generating strategies for solving unfamiliar problems and an inflexibility in the use of strategies since there is often a rather rigid perseveration with unsuccessful approaches. Tasks requiring a shifting of one problem-solving approach to another are especially taxing for the aged. It is still not clear whether this is because they do not have the cognitive ability to do so or whether it is due to some of the motivational and personality factors outlined below. Similar doubts cloud the interpretation of studies of learning decrements in the elderly. Although many of these have apparently demonstrated consistent age-related declines in learning ability, there is a growing feeling that this is a performance decrement rather than a loss of learning ability. If learning tasks are slowly paced or self-paced and if older people are appropriately motivated or aroused then there is increasing evidence that they are quite able to learn a range of new skills.

e. Perception

Apart from the reductions in sensory acuity there is some evidence that perceptual processing changes with age. In scanning tasks, older people have been found to be less able to ignore irrelevant information and selectively attend to specified information. It has also been found that with advancing age people become slower and more cautious in perceptual judgement tasks. Thus in an experimental situation in which one is required to say which of two lines of similar length is the longer or shorter, older people take longer to make such a decision and tend to be less confident about the accuracy of their responses. All of this might be explained in terms of a change in the speed–accuracy trade-off with increasing age. In most psychomotor tasks there is a balance between speed and accuracy in that there is an element of mutual exclusion between the two. Very fast performance may become quite inaccurate and correspondingly total accuracy may only come about by slowing. It has been found that people are able to trade speed for accuracy and vice versa according to the demands of any given situation but that there appear to be personality differences in this respect. Thus the impulsive person opts for speed at the cost of accuracy while the obsessional makes few errors working in a painstaking fashion. In this sense then the slowing in ageing may also be part of a general transition in speed–accuracy preference which is partly determined by cognitive slowing and partly by such non-cognitive changes as increased caution.

f. Factors affecting age-related changes

It has already been pointed out that there is a great variation in the extent to which these cognitive changes will occur in any older individual. Genetic differences in rates of ageing may account for some of this variation but there is also evidence that a number of environmental factors play an important role. Individuals who have been mentally active and who continue to be into old age have been found to show much less of a cognitive decline. Moreover, various training procedures have been found to modulate and even reverse cognitive deficits in the elderly. Interestingly it has also been shown recently that physical exercise can significantly influence both physiological performance and speed of responding. For example, programmed exercise can lead to improved cardio-vascular and respiratory functioning and to faster reaction times. In fact, in the latter study men in their sixties showed reaction time performances comparable to men in their twenties (Spirduso and Clifford, 1978). For these reasons many now believe that the notion of an irreversible decrement of intelligence is no longer tenable.

The fact that favourable or unfavourable environments may modulate levels of cognitive functioning is apparent at any age level but appears to be critical at the earliest and latest years of life. The importance of the early years in child development was discussed in the previous chapter and similar points can be made with respect to the elderly. As with development, a clear pattern of biological changes is associated with the ageing process but the effects of this on individual functioning are to some extent dependent on the environment. Findings of this type have clear implications for social policy with respect to the aged, particularly in relation to environmental conditions in geriatric hospitals and old people's homes.

g. Changes in personality and behaviour

There appear to be some personality and motivational changes which are associated with ageing but these are more difficult to define than the cognitive changes. It is probably true to say that people's personalities do not change in any radical way with advancing years, although in some of the dementias, described below, there can be marked behavioural changes. The majority of old people probably continue to be, in type, what they have always been. That said, some studies have revealed that a cluster of behavioural changes can be detected although these are neither universal nor inevitable. An increase in rigidity and caution has been one of the more consistent of these findings. This was alluded to in the discussion of cognitive changes above and may tie up quite closely with these. It has also been found that older people are less sociable and emotional and more apathetic.

Some writers have claimed that such changes are part of a general lifestyle adopted by the elderly. They have referred to this as 'disengagement' since it comprises a withdrawal and loss of interest together with the sorts of personality factors already described. There is certainly evidence that something correspond-ing to disengagement is more prevalent in the elderly but it is unclear whether this is an active preference or is socially determined. Various social factors, such as retirement and isolation which are outlined below, may mean that the older person will have greatly reduced opportunities for social contact and will adapt to this. Again there is now quite good evidence that older people who are in a more favourable social environment do not appear to disengage in the dramatic way which has been suggested. Similarly it has always been assumed that sexuality diminishes greatly with age but recent studies have shown that this is dependent on opportunity and on health. Although there is some decline in sexual activity, sex continues to play an important role in the lives of most older people, at least up to 75 years.

It is probably becoming apparent from the discussion above that it is hard, if not impossible, to disentangle the biological, psychological and social aspects of ageing. As with a number of phenomena in this book, such as pain, there are clear biological changes but the impact of these on the individual will depend on the social conditions surrounding the older person.

9.4. The social context of ageing

In addition to biological and psychological changes it is also important to note that in industrialized societies, ageing is very likely to be accompanied by a range of social changes which have an undoubted effect on individual functioning.

The elderly are increasingly likely to live alone. About one-third of the pensionable population in Great Britain now live alone and it is estimated that this figure will get larger. This trend is more marked among women because of their greater life expectancy. One reason why an increasing number of people live alone can be found in the increase in the housing stock during the twentieth century. In one sense the elderly have benefited from this development in that they are now more likely to live in the uncrowded and familiar environment of their house as opposed to living with relatives or in institutions. However, this trend also brings problems as the housing conditions of many older people are more likely to be lacking modern domestic facilities. For example, an official study in 1981 showed that a small proportion of the elderly are still without an inside toilet and a bath whereas all younger householders have these facilities.

The picture is equally bleak when considering the consumer durables, or the lack of them, possessed by older people. Less than one-third of men over 65 have central heating as compared to approaching 60 per cent of the rest of the population. The elderly are also less likely to possess a telephone. The lack of these two provisions can obviously contribute to many of the problems experienced in old age and which may have clinical consequences. For example, the problems of hypothermia among the old are now well documented and the desolation and depression which can arise from isolated living may be diminished by the telephone, particularly in bad weather.

Improving the standard of accommodation could play a significant part in ensuring that the elderly can maintain their social independence. With this in mind one recent writer in this area commented:

> It is often the inconvenient, insanitary and hypothermia-inducing circumstances which provide the straw which eventually breaks the camel's back and induces elderly people or their relatives to seek institutional accommodation. Such circumstances may also make it impossible to welcome back into their own home those who have been admitted to hospital during an episode of acute illness and have since recovered but may not be able to face the rigours of life alone in a house which even able bodied adults might find daunting. (Jefferys, 1978)

Providing the facilities for as full and independent an existence as possible would appear to be an important aim in determining social policy for the elderly, particularly when some of the factors in the last section are considered. In this respect, the older approach of the almshouse may provide something of a model for the housing needs of many older people. Nowadays this would take the form of a small development of minimal but adequate accommodation with links to helping facilities and overlooked by a warden. This type of protected living unit with access to services gives all the possibilities of individual existence but allows for special needs.

The possibility of an independent existence in old age also depends on having a minimal level of income and again this can be a problem area. There have been major changes in the proportions of the elderly doing a paid job. Between 1960 and 1980 in Great Britain the number of men aged 65 or more in paid employment has dropped from about 25 per cent to about 15 per cent. This figure is likely to reduce even more when taking into account current economic predictions and such factors as increased automation and the adoption of microprocessor techniques. Paradoxically the proportion of older women in employment has risen in recent years but the work they are engaged in tends to be part-time and poorly paid. Thus the main source of income for the majority of men and women aged 65 or more in Great Britain is their state pension. The net result is that the total income of elderly households is well below that of other adult households, although there is a great range in this. However, it is unfortunate to note that income decreases with age in that those aged 75 or more have a substantially smaller weekly income than those aged 65 to 69. Poverty is more widespread among the elderly than in any other age group.

Contrary to popular belief, only a relatively small number of older people are institutionalized. Most live and die at home. For the 5 or 6 per cent who are in hospitals or homes, the outlook is not particularly encouraging. The lack of resources and apparent reluctance of skilled medical staff to work with the elderly inevitably mean that the quality of life may leave much to be desired. In the better homes there is an emphasis on the needs of the individuals and an attempt to provide sufficient stimulation and possibilities for independent functioning. However, it is still probably true that far too many older people in institutions are in relatively impoverished environments, in both the psychosocial and physical sense, and where the emphasis is on orderliness and routine rather than individual needs. In view of the problems of institutionalization which are described in Chapter 12, such environments are only likely to exaggerate and accelerate patterns of psychological decline. There is sufficient evidence now to demonstrate that where older people are moved from an unsatisfactory residential setting to a more favourable one, then apparent declines in function can be minimized or even reversed.

For some time now the World Health Organization has recognized the importance of social conditions in mediating the effects of ageing. They also recognize that the provision of a satisfactory economic level is essential for the mental and physical health of older people. Possibilities for continuing employment together with approaches to retirement based on an individual's capacity rather than chronological age are among the other WHO recommendations. Although medical science may have helped to increase the numbers of people living into old age, it is becoming clear that Western societies are, by and large, poorly equipped to deal with the needs of this growing population. Changes in social priorities are necessary to ensure at least adequate social conditions for older people, whether at home or in institutions.

9.5. Clinical considerations

There is a whole branch of medicine given over to the treatment of the elderly and it is not intended to summarize all the aims and scope of geriatrics. However, two areas are mentioned in the light of the other issues which have been raised. First, it seems sensible to consider some of the possible clinical implications of the psychological and social factors associated with the ageing process and, second, there is a brief outline of the problems associated with 'premature' ageing or dementia.

a. General clinical implications

At the outset of this chapter, some mention was made of the great range in the psychological changes which are associated with ageing. This is clearly an important point to keep firmly in mind in one's dealings with the elderly. Stereotypes and assumptions of incompetence are pointless and ultimately insulting. As in the handling of all patients and perhaps more so with the elderly, it is obviously necessary to adapt one's approach to the level and needs of the individual. The sort of problems in communication which are described in Chapter 10 are particularly likely to occur with older people if care is not taken to relate at an appropriate level. It may be necessary to explain things more slowly and to structure information more carefully to avoid forgetting by the elderly patient. Repetition and the use of frequent reminders may also be helpful in this respect.

At least part of the variability in cognitive and social functioning among the old is attributable to social factors, which points to the importance of not overlooking the treatment environment. The physical environment of the hospital or home should be appropriately matched to the needs of the older patient. Minimizing hazards through the implementation of such factors as good lighting and flooring and stairways which facilitate mobility and maximize self-reliance are desirable aims. In psychosocial terms there should be an emphasis on the provision of opportunities for as stimulating and varied activities as possible.

b. Psychological problems

There is a tendency for neuroses and depressive disorders to become more prevalent with age and this may well be a response to the social and psychological changes outlined earlier. Many old people must experience a great deal of isolation, if one bears in mind the fact that a large number live alone. This may be of particular significance for older women who are much more likely to be widowed, if the respective life expectancies for men and women are considered.

Two further potent reasons for depressive reactions in the elderly stem from loss of esteem and bereavement. The former may be associated with retirement and subsequent feelings of worthlessness, which can easily be exacerbated by social isolation or indifference. The depression which is frequently associated with bereavement will be brought about by the loss of spouses, relatives or close friends. Moreover, it is not uncommon to find older people increasingly preoccupied with their own death. Although this can be of positive value in a retrospective and preparatory sense, if it becomes too much of a preoccupation it can be a source of anxiety and depression.

A number of studies have reported an increase in paranoid reactions in the elderly. However, it seems most unlikely that this is an inevitable consequence of ageing but may well be an indirect result of other factors such as social isolation and sensory loss, particularly deafness. When individuals are cut off in this way, there is always a chance that some will develop paranoid feelings and it has been found that frequent home visits to elderly people living alone are of great value. Also such factors as the provision of good hearing aids which do not cause discomfort can also make a considerable difference in this respect.

It is a sad observation that many students in the health sciences unquestionably accept that ageing gives rise to an inevitable decline in function and that this is associated with increased passivity and helplessness. As was indicated above, more recent studies have shown that this position is untenable and can give rise to self-perpetuating truths in that if the elderly are treated as such then it is more likely that these negative aspects will prevail. Fortunately geriatric medicine has begun to recognize these issues and there are attempts to incorporate them into treatment programmes. Geriatric care should predominantly involve a holistic and multidisciplinary approach to the patient since it requires that the skills of the nurse and doctor will be complemented by those of the psychologist and social worker.

c. Senile dementia

It is estimated that approximately 10 per cent of the population over 65 years can be said to have senile dementia. In structural terms this appears to involve an acceleration of the changes which occur in 'normal' ageing. The principal neuropathological changes found in post-mortem studies are a shrinkage of brain substance and a disintegration of grey matter. More detailed morphological studies have revealed other characteristic structural and biochemical changes. These include the presence of plaques and neurofibrillary tangles, particularly in the neocortex and hippocampal regions, and a reduction of activity in the cerebral cortex of choline acetyltransferase, suggesting an interference with neurotransmitter processes. Although these do not show a one-to-one correlation with functional changes, there appears to be overall agreement that the more severe the cerebral atrophy the more likely it is that a person has been demented.

The corresponding behavioural changes are in many ways an accelerated and extreme form of those described earlier and principally entail failing memory, intellectual deterioration and behavioural disturbance. The speed with which these changes occur can vary enormously but the end-result is that of a diminishing capacity to meet the demands of day-to-day living. So much so, that in severe dementia considerable help may be necessary to cope with basic functions and to minimize behavioural problems. These patients present a separate problem group with quite special needs, many of which lie in the psychosocial area. In this respect, it is important to note the recent emergence of psychogeriatrics as a separate specialty, in which psychiatrists and psychologists are turning their attention to the mental health needs of the elderly, particularly those with dementia.

● **Recommended reading**

Birren J. E. and Schaie K. W. (1977) *The Handbook of the Psychology of Aging.* New York, Van Nostrand Reinhold.

Brocklehurst J. C. (ed.) (1985) *Textbook of Geriatric Medicine and Gerontology*, 3rd ed. Edinburgh, Churchill Livingstone.

10

Patients and doctors

The meeting between the patient and the doctor is in many ways the focal point of all medical practice. Many studies have investigated the nature of this interaction and its effects on the eventual outcome. These studies have provided some revealing insights into the behaviour of the doctor and patient during the process of the consultation and the main findings from these studies are described later in this chapter.

This chapter begins with a consideration of some factors which clearly influence the consultation, namely the attitudes and beliefs held by patients and doctors. In patients these are collectively referred to as 'health-related attitudes' and there is evidence that these can influence many health-related behaviours such as the decision to seek medical help or to take the prescribed treatment. Doctors too differ in their views about their own role and the way in which they work and these differences can influence the consultation in many ways.

● 10.1. Factors influencing the behaviour of patients and doctors

a. Determinants of patients' health-related behaviour

The term 'health-related behaviour' is used to cover a wide range of behaviours concerned with aspects of health and illness. It includes daily behaviours with health implications (e.g. diet), preventive behaviours (e.g. attending dental check-ups, screening, etc.), risk avoidance (e.g. giving up smoking; limiting alcohol consumption) and specific behaviours in relation to symptoms and illnesses (e.g. self-medication; seeking medical help; adhering to treatment advice).

One very striking characteristic of these behaviours is how much they vary from person to person. This variation has prompted psychologists to search for explanations in an attempt to understand, for example, why some people seek medical help more than others or why many people do not follow medical advice or treatment.

The simple answer to some of these questions is a biological one. If this were true then more frequent attenders would be expected to have more symptoms or more severe ones. The evidence fails to support this since there is very little difference in the health status of attenders and non-attenders at general practice surgeries. Moreover, many people attend with relatively 'mild' symptoms whereas others may not attend with much more severe ones. Similarly the level of compliance in attenders is not related to the severity of their illness.

An alternative explanation is based on the individual's past experiences and the way in which these influence later behaviour (e.g. an unpleasant experience at the dentist causing avoidance). A number of studies have shown that learning and previous behaviour are good predictors of future behaviour in the health setting. However, each individual will inevitably encounter many entirely new health-related experiences for which no past experience is available. Also it is possible that past experience might influence future behaviour more indirectly by influencing attitudes and beliefs.

Although some health habits and behaviours may be learned from specific experiences, many of the important influences may operate via beliefs and attitudes rather than by triggering specific behaviours. This type of explanation has been most favoured by psychologists researching in the health field. Thus they have attempted to identify differences in health-related attitudes and beliefs as predictors of health-related behaviours. A more detailed account of the evidence from these studies now follows.

Health attitudes and health behaviour
Psychologists use the term *attitude* to describe the reactions that people have to people, objects, situations or issues in their environment. They are all assumed to have three components, namely *beliefs, feelings* and *behaviours* or behavioural intentions. Thus some people who believe that doctors are aggressive may feel dislike or fear in the presence of a doctor, which in turn will influence their intended or actual behaviour with doctors. Most of the research in this field has attempted to identify *health beliefs* which can predict health-related behaviours.

A great deal of this work has involved the *Health Belief Model* (HBM) which is a general theory developed to explain variations in health behaviour. According to the HBM, individuals will only take health actions if certain conditions are present. First of all, 'cues' or 'triggers' are necessary to create situations in which individuals may consider taking action for health reasons. Thus some people may consider giving up smoking or cutting down on their intake following the onset of an unpleasant cough or the provision of a programme for giving up smoking at their local doctor. The model proposes that whether they then take this action will depend on their perception of the threats and benefits involved. Their perception of threat is a function of how susceptible they perceive themselves to be to a particular disease (e.g. lung cancer) as well as their perception of the severity of that disease. Their willingness to take action also depends on the relative balance of the perceived advantages (e.g. being fitter; avoiding major illnesses, etc.) and the perceived disadvantages (e.g. the time, inconvenience, discomfort involved) as well as the perceived efficacy of the treatment or action involved.

The theory was originally developed in the 1950s and has been modified and developed over the years to incorporate more factors. It has been used extensively in studies of health-related behaviour as well as in health education and other programmes. Although some of the health beliefs that form part of the theory have been found to predict particular health behaviours, it is being recognized that it is often too general and unwieldy both for research and practical applications since an individual's health behaviour can vary enormously from situation to situation. Moreover, there are often considerable disparities between people's measured attitudes and their actual behaviour.

Although the HBM has been justly criticized on a number of grounds, it has at least identified some of the important attitudes and beliefs which are associated with health-related behaviours. These include the following:

    i. The degree of interest in and concern with health (health motivation).

    ii. Beliefs about one's susceptibility to a particular illness.

    iii. Beliefs about the severity of a particular illness.

    iv. Beliefs about the benefits and costs of a particular health action.

    v. Beliefs about the efficacy of particular health actions.

All of these beliefs have been found to be associated with particular health-related behaviours, particularly preventive behaviours and adherence to recommended treatment or advice, but the evidence is not consistent. The beliefs in the efficacy of treatment are similar to another set of health-related beliefs which have been studied, namely beliefs as to whether one's health can be significantly controlled by oneself or one's doctor.

This tendency to see events and situations as being under one's own control or subject to chance or uncontrollable factors has been labelled *locus of control*. Thus individuals with an internal locus of control believe that they are responsible for what happens to them whereas those with an external locus have a more fatalistic view. This concept has been applied to the health setting by Wallston and Wallston (1978) who have derived a health locus of control questionnaire which provides three measures to assess the extent to which people believe their health can be controlled by themselves, by 'powerful others' (e.g. health professionals) or is due to chance. Experimental studies using these measures provide mixed support for their ability to predict different health-related behaviours. They do not seem to be particularly useful as general measures but are more successful when they are amended to apply to specific behaviours (e.g. beliefs about one's ability to control a specific health problem, such as diabetes).

These formal approaches to the study of health attitudes and behaviour have had mixed success. Although they have identified certain beliefs and attitudes which can predict health-related behaviours, perhaps one of their inherent difficulties is that they are too structured. People's beliefs may be more idiosyncratic and personal. Thus the use of formal measures may fail to reveal beliefs or ideas which are particularly important for the individual and which guide his or her own behaviour. There is some support for this view and recent work has attempted to look at the views or theories that people have about their own health (Tuckett et al., 1985). This work has indicated that a primary task for the doctor in the consultation is to identify patients' own views about their condition as a basis for good communication.

A great deal of psychological research has been devoted to the study of attitudes which can predict subsequent behaviour. This work has not been entirely successful and more recent theorists have argued that it is only possible to use attitudes or beliefs to predict one's intention to behave in a certain way rather than the behaviour itself. Nevertheless this work has highlighted the fact that patients bring more to the doctor than a particular symptom. They bring general attitudes and expectations about health and the role of the doctor, together with more specific ideas or beliefs about their current condition. Recent research indicates that the doctor will need to be aware of these both in order to understand why the patient has come and to communicate satisfactorily.

b. Differences between doctors

A limited amount of research has indicated that, despite having had a common basic training, doctors may show consistent differences in their approach to patients. Older studies distinguished between those doctors who were more concerned with technical aspects of illness and treatment and those who were interested in psychosocial aspects of illness. Clearly these two positions are not mutually exclusive but there do appear to be doctors who fall into one of these two camps. Some specialties are more likely to attract the more technically or the more socially orientated doctors but in areas such as general medicine and general practice both 'types' have been identified. Thus for any patients the process and outcome of their consultation may be determined by the sort of doctor they happen to encounter.

Differences in consulting style among general practitioners have been investigated in some detail by Byrne and Long (1976). These researchers worked from transcripts of consultations which they analysed in great detail and demonstrated consistent differences in the way consultations were run. They found some doctors whom they described as 'patient-centred' in that they allowed patients to raise issues for discussion and responded to these. In contrast they identified others as 'doctor-centred' since they clearly determined the shape and form of the consultation and did not appear to be interested in the patient's own views or concerns.

These differences in consultation style probably reflect more pervasive attitudinal differences between doctors and their perceptions of their role. There is little evidence as to the origins of these differences. Some probably stem from personality differences and others from specific learning experiences within medical school and later medical training.

Whatever their origins, doctor differences of this type will not only influence communication patterns in the consultation, but also have effects on the diagnostic process and the approach to treatment. In addition, very specific 'past' experiences can have quite powerful influences in particular consultations. For example, if a doctor has missed a serious problem (e.g. a heart problem in a patient presenting with chest pain) on one occasion, his/her future response to patients presenting with a similar picture may be excessively cautious and overdependent on investigations even when the problem is more likely to be quite straightforward. Even more specifically the doctor may have had a frustrating or harrowing surgery and then found that his or her patience is limited in later consultations.

These various differences between doctors have been seen most strikingly in studies comparing the diagnosis and management of similar clinical problems. In the next chapter there is an account of the processes involved in making a diagnosis and this highlights the influence of these differences in the diagnostic process.

● **10.2. Communication problems and their effects**
The following quotation sets the scene for this section:

> The quality of medical care depends in the last analysis on the interaction of doctor
> and patient and there is abundant evidence that in current practice this interaction
> all too often is disappointing to both parties. ... Of the various factors that
> contribute to this discontent certainly one of the most important is poor
> communication between doctor and patient. (Korsch and Negrete, 1972)

These comments come from a study of doctor–patient communication
which looked in detail at 800 consultations in a paediatric outpatient department.
Some of the evidence which is put forward in the following section is taken from
this study and the reader is encouraged to read the original article.

The communication problems which have been identified can be
subdivided into those problems which are primarily viewed from the patient's
perspective and those which come from the doctor as may be seen in *Table* 2.

Table 2.   Problems in patient communication

A.   *From the patient's perspective*
   i. Lack of information
   ii. Communication 'gap'
   iii. Poor recall
   iv. Low empathy
   v. Activity/passivity

B.   *From the doctor's perspective*
   vi. Low compliance
   vii. Poor information

a. Lack of information
A very large proportion of patients complain that they are not given
enough information by those who are treating them. In particular they appear to
want to know what is actually wrong with them and what will happen to them, in
terms of the type of treatment and the sorts of changes that will occur. For
example, in the Korsch and Negrete study one-fifth of all the mothers were not
given a clear statement as to what was wrong with their children and nearly half of
them were uncertain as to what the course of the illness would be. It is significant
to note that this was not related to the length of the interview since these
complaints were found as frequently in those who had quite long interviews.

A very similar pattern of results has been found with hospital patients (*see*
Chapter 13) and with patients receiving other types of treatment such as dentistry.
Even the great majority of those with very serious or with terminal illnesses
appear to want to be told about their situation but in most cases this does not
happen. This point has been emphasized by one writer who noted that 80 per cent
of dying patients know that they are dying and want to talk about it while 80 per
cent of doctors deny this and believe that patients should not be told. There are
now results from many studies which show that the majority of patients with fatal

conditions want to be accurately informed about their illness so they can prepare themselves and die in a dignified fashion. Unfortunately it is still probably true that many of those who deal with patients believe that they should only give good news and if there is none, say nothing. This may be easier for them to handle personally since giving bad news is a difficult and often emotional matter.

For the patient then 'no news is not good news, it is an invitation to fear' (Fletcher, 1973), which gives some indication as to why lack of information can be so problematic and why providing clear information can be of value. If patients remain in the dark and yet, because they are suffering or are in hospital, know that all is not well then this is most likely to make them much more anxious. The uncertainty and helplessness which are often generated in this situation can both be potential precursors of anxiety and depression. As is indicated in later chapters, there is often a psychological reaction to illness and hospitalization and a degree of anxiety is both understandable and 'normal', in the sense that perhaps most people would react in such a way. However, raised anxiety levels can have significant adverse effects on both the perception of symptoms and the response to treatment.

One study of surgical patients has shown that those who are either indifferent or over-anxious preoperatively will tend to respond badly postoperatively. Those who showed a moderate, but what was deemed to be an appropriate, level of preoperative concern were the ones who adapted best postoperatively. Further investigation of these three groups of patients showed that an important factor which differentiated the indifferent and moderately anxious group was how well informed they were about their operation and the outcome. The indifferent group were found to be very poorly informed and were just not prepared for the trauma and subsequent pain from the operation. This type of finding has been replicated and extended in a number of other studies in which the effects of preoperative information on postoperative recovery have been investigated. All of these have shown that not only are the patients' psychological states better, as evidenced by less distress and anxiety, but also there are benefits to their physical state when clear information has been given before an operation. Thus in one study those patients who had received information about their operations were found to request significantly less analgesia and to be able to leave hospital between two and three days earlier than a control group.

One objection to findings of this sort has been that it takes time to inform patients and that this time could be better utilized using 'real' medical skills on other patients. However, if the gains from supplying information can be as great as those described above then this rather weakens the strength of any such objection.

Another objection that is sometimes raised is that some patients may not want to know very much about their condition and that routinely informing them may be stressful and counter-productive. This may be true for a small group of patients if information is given in a mechanical fashion. The real point to be made here is not that information should be rammed down people's throats regardless but that the approach to the patient should be one which allows areas of uncertainty to be mentioned and dealt with in a satisfactory way. In doing so it should be possible not only to determine whether someone wants to be given information, which will probably be the case, but also how much detail should be specified. In this context there is evidence that the personality of the patient has an influence on the way such information should be presented so as to allay anxiety best (*see* p. 101).

Allowing patients to determine and specify what they would like to know also appears to provide a satisfactory basis for the care of the dying. It is very often with these patients that the greatest and most contrived silences are maintained by medical staff. Those who work with dying patients in hospices emphasize the importance of allowing patients to divulge their fears and expectations as well as indicating what they would like to be told about their condition.

From all this it can readily be seen that failure to provide sufficient information can have direct and indirect consequences on how patients feel and respond.

b. Communication gap

The second problem area described quite commonly is that of the 'communication gap'. This refers to information which passes to and from the patient but which is either not understood or understood in a different way by the doctor and the patient.

It has been found that doctors and other health professionals are very fond of using jargon which is often not understood by patients. These technical terms may be either meaningless to patients or quite often incorrectly interpreted, as Korsch and Negrete (1972) have demonstrated. They gave the example of one patient who thought a 'lumbar puncture' was an operation to drain the lungs and another who took the term 'incubation period' to refer to the length of time a child was to be kept in bed. Another mother did not realize that her child was to be operated on when the doctor said he would have to 'explore'. In this study it was reported that this type of jargon was used in more than half of the 800 interviews which were investigated.

The use of this type of jargon did not necessarily leave patients dissatisfied. On the contrary many were rather flattered and impressed by the technical terms. However, for many of the mothers in this study it was as if no information had been given since they were still effectively no wiser as to what was going on. Apart from being flattered, other reasons for not requesting clarification are also given. Typically patients also say that they do not want to look stupid by admitting ignorance or that they do not want to cause trouble by asking for things to be explained. These sorts of reasons obviously reflect the effects of perceived role differences on the part of the patient, as well as differences in social class and expertise. It should therefore be the responsibility of those who deal with patients to ensure that information is clearly presented in a manner which can be understood. Failure to do this is not merely bad communication, it may effectively be non-communication.

In a sense, many patients also use a type of jargon in that they will use terms, the meaning of which will need to be clarified by the doctor. Over the years a patient will pick up and use particular phrases such as 'my nerves' or 'feeling run down' to describe states that are familiar to themselves. However, it has been shown that such phrases do not carry universal meanings and it may be important for the doctor to request a more precise description of the changes that have been experienced by the patient. Failure to do so may result in a misleading picture as to the true nature of the patient's problems.

IN THE PICTURES BELOW PUT A TICK UNDERNEATH THE DRAWING
THAT SHOWS THE CORRECT POSITION OF THE BRAIN

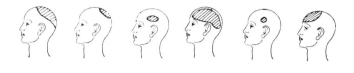

							Total	Rating
Doctors	0	0	0	53 (100%)	0	0	53	Good
Patients	11 (5·9%)	9 (4·8%)	17 (9·2%)	122 (66·3%)	4 (2·1%)	21 (11·4%)	184	Fair

IN THE PICTURES BELOW PUT A TICK UNDERNEATH THE DRAWING
THAT SHOWS THE CORRECT POSITION OF THE SCIATIC NERVE

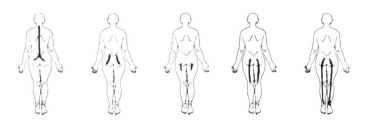

						Total	Rating
Doctors	0	1 (1·8%)	2 (3·7%)	29 (54·7%)	21 (39·6%)	53	Fair
Patients	37 (22·8%)	25 (15·4%)	8 (4·9%)	36 (22·2%)	56 (34·5%)	162	Poor

Fig. 15. Examples of the differences in the use of anatomical terms by doctors and patients. (From Hawkes, 1974.)

Another widely reported aspect of this communication gap is the finding that doctors and patients may use the same terms in different ways. Perhaps the clearest examples of this are the studies in which doctors and patients were tested for their interpretation of various anatomical terms (Boyle, 1970; Hawkes, 1974). Examples from one of these studies are shown in *Fig.* 15.

What these examples demonstrate is that there may often be some misunderstanding by both doctors and patients when anatomical terms are used. Patients may incorrectly ascribe pain to a particular anatomical area or may misconstrue an explanation from the doctor by confusing parts of the body.

A similar pattern of misunderstanding by patients has been found in relation to medical advice given to them. Two examples from one study illustrate this point. First it was found that in response to the advice to avoid aspirin-containing substances:

9 per cent of the sample still thought that Aspro could be taken;

17 per cent of the sample still thought that Disprin could be taken;

20 per cent of the sample still thought that Anadin could be taken;

72 per cent of the sample still thought that Alka Seltzer could be taken.

The second example was concerned with the advice to avoid foods containing starch or sugar and found the following responses to these high-carbohydrate foodstuffs:

12 per cent of the sample thought that sweetened condensed milk could be consumed;

38 per cent of the sample thought that cream cakes could still be consumed;

59 per cent of the sample thought that butter beans could still be consumed.

All the examples again emphasize the need to check that not only has information been understood but that there is a communality of understanding between doctor and patient.

c. Poor recall

The third problem area for patients is that of poor recall of information and advice given to them. In view of what has already been described, it is perhaps not surprising to find that around half the information which has been presented cannot be recalled within 5 minutes after leaving the surgery. From the earlier chapter on human memory functions it was seen that only a limited amount of information can be retained for a fairly short period of time and that for information to be held for longer periods it needs to be encoded in a form which is meaningful to the individual. From what has already been said in this section, it is clear that much of the information given out in the surgery will not be easily encoded by the patient but there do appear to be a number of quite successful ways of improving this situation.

Information is more easily forgotten when patients are anxious and so this offers one way of reducing memory loss. More specifically it is found that advice and instructions, particularly when they come at the end of a consultation, are forgotten more readily and that information which is considered by the patient to be less important is also retained less well. Thus it has been found that if advice is presented before other information and if its importance is sufficiently emphasized there is a significant increase in its chances of being remembered (e.g. an increase from 44 per cent recall to 75 per cent recall in one study). Similarly if care is taken to ensure that information is comprehensible and is organized into identifiable categories then recall also significantly improves. Finally, it has been convincingly demonstrated that the use of specific rather than general advice greatly aids memory. One study showed that the recall of specific instructions (e.g. 'lose half a stone in the next 2 weeks') is some three times as great as for general instructions (e.g. 'try and lose some weight'). Once patients are given quite specific and comprehensible information, it would appear that this can be retained and acted on whereas general advice is easily misconstrued and more commonly just forgotten.

d. Low empathy

A frequent complaint from patients is that many doctors just do not seem interested in their problems. In the Korsch and Negrete (1972) study it was found that while mothers had expected that an interest would be shown in their concerns, the recordings showed that only 5 per cent of all the interactions were friendly and empathic in nature. The great majority of the dialogue dealt with technical aspects of the illness and tended to ignore the patient's view of the problem. About one-quarter of the mothers had not been able to mention what really concerned them about their children because they were not given the chance or encouragement to do so. Sometimes this leads to a complete breakdown in communication since patients become so preoccupied with their own unexpressed worries that they stop paying attention to the doctor. The effects of this can be more far reaching than just interfering with communication since it may affect subsequent behaviour. For example, Korsch and Negrete concluded that 'the disregard of the mother's concern must be considered as an important hindrance to communication in the light of the fact that in the post-visit interviews, 300 out of the 800 mothers held themselves in some way responsible for the child's illness'.

Patients also report that if a doctor is perceived as unsympathetic this will affect a number of aspects of their consulting behaviour. They may visit less often but, more commonly and more seriously, they will be less likely to discuss more personal problems. Findings of this type provide good evidence for the two-way nature of the doctor–patient interaction. The patient appears to be monitoring the doctor with respect to both the doctor's technical competence and to his or her empathy. Those who feel that their doctors have understood their concerns are much more likely to express satisfaction with communication and hence to follow advice as is seen below.

The effect of the doctor's attitude on the patient's subsequent willingness to present certain types of problems is seen clearly in a survey of the presentation of sexual problems. All the doctors in this study were initially rated for their 'comfortableness' and interest in discussing their patients' sexual problems. It was found that those who appeared disturbed or indifferent to the subject were hardly ever consulted about sexual problems whereas those who routinely asked about sex in a relaxed and open manner were consulted more frequently. From studies of this type there is a strong indication that the extent to which personal problems can be discussed will depend as much on the characteristics of the doctor as on the severity of the problems.

Part of this failure to be aware of the patient's particular concerns would appear to reflect the differences in the perception of clinical problems which exist between doctor and patient. For the doctor the problem is typically construed in terms of certain biological changes but for the patient the experience of a problem will also have intrinsic psychological and social facets. It is therefore important to be aware of what any problem means to the patient since this awareness is not only necessary for facilitating communication but also may be of therapeutic value in itself.

e. Activity/passivity

The last of the problems from the patient's viewpoint was listed in *Table* 2 as activity/passivity. This is in some ways related to the previous problem and refers to the complaint about the relative roles which are pursued by doctor and patient. The analysis of the taped interviews in the Korsch and Negrete study showed that, although the doctors felt that they had been 'democratic' in their approach to their patients, they had actually adopted a very active role and had done far more talking than the patients, who had a far more passive role virtually forced on them. This type of approach is engendered and maintained by use of interviewing styles which are characterized by the use of 'closed' questions. These are discussed more fully below but consist of questions to which only simple yes/no type answers are possible. In this framework the patient will become a passive respondent to a string of questions which are determined solely by the doctor. While such an approach is obviously necessary at some stages of the interview in order to get a clear picture of all the details of a problem, it brings certain difficulties. First, it may mean that whole problem areas may be missed because the interview has taken a very specific direction at an early stage. Second, it necessarily means that the clinical problem will become defined primarily in the doctor's terms as this is where all the questions are coming from. Such an approach is quite contrary to the old medical advice to 'listen to the patient and he will tell you the problem'.

Some patients appear to prefer this type of passive role and find it important that the doctor is in complete control. Many others, however, value a much more reciprocal relationship since it allows them to describe problems in their own terms and gives them a chance to bring up problems in addition to those which have already been pursued by the doctor. Thus in situations where there is a complex of problems and where the patient has chosen a particular one as the 'ticket' for admission to the surgery, such an approach may be very necessary.

f. Low compliance

One of the most direct effects of poor communication which have been demonstrated by the various studies has been on compliance rates in patients. From a whole range of studies with different types of clinical problems and medications, it has been shown that between 40 and 50 per cent of patients do not comply with treatment. Some details are shown in relation to specific treatments in *Table* 3 and overall they show a consistent picture of patients not following advice or treatment.

The reasons for this are almost certainly many and complicated and it might be thought that total compliance is an even more serious problem but some

Table 3. Percentages of patients who did not follow treatment or advice (from Ley, 1974)

Type of advice	No. of studies	Percentage of patients who did not follow the advice	
		Range	Average
A. Medicine taking			
i. PAS and other TB drugs	20	8–76	37·5
ii. Antibiotics	8	11–92	48·7
iii. Psychiatric drugs	9	11–51	38·6
iv. Other medicines, e.g. antacids, iron	12	9–87	47·7
B. Diet	11	20–84	49·4
C. Other advice, e.g. child care, antenatal exercises	8	30–79	54·6
D. All advice	68	8–92	44·0

explanations are possible. Poor recall due to the complexity or vagueness of the instructions given has been shown to provide one of the reasons why treatment is not followed. Additionally the patient's own views, as to the nature of the problem and the best type of treatment, can play a role in determining whether the given treatment is deemed appropriate and hence followed or not. However, a more universal explanation and one which may partly encompass both of these is that of dissatisfaction with communication. One of the most striking findings to come from the Korsch and Negrete study was that there was a direct relationship between patient satisfaction with communication and compliance with treatment. They found that of the patients who were satisfied with the communications aspects of the interview 54 per cent complied totally with the prescribed treatment whereas the equivalent figure for the dissatisfied group was approximately 16 per cent. This is a very large and very real difference, particularly in such a big group and highlights the importance of good communication in medicine.

From the preceding account of the communication problems and their effects, it can now readily be seen that communication skills should not be dismissed as an 'optional extra' for successfully handling patients. Clinical knowledge and expertise may be entirely wasted if patients have failed to understand instructions or feel that their problems have not really been mentioned or understood. Many ways of dealing with these problems were described above and are often quite specific in relation to a particular problem. However, there are two underlying themes which merit further discussion. First, it is clear that good interviewing skills are a fundamental part of clinical practice and that many of the communication difficulties would not arise if these were adopted. Second, patients and doctors may see the same problems in quite different ways and this discrepancy may in turn contribute to communication difficulties. There is a consideration of the nature of clinical problems in the next chapter and this also indicates the usefulness of looking directly at the underlying processes associated with diagnostic problem-solving.

● **10.3. Patient interviewing: some general guidelines**

The purpose of most consultations is to discover why the patient has come and to decide on an appropriate course of action. Stated as baldly as this, the interview is made to sound a rather straightforward and perfunctory process in which information is systematically collected. This picture of the interview also tends to encourage the notion of the patient as a somewhat passive respondent who provides information to order. A number of rather glaring contradictions exist which force a rethink of this rather simple picture.

First, clinical problems may not always be simple entities which can be discovered from a sequence of logical questions. In any one patient there may be a range of symptoms which may or may not be inter-related. This potential multiplicity of symptoms has been recognized by the advocates of the problem-orientated medical record (Weed, 1969), which is described in Chapter 11.

Second, the patient is rarely, probably never, a passive respondent. As was made clear in the previous section, the patient monitors the doctor and the information that emerges will in part reflect reactions to the doctor's attitude and approach to the interview. Third, it may be as important to know why the patient has come at this particular time rather than merely documenting the perceived clinical changes which have pre-empted the visit. This is particularly true for the large number of patients with longstanding chronic problems and where there is not a recent onset of illness.

As soon as factors of this type are considered the nature of the clinical interview takes on a new complexion. Rather than being a mere mechanical extraction of facts, it becomes much more meaningful to see it as a dynamic process since it consists of an interaction between two individuals. The information that emerges will depend on the nature of this interaction, on the sorts of questions which are asked and particularly on the way they are asked. If the same patient is interviewed separately by two different interviewers it is often found that two quite distinct interpretations of the patient's problem will emerge. It is not too difficult to see how such views are reached when an analysis is carried out of the types of questions which were used.

In this section, then, there will be an account of some different types of interviewing strategy and their effects on the outcomes of the intertiew. The emphasis here is not on what information should be obtained but on how to obtain it. Important features of this approach include the role of rapport, the development of the doctor–patient relationship and an overall attempt to facilitate the emergence of facts rather than their extraction from the patient. Thus the purpose of this account is to provide guidelines about those approaches which maximize communication between doctor and patient.

The overall atmosphere of the interview is of great importance in determining how the consultation will progress. The interview should obviously take place in a quiet room which is comfortable and in which privacy can be ensured. The behaviour of the interviewer should encourage communication in that there should be attentiveness and a sensitivity to the direction which the interview should take. Attentiveness should be towards the patient's non-verbal behaviour as well as what is being said. This should allow the interviewer to recognize areas of subjective importance and to detect discrepancies between what has been said and the emotional state of the patient. The importance and recognition of these non-verbal clues are discussed more fully in the next section. Finally, it is generally found that communication is best facilitated by starting with a relatively low use of control and gradually proceeding to a more directive approach by homing in on specific areas of relevance.

A range of interviewing techniques is available and these will be of value at different stages in the interview.

a. Opening the interview

This is clearly an important stage of the interview when impressions are formed which can persist and affect the attitudes of both parties. On the doctor's side it would appear important to greet the patient and, if necessary, to introduce oneself at the very beginning of the interview. There may be some value in having a relatively brief neutral chat at this stage in order to relax the patient and establish rapport. However, this should not go on too long as the patient has come for a purpose and may be bewildered if this is not discussed for some time.

Questioning about the clinical problem should be initiated by using open-ended questions. These are questions which do not necessarily produce a specific answer but let the patient indicate the problem area or areas. Such questions typically take the form, 'What seems to be the problem?' or 'Why have you come to see me?' The value of these questions is that they allow patients to describe the problem in their own terms and, in doing so, are likely to create a climate in which communication is encouraged. The early use of direct questions may close off whole areas of important information from discussion. A further criticism of the early use of directed questioning is that it can result in a style of interview where the patient passively responds to very specific questions and it may be difficult for further areas to be raised and discussed. Thus the early use of directed questions may well force the interview into a cul-de-sac from which it may be difficult to emerge.

Once the initial open-ended questions have indicated the areas of importance, these can be pursued in detail and this is where the use of directed questions is valuable to provide precise details. New areas can also be explored by the use of further open-ended questions, such as 'Is there anything else bothering you?', later in the interview. If there are a number of problems and if some of these may have been difficult to discuss at the beginning of the interview, these can now be discussed.

Sometimes patients will not be able to make full use of these initial open-ended questions and if this happens there will be a temptation to resort to direct questioning immediately. This temptation can be avoided by using less controlling strategies such as silence, facilitation and confrontation to encourage the patient to talk rather than dragging out information with direct questions.

b. Encouraging and prompting the patient

Sometimes the patient will become silent or find it difficult to continue describing a particular problem. Here again the temptation is to try to pre-empt what would have been said with a direct question but at this stage silence by the interviewer may be very valuable.

Many medical students become embarrassed when silences occur during the interview, feeling that this reflects badly on their perceived competence and may grasp for any question or diversionary tactic. However, silences can take many forms and if silences by the patient are countered with silence by the interviewer, accompanied by the appropriate non-verbal cues of interest, then this may be sufficient encouragement to the patient to start up again. This use of silence can be very productive since it provides patients with the message that there is time and interest for anything that they would like to say. Generating the feeling that there is no need to rush and that there is a willing listener present can be greatly valued by patients in the early stages of the interview and may facilitate the discussion of a completely new and relevant area.

Long silences are generally uncomfortable and should be avoided. There are also some patients who will feel uncomfortable with any silence and in this case there is no sense in persisting with this strategy.

During the interview it is important to encourage communication in any way possible. Typically this type of facilitation will involve the use of verbal and non-verbal cues which indicate to the patient that the doctor is interested, listening and wishes the patient to continue. Nods, small grunts or appropriate phrases and sufficient eye-contact are all facilitatory for the speaker. During conversation the speaker will routinely make brief glances at the listener to check what impression is being made and this will determine how much is subsequently said. It has been found that facilitating gestures are indeed reinforcing in that they encourage communication of the particular topic being discussed at the time. A combination of attentive silence and facilitation following an open-ended question will often allow much of the relevant information to emerge but if the patient is not speaking freely, a more directive approach will be needed.

The most directive approach available to the interviewer is to fire a series of direct questions and this will entirely dictate the flow of the interview. As was indicated earlier, this is a necessary way of collecting the vital details about the nature of the clinical problem. However, if the interviewer suspects that there might be another problem lurking below the surface and that the patient is having difficulty in raising this, then a different type of directive approach is available for getting at this. This technique is known as confrontation and the object is to take something which the patient has said or to refer to some aspect of their non-verbal behaviour so as to direct more attention to it. The following statements are an example of this type of approach: 'You seem upset', 'You sound angry' and 'You seem to be finding it difficult to tell me about this'.

Confrontation is usually a statement about the interviewer's perception of the patient rather than a totally direct question, which might put too much pressure on the patient. This can be particularly valuable when the patient's non-verbal behaviour either communicates something which is not being overtly discussed or is actually incongruous with what is being said. Thus, if the patient appears to be tense or depressed but is not actually discussing a psychological problem, a confrontation-type of question can be used to indicate that the interviewer has recognized this. Yet the structure of the question still allows the patient to decide whether the interview will take a new direction or not. This type of questioning can be very valuable and offers possibilities for approaching new problem areas but care should be taken to ensure that it is not used in too critical or hostile a manner and is not used repeatedly about the same point, in an interrogatory or nagging fashion.

c. Support and reassurance

It is becoming clear that the interview does not just consist of an exercise in data collection but is a forum in which problems are raised and discussed by two people. Quite often when chronic or difficult problems are discussed and when the climate of the interview is such that patients feel able to express emotion, then the interaction may well take on a different form. At times like this the interview will cease to be of the strict question–answer format and becomes a situation in which the interviewer will have to respond to the feelings of the patient and be aware of what they mean.

If patients do raise psychological problems or show a psychological response to other problems, it is necessary for the interviewer to recognize this and to be supportive to the patient. This can be valuable in indicating the interviewer's interest, understanding and empathy with the patient. Thus statements such as 'I understand' or 'That must have been upsetting for you' fulfil this function. Also a sympathetic summary of what the patient has said has the joint value of conveying that the problem has been correctly understood and that there is someone who appreciates the patient's own reality of the problem. One of the most important times to show support is after the patient has expressed strong feelings, possibly after a confrontation. Supportive words must also be accompanied by an appropriately supportive attitude in order to be effective since a perceived incongruence between supportive words and an indifferent non-verbal response might be counter-productive.

Showing interest and concern with patients who are going through a bad time, psychologically or physically, can be of great value as a supportive mechanism. This does not usually involve interpretations of the patient's emotional changes since the origins of these are usually fairly obvious, nor does it depend on the complex role relationships necessary for other psychotherapeutic approaches. It is essentially a maintaining technique which allows the patient to work through a difficult time with a sympathetic person and, as such, a supportive approach on the clinician's behalf can be of tremendous value. This type of approach to the patient is discussed again in Chapter 14 where the value of talk as treatment is discussed.

One other important component of the supportive role which may have to be employed in the interview is that of reassurance. Patients may be very anxious or guilty about their feelings and it can be of great value to indicate that such feelings are understandable and to give some idea what the outcomes might be. Any communication which results in restoring the patient's sense of self-esteem or confidence will meet this need and this can be particularly helpful if the patient is frightened or anxious. As with any supportive approach, reassuring words must be accompanied by an appropriate attitude and should also be based on reasonable evidence. Clearly reassurance should not be given in a way that creates unreasonable expectations nor should it appear to indicate that nothing is wrong when there is a serious problem. This 'head in the sand' dismissiveness may be comfortable for the clinician and may bring temporary relief to the patient but in the long term it will not make it any easier for the patient to come to terms with a difficult problem such as a chronic or terminal illness. Indeed there is some evidence that a dismissive approach in these situations is actually worse for patients in the long run because they will have been given the message that everything is meant to be alright whereas they can see and feel that it really is not the case. Reassurance must therefore stay close to the known facts and must work through the patient's feelings. By allowing patients to express their fears and reactions it should be possible to ascertain the extent to which these are accurate in order to correct any misconceptions and provide information about clinical facilities, such as pain relief. Such an approach will have the combined advantages of allowing patients to express emotions, of locating particular anxieties and of dealing with these with understanding and realistic information.

This account of interviewing strategies has described some fairly simple ways of ensuring that communication problems can be avoided and that patients are given a sufficient opportunity to describe their problems. Obviously specific types of directed questions will be necessary to get the fine details of any condition. Even so, understanding the patient's problem may be more than a question of documenting the exact nature of recent biological changes. It may involve an awareness of the patient's perceptions of those problems and the role of psychosocial factors in this. In these terms, an approach of the type outlined above, which is essentially open ended in nature, is one which should provide the basis of a good interview.

● **10.4. Non-verbal communication**

We have seen that one criterion of skilled communication is the ability to recognize and act on non-verbal changes in the patient. In addition to this there are skills associated with the transmission of appropriate non-verbal signals to the patient. These can indicate interest, concern and empathy and be of great value in facilitating communication. From the moment the patient enters the surgery, a range of non-verbal cues is available which can influence the atmosphere and shape of the interview. The position of the chairs, the initial behaviour of the doctor and the type of greeting can all play an important part in determining attitudes and expectations in the patient. Similarly the patient's appearance, entry and initial dialogue may all provide important indicators of mood, emotion and personality which might be of great value in understanding the nature of the clinical problem. Here a fairly brief account of some of the more familiar non-verbal aspects of communication is presented. This is not in any way an exhaustive account but one intended to indicate the range of those cues which can be of importance in communication.

a. The nature of non-verbal cues

The particular value of being able to recognize and interpret such cues in the clinical interview is that they may often allow some insight into emotionally charged areas which are not or perhaps cannot be revealed verbally. Most of this type of information will tend to be revealed by the dynamic cues as indicated in *Table* 4, particularly the facial changes, body movements and paralinguistic data.

The *static cues* may reveal useful information and may play an important part in forming initial impressions both by the doctor and patient. Clothes and hairstyle will give some idea of the sort of image the individual will try to present to the world and may also indicate aspects of psychological disturbances. Severe depression is sometimes accompanied by the tendency for self-neglect and this can be readily perceived. However, none of these cues is absolute in the sense that they convey a universal invariant meaning. Static cues particularly reflect a range of cultural and contextural determinants, and impressions that might be initially formed from static cues may be hastily modified once more data are available from conversation. The so-called dynamic cues do deserve a little more detailed consideration as they may supply a rich source of information in the interview.

Table 4. Non-verbal cues in communication

Dynamic cues	Static cues
Orientation	Face
Distance	Physique
Posture	Voice
Gesture	Clothes, glasses, etc.
Body movement	Make-up
Facial expression	Hair style
Eye movements and eye contact	
Tone, rate and fluency of speech	

i. Orientation and distance

Two cues which play an important role in the initial part of the interview are orientation and distance since the positioning of the chairs in the surgery will provide information about these. The position one person takes up with respect to another in conversation has been shown to depend on what sort of encounter they are expecting or wanting. If a friendly or intimate encounter is expected then the people involved tend to choose positions which allow for greater closeness, even for physical contact. In contrast, an unfriendly or more competitive meeting will be signalled by sitting opposite the other party so as to see them more clearly.

Touch and body contact represent a powerful means of emotional expression and an effective source of comfort in a social interaction. Obviously the effect of physical contact will ultimately depend very much on the age, sex, relationship and status of the two people involved. There are also quite significant cultural differences in the use of body contact and in the preferred distances that are maintained in social situations. This is best illustrated by the example of the 'embassy shuffle', a dance-like manoeuvre which can allegedly be seen at social functions in embassies and other situations where people from different cultures meet. The shuffle typically takes place during conversation between somebody from one culture who prefers a reasonable distance in conversation (say 5 feet apart) and another for whom it is culturally normal to talk at a distance of 1 to 2 feet apart, a distance which the former would regard as intimate rather than functional. The end-result is that while the conversation progresses one speaker perpetually backs off and the other closes up in an attempt to maintain their respective preferred distances for conversing. Hence the embassy shuffle.

ii. Eye contact

The distance between speakers also has an important effect on the amount of eye contact that occurs between them. The closer two people are together, the tendency is for eye contact to decrease, as if there is a balance between these two variables which individuals can manipulate in order to maintain a psychologically comfortable interaction. Other important factors can also determine the degree of eye contact between individuals. For example, more eye contact is showed by those who are listening than those who are talking during a conversation. The speaker will make much shorter and less frequent eye contact with the listener in order to check how the message is being received. If a person is disliked or found to be unattractive, there will be less eye contact and the same will be true if a topic is very embarrassing or difficult for the speaker. Prolonged eye contact is usually inferred to be a sign of a strong emotional response which can be either positive or negative (i.e. either affection or anger) whereas averted eye contact may be indicative of guilt, fear or rejection. On the diagnostic side it has been claimed that depressed patients show a decrease in the frequency of eye movements whereas an almost total lack of eye contact has been suggested as one indication of autism in children (*see* Chapter 8).

In addition to this expressive function eye contact can also play an important part in regulating the conversation between speakers. When one speaker has finished or is coming to the end of an utterance, there will be a tendency to look towards the other speaker, who then can start to reply. In a study where speakers were specifically instructed not to do this or were not able to see each other, it always took longer for replies to occur since the signal to do so was not available. In these situations conversation becomes much less fluent, more jerky and filled with unnecessary pauses. This type of regulation of conversation is also facilitated by such paralinguistic cues as the intonation of speech and use of pauses.

iii. *Paralinguistic cues*
These comprise such features as tone, rate and fluency of speech and can provide useful information about the patient's emotional state and intentions. Studies using actors have shown that, with exactly the same standard sentence, it is possible systematically to manipulate these cues to convey a range of emotions from hate and despair through to amusement, admiration and affection. Typically a person who is anxious will be found to make more hestitations and errors in speech. With states of anxiety and excitement, speech is also likely to be faster and more body movements are made. In contrast, depressed patients will tend to talk in a slow, rather soft and monotonous voice. Indeed such different modes of speech as shouting, giggling and whispering are all suggestive of different mood states. Perhaps the most dramatic example of the effect of emotional state on paralinguistic aspects of speech is to be found in the speech of some severe stutterers. With these, the severity of the stuttering can reflect the degree of anxiety or relaxation.

One potentially important source of information can be the degree of congruence between the verbal and non-verbal aspects of speech. It is possible for a person to describe something about themselves and yet for the paralinguistic cues to indicate something quite contrary. For example, patients may say that they are not depressed or anxious on direct questioning but aspects of their speech may indicate otherwise and that they are unwilling to admit this. Recognition of such incongruences should not provide ammunition for an attack on the dishonesty of the patient but should be carefully noted since they may be of some importance in understanding the particular clinical problem.

Consistent incongruences between the spoken and emotional content in the speech of mothers towards children have been implicated as a potentially harmful source of later problems in relationships. In childhood very important lessons about human relations are learned from interactions with parents or those close at hand. If these are continually ambiguous, in that there is a clash between verbal content and emotional tone, the child may have great difficulty in knowing how best to relate to that person. This, in turn, may provide the basis for a lifetime of failures in personal relations but this is not always the case. This explanation of adult difficulties in relations and of later schizophrenic illness is known as the 'double-bind' hypothesis. The argument roughly goes that the young child gets caught up in the conflict of the double-bind between emotional tone and verbal content and that this lays the foundations of later psychopathology.

iv. Body movements

Body movements also carry information about the emotional state of the individual but in a relatively crude form, when compared with the detail of information which can be gleaned from facial expression. Ekman and Friesen (1977) have suggested that body movements provide an indication of the intensity of emotion whereas the face actually identifies the nature of the emotion. Thus the movements and posture of the body may express the level of arousal, tension or relaxation and whether this is positive or negative but the facial changes will indicate more exactly the nature of this. Moreover, body movements will also indicate how someone is coping with an emotional state which is signalled by the face. Thus if there are facial signs of anger, the body may move forward to attack or tense up and withdraw depending on the way the individual is able to express the anger.

The willingness of the individual to participate in communication can be indicated by posture. For example, someone who is leaning away with arms and legs crossed is probably relatively unwilling to talk and is also likely to be tense and uninterested. If a patient assumes this type of posture during a consultation, it may be an indication that a difficult area has been reached and that further conversation may be difficult or non-existent. It is probably fair to say that, although a rough indication of the person's intentions and emotions may be inferred from postural cues, these are not precise or universal in the sense that they always convey quite specific information. They must be interpreted in the particular context in which they occur and in conjunction with other verbal and non-verbal cues.

There is a whole range of postural and movement cues and it is not intended to describe all of these. Some aspects appear to be totally under conscious control and are non-verbal equivalents of words. Two simple examples are the use of shoulder shrugs to indicate uncertainty or head nods to indicate agreement or disagreement. Others are more unconscious and appear to illustrate or underline what is being said. These are more apparent in sociable and outgoing individuals and also show marked cultural differences in their frequency and intensity. Moreover, clinical studies have shown that this illustrative type of body movement is more commonly seen in neurotic as opposed to psychotic patients on admission to hospital and that low rates of such movements tend to be judged by psychiatrists as evidence of withdrawal. Finally, there are movements which usually appear to be unconscious and involve the movement of one part of the body together with another part, such as scratching, picking, rubbing, wringing hands and licking lips. High rates of such 'self-manipulative' movements tend to have the effects of making patients be judged as anxious or guilty, from videotaped studies of therapists and patients. Overall they seem to provide some sort of index of discomfort and typically arise when a person is ill at ease, tense or anxious.

With all these non-verbal aspects of communication there can be very large cultural differences in their quality and quantity. Indeed some interesting misunderstandings can occur because of cultural differences in interpretations of gestures. It has been shown that sticking out the tongue indicates an apology in parts of China, the evil eye in India, deference in Tibet, a rude sign in England and just means 'no' among the Marquesans. The same gesture in England can also have a number of connotations such as cheekiness, rudeness, sexual provocation or bewilderment depending on the particular context in which it occurs. In contrast some facial expressions are almost universal and appear to be reflex-like in their expression. Ekman and Friesen (1977) note that facial nerves are connected to both the very old and new brain areas. Thus some are at times involuntary, automatic responses and at others are voluntary and well controlled. These rapid contractions of the facial musculature can signal temporary changes in feelings, reflecting emotions such as fear, surprise, anger, disgust, sadness and happiness. However, being able to recognize them and use them for clinical purposes may be difficult since they are often quite fleeting and may only be localized to part of the face. For example, the upper half of the face, particularly around the eyes, is especially important for expressing surprise or fear. Another difficulty in detecting such changes lies in the fact that the listener may be paying attention to other messages including the verbal content and body movements.

b. Using non-verbal information

Although it is initially difficult to pick up the full range of emotional expressions which the face can convey without the aid of sophisticated videotape equipment. it is possible to learn and improve these skills. There are some quite good books which provide detailed guidance for acquiring these sorts of skills and the interested reader is referred to the recommended reading at the end of the chapter. It may not be necessary to go to such lengths since an awareness of and a sensitivity to the sorts of non-verbal changes which can occur should be sufficient for detecting some of the more important messages which are available.

One final and interesting related issue here is the way in which training in non-verbal communication skills is being used for therapeutic purposes with some psychiatric patients. It has been recognized that one behavioural feature of a number of psychiatric patients, particularly those who are more introverted and neurotic, is that they are deficient in social skills. This means that they are poor in social situations, finding it difficult to initiate and maintain conversations with the result that they may withdraw and avoid social contact, which in turn will tend to compound their psychological problems. With these patients it has been found that part of their problem may consist of deficiencies in both the reception and expression of non-verbal cues. For example, they may be quite poor at recognizing and generating the eye contact and head movement cues which are necessary for regulating beginnings and ends in conversations. Thus conversations will lack fluency and speakers will be uncertain when to start and stop speaking. In addition they often fail to show the appropriate postural cues of interest and social involvement, with the result that they give the impression of being withdrawn and disinterested.

Recent therapeutic techniques with such patients consist of specific training in social skills, which includes training in both the recognition and the expression of non-verbal cues. This has produced some remarkable results and has helped enormously in allowing patients to benefit from greater social contact and in breaking the vicious circle of social withdrawal and further psychiatric difficulties. Furthermore this important clinical work provides a very concrete answer to those critics who claim that communication ability cannot be taught or learned on the grounds that either you have it or you do not. Work of this type shows just how much it can be thought of as a skill and that different levels of expertise reflect environmental opportunities rather than some innate facility.

Finally, it provides a reminder of a point made by Fletcher (1973) that good communication ability nearly always has to be learned and that such learning should form an integral part of clinical training.

● Recommended reading

Dimatteo R. M. and Dinicola D. D. (1982) *Achieving Patient Compliance*. New York, Pergamon.

Ley P. (1977) Psychological studies of doctor–patient communication. In: Rachman S. (ed.) *Contributions to Medical Psychology*. London, Pergamon.

Pendleton D. and Hasler J. (1983) *Doctor–Patient Communication*. London, Academic Press.

11

Diagnosis as problem-solving

In effect, each new patient constitutes a problem-solving task for the clinician. The prime purpose of the initial interview is to identify the nature of the patient's problem and to make an appropriate management decision. In the previous chapter there was a consideration of the communications aspects of the interview in terms of the interaction between clinician and patient. The way in which questions are framed and the general approach to the patient are all manifestations of the general attempt to solve the problem—what is wrong with this patient? In this chapter there is an account of the problem-solving processes which typically occur as part of the diagnostic process. First, there is an outline of some of the more salient features of human problem-solving behaviour, as revealed by experimental work. Following this there is an attempt to describe diagnostic decision-making in these terms to understand the way these decisions are reached and the sorts of factors which may help or hinder this process.

- ### 11.1. Human problem-solving: some general characteristics

a. Approaches to problem-solving

In many ways the investigation of thinking and problem-solving has been one of the most difficult and least fruitful areas for experimental psychology. Older theories of problem-solving tended to rely on rather mechanistic models whereby one proceeded through a number of fixed stages such as preparation, incubation and inspiration. There was a fair amount of effort put into trying to define the effects of various conditions which could affect problem-solving success and these included such factors as the structure of the problem and the role of past experience. However, the very nature of problem-solving as an essentially private and inaccessible process has made it difficult to study and has also meant that there is relatively little agreement as to the best method of investigation.

In recent years, the advent of the digital computer has had an important influence on the direction and structure of research in this area. Computer scientists have produced programs which can solve a range of problems. The significance of this work is not that computer problem-solving is an exact replica of human performance but that every process must be exactly specified for the program to operate successfully. It is for this reason that the computer approaches can be of value in studying human thinking since one can begin to see what sorts of processes are necessary to solve problems and to compare human and computer performance on specified problems. In order to write a computer program to solve problems one has to instruct the computer step by step and no woolly thinking is allowed. This can give the experimental psychologist the chance to simulate the problem-solving processes used by humans on a computer. In order to do this, data about human performance have to be obtained and these are used to construct a model of the likely processes which occur. The human data are translated into a computer program so that the program is now a simulation of human problem-solving and as such actually constitutes a model in itself.

However, two major problems still exist with this computer-based approach. First, it is still not a trivial task to study human problem-solving in order to obtain the appropriate data to construct a simulation program. Much recent work has used 'protocol analysis', which effectively has meant that subjects have to describe aloud every step used during problem-solving and the psychologist has to analyse these protocols and convert them into a model. There is no guarantee that verbal descriptions actually correspond with underlying cognitive processes. Moreover, asking subjects to do this may actually interfere with or distort these underlying processes. This difficulty of externalizing the problem-solving process still remains but a number of investigators have used a range of ancillary techniques such as the study of eye movements (see Chapter 2) in order to provide confirmatory evidence. The second problem with computer simulation studies is that of how to compare the performance of human and computer in order to test the accuracy of the computer model. The conventional way of testing the computer model has been to present computer and human with a new set of problems and compare the performance of the two. This can give some indication of the similarity of the two systems but still leaves considerable problems in determining the degree of similarity and the nature of the discrepancies.

Although these newer approaches have still not resolved all of these difficulties, they have offered the psychologist some new and exciting methods of investigating human thinking. The best known and most comprehensive example of this work is that of Newell and Simon (1972) and since the theory which they have derived is the most accepted of current models, it will provide the basis for the present description of problem-solving.

b. A model of problem-solving

What happens when a person solves or tries to solve a problem? Obviously many things will determine the exact processes which take place and not least of these will be the nature of the problem itself. The problem may be relatively well defined, such as an endgame situation in chess where it is possible to mate in a specified number of moves whatever the opposing player does. In contrast the problem may be very open ended and many different types of solution may be possible. It is clear that many real-life problems fall into this second category, which tends to reduce the validity of many experimental studies which usually make use of rather more structured problems. Even so, there do appear to be a number of stages and processes which are relatively common to all types of problem-solving.

An important and often overlooked first step in problem-solving is to understand the nature of the problem and derive an 'internal representation' of it. Problem-solving has to take place inside the head and in order to do so the key features of the problem must be processed and stored internally so that they can be acted on. Deriving an internal representation may be relatively straightforward for a well-specified problem but for more diffuse problems this may be a complicated stage and one which can have an important influence on the structure of later problem-solving. At this stage the problem-solver must understand the goal, the particular conditions which are imposed and the nature of the data which are available.

Having done this, a plan must be devised which will guide the solver towards a solution. In this respect Newell and Simon have made an important distinction between two types of plan, namely *heuristics* and *algorithms*. An algorithm is a set of rules which, if applied correctly, will guarantee a solution. For example, the rules for multiplication are algorithmic, since they will always produce a correct answer if they are used correctly. Unfortunately very many problems cannot be tackled by using algorithms either because algorithms do not exist or because they would be too unwieldy or difficult to apply. Hence human problem-solving relies predominantly on heuristics, which are strategies or rules-of-thumb. These are usually much less painstaking and exhaustive but provide direction and guidance towards a solution without necessarily guaranteeing success. Typically heuristics are based on previous experience in problem-solving, particularly with a similar class of problems to the current one. One commonly used and powerful heuristic is therefore to find analogies between the present problem and previous ones which had been successfully solved.

A critical stage in problem-solving is that of generating hypotheses as to how a solution can be obtained and of devising and using strategies to that end. For many problems there may be too much information to hold because of normal memory limitations and so solvers often reorganize the overall problem into components or subproblems which can be tackled as units. At any given time during problem-solving, progress can be gauged by the state of knowledge or information which has been accumulated up to that point. In these terms, problem-solving consists of progress from one state of knowledge to another via the application of various heuristics. If heuristics are successful, new information is obtained and progress is made towards a solution but this course can be quite erratic and not necessarily linear since back-tracking may occur when a dead-end is reached.

At each step in problem-solving, Newell and Simon maintain that something which they call a 'means-end analysis' must be applied to the outcomes of strategies in order to evaluate whether progress has been made towards the solution. A similar type of analysis is often necessary to determine whether an acceptable solution has been reached. For some problems this will not be necessary since the solution state will have already been defined but for other problems there may be many possible solutions and there is a critical point at which the acceptability of a solution must be determined. The specific heuristics or strategies which are used will depend on the nature of the problem but from a range of studies there is some agreement that the processes outlined above are common to a range of problem-solving situations.

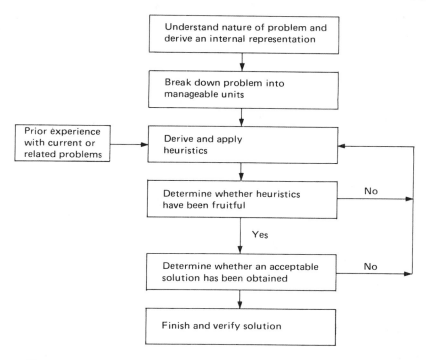

Fig. 16. A simplified flow chart of some of the likely processes involved in problem-solving.

With any problem subjects appear to adopt a relatively small set of strategies which are used repeatedly rather than creating a diverse range of strategies. Thus the typical stages in problem-solving can be represented diagrammatically in *Fig.* 16.

One further point to be made about this model of problem-solving is that it is essentially a dynamic model in which hypotheses are being continually generated and tested in order to work towards a solution. This contrasts with some of the older, mechanistic notions which maintained that all the information about a problem is first accumulated before hypotheses are formed. An information-processing model of the Newell and Simon type places an emphasis on the early formulation of hypotheses as something which is particularly useful since it converts the problem from an 'open' one, in which the end point may be unknown, to a 'closed' one which consists of the successive testing of hypotheses. Another way of characterizing this type of model is as a 'heuristic search process' in that the hypotheses which are generated will determine what information will subsequently be processed and problem-solving becomes a directed search process rather than a mechanical collection of data.

Another important feature of this model is the way in which hypotheses are initially generated and then evaluated. This goes back to a point made earlier about the so-called internal representation of a problem since the way a subject processes and stores the problem in his head will play a very important part in determining how he goes about solving it. A simple example illustrates this point:

Problem: Where would you place the next six letters in the alphabet?

A   EF HI K   _____

      BCD   G   J

(i.e. above or below the line)

The answer to this is that L, M and N go above the line and O, P and Q all go below, the rule being that all the letters made up of straight lines go above the line, and those with curved components go below.

If this problem is construed as a letter series problem and tackled as such, the sorts of hypotheses which are generated and tested will be related to various series of letters. As soon as the letters stop being considered in terms of their alphabetic connotation and as visual shapes which can be classified in terms of having curved or straight components then quite different hypotheses come to mind and can easily be evaluated.

For the purpose of the present discussion, the point to be made here is that solution strategies and hence solutions will reflect how a problem is construed and internally represented. A similar point was made in relation to memory storage in Chapter 2. There it was shown that the way in which information is encoded and processed will directly affect the way it is stored and consequently how well it is retained. This 'levels of processing' explanation would also appear to hold good in understanding this aspect of problem-solving since it can be shown that the way a problem is encoded will determine the choice of strategy and hence the type of solution which is finally produced.

One important determinant of strategy choice will be the previous experience with particular problems. One reason why many people might get stuck on the problem given above is that previous experience of similarly structured problems has always been associated with solutions which are derived from knowledge of properties of the alphabet or from number series problems. Finding similarities between current problems and previous ones and being able to make use of prior experience is usually a very useful and powerful heuristic device. Arguably one might maintain that such skills are the cornerstone of our intelligence. However, this dependence on experience and habits can have negative effects since there have been many studies which have shown that once subjects have discovered a successful strategy they will persist with it even when a much simpler approach or a quite different one would have been more fruitful.

Finally, there must be a brief mention of the way in which hypotheses are tested and the information which they produce is evaluated. When a hypothesis is generated, the natural tendency appears then to be to seek confirmatory evidence. If this is found, then more and more confirmatory evidence tends to be sought until it appears that the hypothesis has been proved beyond doubt. However, the real test for any hypothesis is to apply a negative test in order to exclude the possibility of other hypotheses. In a series of studies investigating this issue, Wason (1974) has showed that most subjects will confirm hypotheses in order to reach a solution and find it difficult to think about investigating alternatives. Studies in this area have shown that when it comes to evaluating evidence in problem-solving most subjects become blinkered by their own hypotheses and adhere rigidly to one way of working. Even when a dead-end is reached subjects very often attempt to persist with the same strategy and may be reluctant to abandon it until it becomes blatantly obvious that another tack is necessary.

Human problem-solving would appear to be rather paradoxical in that it can be both highly flexible and skilled in the way strategies can be generated but at the same time somewhat narrow and rigid in the way strategies are pursued and alternative approaches ignored. At least part of this would appear to be a function of past experience, which is necessary to develop expertise but can also ensnare us in time-honoured habits.

● 11.2. Diagnosis as a problem-solving task

When considered in terms of the above account of problem-solving mechanisms, it is clear that diagnosis constitutes one specific type of problem-solving task. In general practice the task is usually a fairly open-ended one in that the clinician must not only find a means of solving the unknown problem but must also recognize when a solution has been obtained. In medical specialties the problem may be more specific by virtue of the fact that a specific referral has been made and that the possibilities have narrowed down. The present account is primarily concerned with what happens in general practice because this is usually the starting point in the diagnostic process.

Older accounts of diagnostic problem-solving seemed to indicate that clinicians collected a large body of data before any hypotheses or guesses were made as to the nature of the problem. What they seemed to suggest was that all the relevant evidence was collected and inspected to see which problems were suggested by the overall pattern of data. More recent studies have shown that this type of approach rarely occurs and that what happens appears to be quite close to the information-processing model which was presented in the last section. In other words, it would appear that clinicians formulate hypotheses early on in the interview and these are used to guide the search for an acceptable solution. In outline the process which occurs may be characterized by the stages shown in *Fig. 17*.

The first open-ended question at the beginning of the interview will elicit a description of certain complaints from the patient and it is most likely that these will immediately suggest certain possible problems to the clinician. If a patient complains of excessive weight loss this will give rise to one group of hypotheses whereas if a patient complains of breathlessness and pains in the chest, a very different set of hypotheses will come to mind. Thus subsequent questioning will reflect what hypotheses are generated at this early stage and further information will lead to these hypotheses being confirmed, revised or rejected. The choice and ranking of these initial hypotheses will be determined by a number of factors:

a. The clinician's own concepts about the nature of clinical problems will exert an important influence on what information is sought and how it is evaluated. This is analogous to the example given in the previous section since the search for and recognition of the problem will depend on the pre-existing notions about the

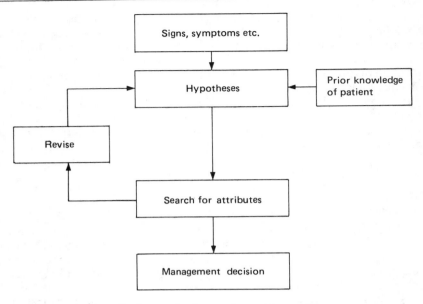

Fig. 17. Stages in diagnostic problem-solving.

nature of problems. Thus the clinician who equates disease entirely with changing biological parameters will seek specific information about such changes. In contrast the clinician who places great store by psychosocial factors and the meaning of the illness to the patient will be more preoccupied with questioning in this area. Similarly in psychiatry, there will be enormous differences between the approaches of behaviourally oriented psychiatrists who believe that psychiatric problems are learned maladaptive behaviours and the approaches of more psychoanalytically oriented psychiatrists who will tend to search for evidence of repressed childhood conflicts and fears.

b. The clinician's estimate of the probability of the hypothesis and disease. For any set of presenting symptoms there will be quite different conditional probabilities of different diseases given the overall frequency of these diseases.

c. The seriousness and treatability of the disease, both of which contribute to the 'pay-off' of the particular outcome of the consultation. The more serious the illness and the more amenable to treatment, the greater is the 'pay-off' in reaching a correct diagnosis. A hypothesis may be ranked high even if it has a low probability. For example, in a child presenting with acute abdominal pain, acute appendicitis will be ranked high as a hypothesis because of the benefits and costs associated with correct or incorrect diagnosis of this problem.

d. Personal knowledge of the patient, including such factors as the past history, previous behaviour and the social environment, may all influence the doctor's judgement. Thus the problem-solving approach may be quite different for the patient who is known to be a frequent complainer or who is known to have a particular environmental situation.

All these factors have been found to contribute to the formulation of initial hypotheses in the diagnostic process. Once these are formulated, the clinician will continue the interview by searching for attributes which support or refute these hypotheses. The attributes which are sought are signs, symptoms and results of tests, all of which can provide positive or negative evidence. Part of this search process should consist of checks for alternative explanations including the possibility of rare disorders. However, it would appear that, in common with all types of problem-solvers, clinicians also find it difficult to search for negative attributes (MacWhinney, 1973). Studies of clinical problem-solving have shown that the strongest search strategy is that of seeking confirmatory evidence. As a result, conflicting evidence or alternative interpretations may be overlooked or ignored. In view of what was said in the previous section, this would appear to be a reflection of human thinking rather than something peculiar to the clinical situation.

As with other types of problem-solving, previous experience will have a significant effect on the direction and effectiveness of clinical problem-solving. It has been shown that the experienced physician will look first for those attributes which can best discriminate between possible hypotheses so as to narrow down the number of possibilities. This is shown clearly in a study of the clinical diagnostic process, as seen in interviews of patients with abdominal pain (Leaper et al., 1973). This compared the skills of recently qualified and skilled clinicians and found that the latter group was able to confirm one hypothesis and reject the alternatives much more quickly and efficiently. With both groups the first few questions did not change the probability levels for the various common causes of acute abdominal pain. By something like the sixth question, the skilled group had managed to isolate a diagnosis whereas the inexperienced clinicians were still no closer to a decision after twelve questions.

The importance of experience and of specialized knowledge has been emphasized in more recent work on clinical problem-solving (Groen and Patel, 1985). It is now felt that the hypothesis-testing type of model described here may be an accurate description of the clinical problem-solving of general practititoners who are confronted by a very wide range of problems. Experienced doctors working in medical specialties seem to use their knowledge base more directly in making diagnoses within the restricted area of their clinical specialty and may only use a hypothesis-testing approach when the clinical picture is atypical.

Two further factors would appear to determine the course of the search and the point at which it is considered to have ended. First, as has been pointed out, the objectives of the interview will vary widely between types of clinician. The way clinicians construe the problem and their own interpretation of their particular role will be important in determining when an endpoint has been reached. Thus there is an enormous difference between the objectives: 'exclude serious illness' and 'establish exact histological prognosis prior to surgery'. In this sense there will be significant differences in the search strategies of clinicians in different specialties and with different sorts of clinical problems. A second determining factor in the course of the clinical search process will be based on the risk, benefit and cost calculations associated with particular decisions.

From all this it would appear that clinical problem-solving has many features in common with other types of problem-solving. Hypotheses are generated and tested as the interview progresses and many of the factors which influence the solution of non-clinical problems have also been shown to operate in the diagnostic process. Above all, it should be emphasized that the likely

Fig. 18. Diagnoses are hypotheses which may be confirmed by the passage of time.

hypotheses which emerge at the end of the interview are not necessarily absolute entities. Unfortunately many clinicians fail to see this point and somehow feel that once they have arrived at a diagnosis then the patient must actually have that particular problem. The hypothesis is an informed guess at what the problem is and will be confirmed or refuted by future events or even just by the passing of time, as is indicated in the cartoon in *Fig.* 18.

This essentially assumptive nature of the diagnosis has been recognized by Hodgkin (1973) when he wrote the following:

> Diagnosis and prognosis are the doctor's prediction of what is likely to happen. This cannot be too strongly emphasized. All too frequently clinicians regard their diagnosis as absolute; such an attitude prevents a doctor from improving his clinical practice by checking his own predictions.

• 11.3. Problem-solving and the medical record

The ways in which a clinical problem is encoded, investigated and treated are all essential components of the diagnostic process and the way this is carried out will be represented in the patient's notes. For this reason it is of interest to note the growing dissatisfaction with traditional methods of compiling patient's notes and an increasing use of the Problem Oriented Medical Record (McIntyre, 1973). This technique of recording notes has as its central feature a list of all the patient's current problems, some of which may be current and urgent and others longstanding and less dramatic. The rest of the record is linked to this problem-list, which also acts as a kind of index. As with more traditional methods there is a data base which contains the background information, reason for referral and previous history. The problem-list is literally a list of current problems which need to be dealt with or considered. This will consist of specific clinical problems as well as other things such as smoking or psychosocial factors which are part of the patient's situation. For each problem in the list, a plan is drawn up which should specify a course of action and a goal. Additional information which covers the results of further investigations is documented within a separate section called 'progress notes'.

From the limited experience which is available with this technique it would appear to have a number of distinct advantages over more traditional records. From the point of view of the present discussion, it would appear that the problem-oriented approach follows more naturally the chain of thought which a good clinician follows. As we have seen in this chapter, this consists of obtaining clear information, locating problems and dealing with them. The problem-oriented approach works in this way and, as such, contains an explicit record of the problem-solving processes engaged in by the clinician. Because there is a logical structure this should help the user to make a proper analysis of all of a patient's problems. This in turn makes this system well suited for teaching how clinical problems should be approached and solved.

Finally, the advent of such procedures as the Problem Oriented Medical Record is indicative of two important points in relation to clinical problem-solving. First, it is apparent that diagnoses are not always single, discrete entities but may well consist of a number of problems at different levels and with different degrees of relatedness. In any case these problems are inevitably related at one level since they are all occurring within the same patient. The problem-list implicitly recognizes this potential multiplicity of problems. Second, as has already been discussed, there is an increasing awareness that the diagnosis is usually only a hypothesis. It represents a best bet which can be confirmed or refuted by future events such as the development of new symptoms and the response to treatment.

- **Recommended reading**

Elstein, A. S., Shulman L. S. and Sprafka S. A. (1978) *Medical Problem-Solving—An Analysis of Clinical Reasoning*. Cambridge, Mass., Harvard University Press.

MacWhinney D. R. (1973) Problem-solving and decision making in primary medical practice. *Proc. R. Soc. Med.* **65**, 934–938.

12

Coping with illness and handicap

This chapter focuses on the reactions of patients to the stresses of physical illness and handicap. Although illness and handicap tend to be defined primarily in terms of physical problems, there is now abundant evidence that there can also be profound psychological and social effects. It is acknowledged that some of these psychological responses are as much a reaction to the treatment and treatment environment as to the problem itself, and these are discussed more fully in Chapter 13.

● **12.1. Coping with physical illness**

Any illness occurs within the context of an individual's life and is therefore likely to have effects on psychological and social functioning. For most patients, major health problems are perceived as stressful events and much of what was said about the nature of stress and stress responses in Chapter 5 also applies here. Thus the 'stressfulness' of an illness and the associated psychological responses will depend primarily on the patient's perception of the illness rather than on the illness *per se*.

The way in which an individual patient perceives and interprets an illness may bear some similarities to the early processes involved in problem-solving which were outlined in Chapter 11. With any problem, first of all it is necessary to derive an 'internal representation' of the problem before it can be solved. Moreover the way in which the problem is perceived and interpreted will then determine the way in which it is dealt with and solved.

Patients construct their own definition or representation of their illness and their subsequent behaviour will then depend on the nature of this representation. Thus the patients' own appraisal of the threats associated with the illness will determine how they feel and the way in which they cope (*see* Leventhal et al., 1984, for a more detailed account of this information-processing or problem-solving model of responses to illness).

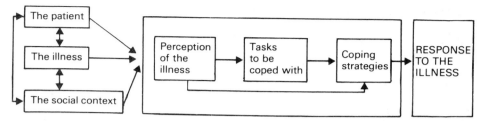

Fig. 19. A conceptual model for understanding the factors influencing the response to physical illness.

If we want to understand how patients cope with the stresses of physical illness it is necessary to take account of the range of factors shown in *Fig.* 19 and to consider the following questions:

    a. How is the illness perceived?

    b. What demands does the illness impose?

    c. What kinds of coping strategies are used?

Each of these issues is now discussed.

a. Factors influencing the patient's perception of the illness

i. Patient variables

As was pointed out in earlier chapters on pain and on stress, there is now a great deal of evidence showing that the way these components of illness are dealt with may vary significantly according to the patient's personality. Even such relatively limited personality traits as extroversion and neuroticism can influence the response to pain.

The patient's age and previous experience can obviously affect the nature of the response. Children's perceptions of illness change with their cognitive and emotional development. Also the effects of an illness in old age can be quite different from its effects on a younger person. Previous experience of similar problems can have a similar effect as supplying information in that the uncertainty will be reduced. On the other hand, if the patient has seen apparently similar but actually more serious symptoms in a close friend or relative then very strong but nevertheless groundless fears may ensue.

The patient's psychological state at the time of the illness can also play a great part in determining its perceived severity. Anxiety can reduce pain tolerance and it is therefore not surprising to find from large-scale studies that anxiety rather than symptom frequency or severity is a critical factor in determining attendance rates at general practice surgeries (Banks et al., 1975).

ii. Illness variables

The actual severity of the illness does not appear to correlate strongly with the psychological responses to it since the patient's own perceptions of the severity and threat are more crucial factors here. Some illnesses such as cancer and heart disease probably do produce more marked psychological responses because of the particular connotations which they have but again there are wide variations in individual reactions to these illnesses.

Sometimes the particular part of the body embodying the clinical disorder can have a particular significance for the patient. Obvious examples here are the impact on active individuals, such as sportspeople, of disorders which limit mobility or exercise. It has been suggested that disabling disorders are perceived as more threatening by men whereas disfiguring diseases are more problematic for women. A number of studies of women following mastectomy tend to confirm the second half of this notion and this probably reflects current cultural expectations about relative male and female roles. However, it is important to bear in mind that operations such as mastectomy and hysterectomy also have a particular symbolic significance for the patient and may be perceived in terms of diminished sex-role identity. Here again the perceived significance of the clinical problem for the patient can be a prime determinant of any subsequent psychological reaction.

The nature of onset and duration of the problem may also determine some aspects of the patient's response. An unexpected and acute onset may be initially quite disruptive but will tend to resolve quickly if the illness is relatively brief. In contrast, a much more slowly developing chronic illness may produce less dramatic psychological reactions but these are likely to be more long-lasting because of the long-term disability associated with the more chronic illnesses.

iii. The social context

An illness of a particular severity may have a greater or lesser impact on the patient depending on the particular social context within which it occurs. It may be perceived quite unfavourably if it occurs at a time when it is likely to be very inconvenient, such as starting a new job. Alternatively, in some situations it can be seen that an illness can be almost accepted gratefully by the patient as a relief from an adverse social situation. The reactions of the people surrounding the patient will also play a role in determining the ultimate psychological impact on the patient. Factors such as these have all been shown to have a direct effect on the perceived severity of a symptom and the delay intervening before medical help is sought. Also recovery from illness tends to be quicker in those who have good social support.

Sociologists have described the operation of a 'lay referral' system in the community. This consists of friends, neighbours or local 'experts' on illness who tend to be consulted when symptoms arise. The effects of such a network can have an important influence on the patient's perceived severity of any disorder. Moreover it has been shown that these perceptions can still persist when medical advice has indicated that they may be exaggerated or misconstrued (Tuckett et al., 1985).

Finally very specific social contexts associated with particular treatments such as intensive care units and haemodialysis provide very specific environmental constraints and demands which can have a marked effect on the patient's wellbeing. Some effects of these particular treatment environments are indicated in Chapter 13 on hospitalization.

b. The demands imposed by an illness

The onset of a major physical illness will affect an individual in many ways and require different sorts of adaptation. Some of the demands which are imposed are fairly unique to illness whereas others are more general and apply to all major types of life stress. These demands are summarized in *Table* 5.

Table 5. The demands imposed by physical illness (adapted from Moos and Schaefer, 1984)

Illness-related demands	*Emotional/social demands*
Dealing with pain, incapacitation and other symptoms	Preserving a reasonable emotional balance
Dealing with the hospital environment and special treatment procedures	Preserving a satisfactory self-image and maintaining a sense of competence and mastery
Developing and maintaining adequate relationships with health-care staff	Sustaining relationships with family and friends
	Preparing for an uncertain future

The main coping behaviours which are described in the next section apply more to the way in which individuals deal with pain, incapacitation and other symptoms as well as with the more general demands. The way in which patients respond to the hospital environment and to special treatment procedures is presented in Chapter 13.

c. Coping strategies

The general statements about coping with stress which were presented in Chapter 5 are also valid here. Two broad categories of coping are applied to the demands imposed by physical illness. *Problem-focused* or *direct* coping behaviours involve attempts to deal directly with the situation in order to make it more manageable or tolerable whereas *emotion-focused* or *palliative* coping is more concerned with managing the emotions generated by the illness.

Problem-focused coping includes such behaviours as seeking information and support, learning new skills and actively participating in treatment. The importance of information for patients has been emphasized in a number of earlier chapters. In the context of coping it consists of obtaining information about the illness as well as becoming more familiar with different treatment possibilities and their likely outcomes. Learning more about the causes of a problem and about the nature and development of a particular illness can be helpful for developing a sense of control and preparation for the impending demands. Also knowing what sort of help is available and how to obtain it can also be of great value. The latter includes enlisting support from family and friends as well as from other sources such as special patient groups which focus on common problems and allow patients to share worries and learn from each other.

Coping by becoming actively involved in treatment may involve the learning of new skills associated with the treatment process (e.g. running a home dialysis machine). Patients may also discover their own helpful ways of dealing with the pain, discomfort or limitations imposed by the illness. Thus they may discover ways of sleeping, walking or sitting which minimize pain. Alternatively, they may be able to rearrange their home environment to maximize their independence. Identifying and participating in new activities and interests provides a further area for active coping.

Coping with the emotional demands or consequences of an illness can be achieved by not allowing onself to be overwhelmed by the associated anxieties and fears. Thus patients may deliberately or inadvertently choose to distance themselves from the potentially overwhelming emotions. They may acknowledge their fears but be able to put them to one side in order to deal with the immediate demands of the illness or the treatment. As we see in the section on coping with chronic illness (p. 197), it is not uncommon for patients to show initial denial as a way of coping which is protective and allows them to get through the early stages of the illness after the diagnosis has been made. Some of the very active coping by participation and involvement in treatment described above can also represent an attempt to 'busy oneself' in order to keep at bay the concerns about the associated threats. Activity can be an effective way of preventing latent anxieties from becoming dominant.

Patients will also need to express emotion and the role of family support and health-care staff is vital here. Many studies have identified the importance for patients not only in expressing fears and related emotions but also in having these recognized and 'allowed' by those around them as part of coming to terms with an illness.

This relatively brief outline of coping strategies has presented only a selection of the types of behaviour which can be seen. As was pointed out in Chapter 5 in the section on coping with stress, it is important to emphasize that patients may use a range of coping strategies depending on the situation they are in and the stage of their illness. Patients' coping can change over time as their perception of their illness changes and as the reality of the illness unfolds.

d. Adverse emotional reactions

With some patients the emotional reaction to their illness may be quite marked and be seen as a problem in its own right. In the light of the comments about the wide range of coping strategies made in the previous section, it is perhaps misleading to regard such reactions as 'abnormal' or 'adverse'. Any emotional reaction can be seen as a particular way of responding to the perceived threats and psychosocial effects of the illness. However, there are occasions when these reactions are sufficiently strong to cause concern for the patient and the health-care team.

One of the commonest reported psychological responses to illness is that of *depression* since it is estimated that in the region of 20–30 per cent of all inpatients suffer from this. This may be relatively mild and transient but it can also be so strong and pervasive that it causes crying, withdrawal and even suicidal feelings.

Depression is most prevalent after the initial stages of the illness when its full implications have become apparent. Thus it may be associated with a sense of loss or the threat of loss to physical or social functioning. It may arise from a sense of guilt associated with the illness since patients may perceive their illness as a punishment for past behaviour. When this occurs patients may adopt a passive attitude, believing that the punishment is justified, and show little motivation towards treatment and recovery. However, this type of 'self-blame' can also be adaptive in the sense that patients may actively try to change their behaviour in the future to avoid a re-occurrence.

If an illness occurs at an unfavourable time in someone's life it may add to a growing feeling of hopelessness and helplessness and result in a very passive and withdrawn response. With these patients it has been commonly reported that they show a poorer physical prognosis and seem to lack the 'fight' or commitment to participate actively in treatment.

At least some of the commonly found *anxiety* which is associated with a physical illness may stem from the uncertainty the patient has about both the cause and outcome of the illness. As was pointed out in Chapter 10, many patients are inadequately informed as to the nature of their disorder and of the ensuing treatment. This state of uncertainty may give rise to anxiety which can be non-specific, in that it is not directed to any particular aspect of the illness. Alternatively, the patient's anxiety in this situation may consist of unnecessary worrying about the cause and severity of the problem. More directed anxiety reactions can also be seen in the phobias which some patients show either towards specific treatments or associated with a particular illness, such as cancer. These illness and illness-related phobias are not an uncommon phobic reaction and account for a fair proportion of all the phobias. For example, one survey of all types of phobias indicated that illness phobias accounted for approximately 15 per cent of the sample (Marks, 1969).

Some patients try to cope with their anxiety by finding out as much as possible about their illness and accumulate masses of information about their disease and the various therapeutic approaches. Patients who react in this way will tend to follow treatment with great care and may sometimes become so involved in the illness and in treatment that all other interests are dropped or avoided. These patients will react particularly badly to lack of information and where such a group has been recognized by doctors then the importance of allowing them to participate actively in the treatment has been stressed.

On the face of it this type of reaction might be regarded as a 'healthy' adaptive response to illness. However, the danger is that it can become a total preoccupation and may ultimately be counterproductive. For example, in one study of postoperative recovery, this type of patient was found to have a prolonged postoperative period and to have more minor medical complications and negative psychological reactions.

Some patients cope with the anxiety aroused by *denial*, as was described in the previous section on coping strategies. For many patients this is an adaptive and useful way of coping with the emotional aspects of a physical illness. Indeed there is evidence that this can have a protective value in a number of treatment situations such as coronary care units (Hackett et al., 1968). However, denial can become dangerous when it prevents individuals from making a realistic assessment of the severity of their symptoms. For example, if the individual denies the early signs of a serious disease, such as cancer, then such denial is clearly maladaptive and potentially dangerous. Thus denial can be instrumental in causing delays in seeking medical help and in doing so may actually reduce the chances of a favourable outcome. For example, in a study of women with breast disease, it was found that those who delayed in seeking medical treatment were considered to use denial as a habitual coping strategy to deal with difficult situations (Greer, 1974). In this context it should be pointed out that denial is not the only reason for late consultation, since such factors as ignorance and the patient's own perception of severity may also be instrumental.

Case history
The following example shows how a patient can react to a clinical problem by denying a great deal of it and also serves to illustrate the importance of understanding this reaction on the part of those who are involved with the patient. A 62-year-old man is admitted to hospital with a second heart attack. He is a man who was once an active sportsman, who still likes to think of himself as physically fit and greatly appreciates it when others tell him that he looks younger than his actual age. On entering the hospital he had a cardiac arrest and had to be resuscitated. When he was told about this some days later it was clear that he was responding to it with a great deal of denial since he denied having a serious heart disease. His actual comments were: 'I feel fine, I don't know that I have anything wrong. If I have any problems, let the doctors prove it to me.'

Obviously this patient is minimizing the severity of his problem as a way of coping with it and may be totally unaware of his denial response. However, for those who have to deal with him it is clearly of great importance to understand this since it may radically affect the way he will follow treatment, the sort of life changes he may or may not make and his willingness to consult on the basis of further tell-tale symptoms.

A rather less common reaction to physical illness is one characterized by *paranoid behaviour*. This may be quite mild and take the form of responding in a somewhat prickly and suspicious way. Thus the patient may place the blame for the illness on someone else such as a relative or another doctor. This may be accompanied by accusations of neglect or incompetence but, if the paranoia is of a more severe nature, these feelings may be expressed more forcibly in the form of an elaborate delusion of persecution. Occasionally this may lead to disturbances in ward behaviour since the patient will act in accordance with the delusion and may aggressively accuse those who are thought to be the persecutors. Moreover, it may be difficult for these patients to accept treatment since this may also be interpreted as something which is intended to harm rather than help.

e. Implications for helping

In view of what we now know about the psychological effects of physical illness, it is clearly necessary for health-care staff to be able to recognize and acknowledge this as part of the process of being ill. An excessive focus on the physical changes may not only result in the failure to recognize the psychological changes but can also have adverse effects on treatment and recovery.

A primary requirement for health-care staff is to acknowledge that physical illness generates changes in emotions and behaviour. Ideally this should also include a willingness to take account of and respond to these changes in an appropriate way. Nicholls (1984) has identified a number of key areas of psychological intervention and the skills which are required. These include *emotional care, informational care* and *counselling*.

Emotional care needs to be based on an understanding that coping strategies and emotional responses are a normal part of illness. Thus staff need to be able to monitor patients and to recognize how they are coping and what worries they might have. Responding to emotions should allow patients to express these in a way which is helpful to them. Nicholls (1984) lists the following skills which are necessary to achieve this:
    i. Making the situation 'safe' (i.e. non-threatening).

    ii. Enabling patients to recognize their own feelings.

   iii. Facilitating the expression of feelings.

   iv. Communicating understanding and acceptance.

    v. Giving time and support.

The value of providing information has been emphasized in many other sections of this book. It is important for responding to patients' questions and for clarifying their misconceptions as well as for preparing for future changes or interventions. Since patients respond and cope in different ways it is necessary to find out what they actually know and what they want to know. If information is wanted then it should be presented carefully and in a way which takes account of the patients' own views and beliefs (*see* Chapter 10). It is also important to realize that a patient's need for information may change over time and that an unwillingness to discuss or receive information at one time does not mean that this will always be so. Further monitoring and feedback will be necessary not only to identify new areas of informational need but also to verify and check previously given information.

The nature of counselling and its uses in the clinical setting are discussed in Chapter 14. The approach described there is based on developing skills in listening and attending as well as those which facilitate the patient's own coping and problem-solving. The task for the helper is threefold. First, it requires the ability to attend to the patients, to facilitate their disclosure of fears and problems and to be able to see the situation through the patients' eyes. Second, having obtained a picture of the patients' situation, it is then necessary to help the patients look at their situation to develop an understanding of their own feelings and responses. Armed with this, patients should then be able to identify areas for change or problem-solving. Thus the third phase of counselling will involve the identification and mobilization of the patients' own coping strategies.

Having specified that this approach to counselling involves three phases or stages of helping to deal with particular problems, the use of the basic listening skills may often be sufficient to identify areas for emotional and informational care. Thus full-blown counselling of the sort described in Chapter 14 may not often be necessary for the majority of patients. However, the component skills are certainly ones which would be valuable to members of the health-care team.

●   **12.2. Coping with chronic illness**

There are many illnesses in which recovery is unlikely to happen and where there may be no change or even a progressive deterioration. With these illnesses, medical interventions may play an important role in pain relief and in controlling symptoms but the ultimate effects of the illness on individuals will depend very much on how they cope. Many of the general statements about coping outlined above are also relevant to understanding psychological reactions to chronic illnesses. Thus patients' perceptions determine not only the impact of the illness but also the patterns of coping with the illness, with treatment and with the associated social disruption.

With long-term illnesses coping often changes over time. Many patients appear to show a degree of denial soon after receiving the diagnosis of a major chronic illness, such as cancer. In many ways this response may be adaptive both in protecting patients from all the implications of having that illness and in allowing them time to adapt. After the initial reaction, both direct and indirect forms of coping may be seen in chronically ill patients. Patients who cope directly seek out and assimilate information about their condition, the treatment and the likely outcomes. In addition they are motivated and active in adhering to treatment and make all sorts of other adjustments in their lives to deal with the illness and related problems in a positive way. Indirect coping consists of attempts to minimize the psychological impact of the illness by such strategies as denial or distraction.

Social factors generally, and social support in particular, have been identified as having a very important influence on the way individuals cope with a chronic illness (Singer and Lord, 1984). The quality of communication and emotional support from within the family and the immediate social environment can have major effects on the degree of physical and psychological distress experienced by patients recovering from such disorders as myocardial infarction and stroke. Support from small group meetings with patients with a similar condition can also be valuable as a forum for sharing worries and for learning information and new coping strategies.

There are often major problems experienced by families in caring for a member with a chronic disease. If the patient is an adult then he or she may well have to depend on others for financial assistance and for help with many aspects of day-to-day living. Chronic illnesses in children can have major effects on family life and have adverse effects on relationships within the family. Thus it is important for the family to be involved in the clinical management and to be adequately informed and prepared for dealing with the long-term demands which chronic illness often imposes.

There are also important individual differences in the effects of a chronic illness, such as cancer. In general, most cancer patients experience considerable emotional distress and social disruption but the extent and nature of this can vary enormously. Some of these differences are due to such factors as the patient's age, personality and social situation. Factors such as the site of the cancer and the type of treatment can influence patients' perceptions and psychological responses. Thus the actual impact of cancer for any individual will depend on many different sorts of stressors and problems, which give rise to different types of coping behaviour. In addition many cancer patients are faced with having to cope with the fact that they have a terminal illness, and a separate consideration of this now follows.

● **12.3. Coping with terminal illness**

There are many important issues which need to be discussed here but this section concentrates on two related topics. First, there is the question of communication with the dying patient and whether patients should always be told about their condition. Second, when patients know they have a terminal condition, how does this affect them and what implications does this have for those involved in caring for them?

a. Communicating with dying patients

There appears to be an interesting phenomenon surrounding the question of whether patients should be told that they have a terminal condition. In a survey of patient groups and of random community samples, it has been consistently found that a very high percentage (i.e. about 80 per cent) of individuals say that they would want to be told if they had a terminal illness. However, consistently fewer people would want a friend or close relative to be given the equivalent message. This double standard also seems to cause problems in clinical practice where the spouse of a dying person may be told about the condition and then request that their partner should not be told. Alternatively the dying person might request that a spouse should not be informed.

There is no obvious golden rule here. The evidence from research studies and from clinicians with experience in hospice care confirms that most people do want to know the truth about their condition and that they cope better when communication has been open and honest. Similarly, openness in communication with close relatives also seems to be associated with a better outcome, both for the patient and for the family. However, there are important individual and ethnic differences and it is clear that communication should be guided by and tailored to the needs of individual patients.

Despite the new climate of openness and truth telling, recent surveys indicate that many dying patients still feel that they have not been given sufficient information or opportunity to discuss their condition and their feelings. It is therefore important for those involved in the care of the dying to be sensitive to the communication needs of individual patients and to be guided by them in what they say and how they say it. Some patients will have particular fears or issues which they want to discuss, and it is noteworthy that there is increasing use of specific psychological interventions with dying patients (e.g. Sobel, 1981).

b. Psychological responses of dying patients

As with the reactions to illness outlined above, the reactions of dying patients to their impending death show wide variations depending on their situation, their personality and their degree of expectation or preparation for the 'bad news'. Some patients, who may have spent months of uncertainty, actually report feelings of relief when given their diagnosis. In contrast others may be shocked or numbed. Not surprisingly most patients show distress but the way in which they show it can vary considerably.

Some writers (e.g. Kubler-Ross, 1969) have claimed that there are distinct phases of adjustment in dying patients. Thus it is maintained that patients will initially respond with denial and then move on to a stage characterized by rage and anger. This, in turn, gives way to a bargaining phase and then a phase of depression before the reality of the terminal condition is finally accepted. Although there is little empirical evidence in support of this fixed sequence of responses, there is agreement both that there is a range of psychological responses of this type and that coping changes over time.

Dying patients have major fears about many issues including pain, loneliness and the unknown as well as fears associated with their own clinical condition. For example, some patients become particularly frightened that they will be racked with intolerable pain or that particular unpleasant physical changes will occur. The role of good communication and adequate pain relief is particularly important in dealing with these fears.

Thus the stages described by Kubler-Ross and others are probably better thought of as different ways of responding which patients may show at particular times according to their concerns and their moods. For those involved in their care, it becomes important to recognize both the range and changeability of emotions and coping behaviours. Similarly the willingness of patients to discuss their condition or to take on board new information will also vary according to their mood and mode of coping.

● **12.4. Psychosocial consequences of physical handicap**

One feature of many physical illnesses is that they are of sudden onset and last for a finite length of time. As a result the consequent psychological changes which may be experienced, and which were outlined in the previous section, are a response to the transient changes in one's life situation. They embody reactions to the pain and physical discomfort, to the social disruption and to the uncertainty of the outcome. In contrast, a large number of medical problems are longstanding and sometimes permanent. Included in this category are chronic illnesses, such as rheumatoid arthritis and emphysema, and physical handicaps, such as spasticity and sensory defects. Although this section is primarily concerned with psychosocial aspects of physical handicaps, many of the findings and implications will also be pertinent to an understanding of patients with chronic illnesses.

As with many of the other topics in this book, it is immediately apparent that the concept of physical handicap is by no means a simple unitary one. It refers to a range of problems with different degrees of severity and incapacity. Moreover the psychosocial consequences of a handicap may be radically different when the handicap has been incurred and disrupts a previously 'normal' life as compared with a congenital disorder, in which the early years may well be the most problematic.

There follows an outline of what may be considered the primary and secondary consequences of handicap. Primary consequences are those which are a direct result of the physical limitations of the handicap whereas secondary consequences reflect the effects of the social context of handicap, particularly the social reactions to it.

a. Primary psychological consequences

All handicaps give rise to some loss of function but the severity of this loss can vary enormously. The problems may range from a slight limp associated with mild spasticity to a total loss of mobility following a severe paralysis. Alternatively, sensory defects can range from a partial hearing loss to very profound deafness and blindness. To some extent, the primary dysfunctions which are associated with the handicap will reflect its severity but not necessarily in a simple fashion. The final effects will depend as much on the social context of the handicap, which is dealt with below, and on the remedial facilities which are available.

The primary defects are the ones which tend to be the main concern for those who treat the handicapped person. Thus for mobility problems, a range of mobility aids and physiotherapy procedures will be employed and for hearing losses, hearing aids together with speech therapy will be used. In essence this is the basis of the traditional medical approach to physical handicap and, as such, it parallels the approach to the treatment of physical illness. This approach consists of diagnosing and quantifying the defect and then attempting to return defective functions to 'normal' levels with selected remedial techniques. However, it is clear that for many handicaps the primary deficits cannot be eliminated or even radically improved with various aids. An in-depth analysis of the effects of any handicap shows that the deficits are often more far reaching and complicated than a specific functional loss. It is not possible to give a comprehensive account of all the primary psychological problems of all physical handicaps here. As a way around this, there follows a detailed consideration of one handicap, namely deafness, which will serve as an illustration of the nature of primary dysfunction.

The example of deafness
When deafness is diagnosed, it can be relatively accurately quantified in terms of the frequency and intensity of the hearing loss. Hearing aids can be provided with particular specifications to attempt to compensate for the loss of auditory input. At a somewhat simplistic level of analysis this might be considered to be the reasonable limit of medical intervention in the treatment of congenital hearing loss but unfortunately the picture is much more complicated.

Congenital deafness
The early diagnosis of congenital deafness is still a relatively difficult procedure. Until the recent development of evoked potential audiometric testing, it was quite difficult to detect and to quantify a hearing loss in the very young baby. Indeed there is recent evidence of relatively severe hearing losses going undetected until 5 and, in very extreme cases, 10 years of age. The linguistic and cognitive implications of such omissions are very profound, as is seen shortly. Furthermore the perception and use of auditory information is not just a question of making this information totally or partly available via a hearing aid but much more one of using higher order mechanisms to decode and interpret this information. The description of visual information processing presented in Chapter 2 should make this point clear and also serves to emphasize the critical importance of early sensory input as a prime determinant of subsequent perceptual ability.

As soon as one starts to think in these terms, it becomes easier to understand the extent of psychological deficits which typically follow profound congenital hearing loss because the developing deaf child will have a greatly restricted input of verbal information. Whereas the hearing child will be surrounded by the spoken word and may well be processing this information from the very beginning, the deaf baby will be denied all this. As a result the most profound effect of congenital deafness is to be found in the area of language development. Instead of being an apparently effortless process, language learning for the deaf is typically extremely painstaking and consequently the great majority of deaf people have a gross language impairment.

To give some idea of the extent of these effects, it has been found that by the age of 5 most profoundly deaf children are only able to use a handful of words well whereas hearing children may typically have in the region of 5000 words at their disposal. Even before the age of formal schooling the whole basis of an individual's spoken language will normally be well established. Moreover, many psycholinguists now believe that the first 5 or so years may constitute something of a critical period for language acquisition, as was discussed in Chapter 8. In these terms, then, the consequences of early hearing loss are very profound.

A great deal of effort is currently put towards both earlier diagnosis of deafness and early language stimulation using appropriate remedial procedures. Even after formal schooling this language retardation is still enormous. A British study of deaf school-leavers of 16 years old found that overall reading competence was at the 9-year-old level and that for those with profound hearing losses the average was at the 7½-year level (Conrad, 1979). Only a very small number of this sample (approx. 5 per cent) could produce speech which was intelligible to objective raters.

Taking this analysis one stage further, it will become apparent that severely restricted language development will have much wider effects on other cognitive functions, such as thinking and memory and in social life. Deaf people will also tend to miss out on many qualitative aspects of communication since non-verbal aspects of speech such as changes in intonation and pitch can convey a range of subtle semantic and emotional information.

On many intelligence tests, in which verbal skills are being directly or indirectly tested, it is not therefore surprising to find that deaf people perform at a lower level. However, on non-verbal tests, such as Raven's Matrices, a very similar distribution of scores is found among the deaf and their hearing counterparts. These findings offer a direct challenge to those psychologists who have maintained that thought is entirely dependent on language, but that is another issue and one which cannot be pursued here. The interested reader is advised to read the work of Furth (1973) and others who have investigated the cognitive abilities of the deaf. What this work does raise is the possibility that as the result of their limited linguistic experience, the adult deaf may actually store and process information in different ways.

Some writers have also claimed that the language retardation and cognitive changes brought about by deafness produce consistent personality differences but the evidence for this is not reliable. It may well be that any such differences reflect difficulties in social adaptation rather than primary consequences of hearing loss. The fact that patterns of social adjustment in young deaf children of deaf parents are consistently superior to those from hearing parents provides indirect support for this view. This also points to the importance of considering the primary consequences of handicap in conjunction with the social context and the secondary aspects.

It is not intended that this description of the psychological consequences of deafness should be taken by the reader to be typical of all handicaps. It has been presented as a model of the way a range of deficits can emanate from a single physical handicap. Any handicap by its very nature brings particular limitations to the individual and these are the ones which spring readily to mind. However, this account has attempted to show that these limitations can ultimately deny the handicapped child a whole range of experiences and have a wider effect on many other psychological processes. The most obvious metaphor here is that of the stone thrown into a pond in that the immediate splash can be taken to represent the immediate loss of function and the outward spreading ripples, the related problems.

Acquired deafness

The psychological impact of an acquired hearing loss in younger adults is usually very profound (Thomas, 1984). The most widespread complaint is a sense of loss and isolation. The person with an acquired deafness has to cope with a number of important losses including the loss of communication, of social roles and of self-esteem. Very many report feeling lonely, worthless and depressed for long periods of time following the onset. There is often a great deal of anger and frustration which is due to the limited social opportunities associated with the communication problems. In addition many people feel that their family and close friends do not really understand what it is like to lose one's hearing. Not surprisingly there are usually two-way problems within families since there are inevitably strains imposed on the hearing members.

For any individual the psychological impact will vary depending on their coping resources and social situation. Interestingly the amount of hearing loss does not correlate with the degree of psychological disruption which again emphasizes the importance of understanding the individual patients and their own particular concerns. This view has been emphasized recently by Thomas (1984) who states that 'it is essential that much more effort should be expended in finding out what it means for each individual to live with his or her hearing loss and what effect it has on those around them, so that a rehabilitation program can be devised which is tailored to his or her individual needs'. Thus the approach to counselling which is outlined at the end of Chapter 14 is particularly appropriate here.

So far we have only dealt with the profound effects of congenital handicap and some attention must be paid to the consequences of handicaps incurred after birth. Incurred deafness can arise as the result of accidents or disease but much more commonly is associated with the ageing process. Hearing losses are relatively common in the elderly and obviously create a range of problems over and above those normally found with ageing. While there is not such a dramatic interference with language as with congenital deafness, there are very real difficulties in communication which can arise. The use of hearing aids is obviously of great value with this group but these are often difficult to adapt to. Thus for those who are unwilling or unable to benefit from an aid, the subsequent social isolation is usually quite traumatic. So much so, that a number of writers have claimed that hearing loss is an important aetiological factor in paranoid hallucinatory psychoses in the middle-aged and elderly (Cooper, 1976). While some of this may be a function of the sensory deprivation incurred by deafness, it would seem to be predominantly a function of the social isolation. The following exemplifies the point:

> *Case history*
> An elderly woman with a fairly severe hearing loss was referred from a medical ward for psychiatric investigation since she was starting to be openly hostile to other patients. During the interview with this woman it became apparent how the hearing loss was an important link in the chain of events leading up to her 'disturbed' ward

behaviour. It appeared that when she arrived in the ward she noticed other patients talking together and strained unsuccessfully to hear what they were talking about. On being unable to hear the topics of conversation she started to fear that the other patients were discussing her and this caused her to stare at these patients in an attempt to lip-read or pick up anything that was being said. Her staring tended to unnerve these patients who then really did start to discuss her and a self-fulfilling vicious circle was set in motion. The paranoid feelings grew and as the woman became more disturbed by them, she started to show hostile feelings towards the other patients. This finally led to psychiatric referral, where this story unfolded and was finally resolved.

What this case history also illustrates is the importance of the social context of the handicap. People with both incurred and congenital handicaps still operate within society and the social response to the handicap may be as problematic as the specific limitations imposed by the handicap.

b. Secondary consequences: the social context

With congenital handicaps, often the greatest amount of stress will be incurred within the home during the child's youngest years. Many workers in this area now feel that the emotional reactions of the parents to having a handicapped child are probably the earliest and most persistent form of stress that the child with a congenital handicap has to endure. The behaviour of parents towards a handicapped child will be determined by many factors such as personality and family size as well as by the facilities which are available both within the home and the community. Although this section is primarily concerned with psychosocial aspects, the contribution of the physical environment should not be underestimated. The demands of bringing up a physically handicapped child in restricted home conditions can be very severe.

Differences in social class and housing conditions can have an enormous effect in determining the impact of the handicap on the family and the resultant stresses on the handicapped child. Within such differences in physical conditions, the personalities and experience of the parents will also be a significant mitigating factor. Even allowing for the influence of such factors, it is still agreed that to a great degree the behaviour of the parents towards a handicapped child will mainly stem from their feelings about having such a child.

There is a wide but consistent range of parental reactions to having a handicapped child and all of these can result in particular attitudes and behaviour towards the child. The presence of a baby with a physical handicap can evoke extremes of what may be called biological feelings of protectiveness and of revulsion. The protective feelings may be quite appropriate but can lead to a highly overprotective type of care which will cause problems later on both for the handicapped child and for non-handicapped siblings. A feeling of revulsion at some level is a normal and not uncommon one although many parents can feel guilty about harbouring such thoughts. If these feelings persist beyond an initial response they can have quite unsatisfactory outcomes in terms of behaviour towards the baby. At one extreme they can result in a very cold and absolute rejection of the baby and at the other in a rather guilt-ridden and lavish over-compensation. Possibly a more common result of such feelings is that of either a rather rationalized rejection (e.g. 'I would like to look after the baby but I think it would be better off with someone with more understanding of these problems') or a rather dutiful care without any real warmth.

Very often the arrival of a handicapped child can evoke feelings of inadequacy in parents both in relation to their own reproductive capacity and their ability to look after the child. The former may have a profound effect on the person's self-esteem and result in depression whereas the latter can have an adverse effect on parental self-confidence in child rearing. Some studies have also indicated that there is a reaction which resembles bereavement behaviour since there is a response to the loss of the 'normal' child which had been expected prior to the birth. Here the family are living with a dual problem. On the one hand they are attempting to care for their handicapped child but at the same time they are, in effect, mourning the normal child they had hoped for and of whom the handicapped child is a constant reminder. Very typically such bereavement responses go through a number of stages starting with initial anger ('Why should this happen to us?'). This may be expressed outwardly towards medical and other people involved in treating the handicapped baby or it may be internalized and have a depressive effect. Later on these feelings may change to a grief type of reaction which will also tend to lead to depression of varying degrees. It has been noticed that where these bereavement responses do occur, adjustment seems to follow quite quickly and parents adapt to the new demands which have been imposed on them.

Obviously for many parents the unexpected arrival of a baby with a physical handicap will come as a great shock and the reaction to this shock may persist for some time. For example, it is not uncommon to find that some parents just cannot come to terms with the full reality and remain in a state of disbelief for months. This can have the effect of causing them to seek second opinions in the hope that a different clinical judgement may be given or to search for a 'wonder drug' that will magically remove the handicap. It is not uncommon for parents to hold themselves in some way responsible for the handicap and all sorts of reasons may be invoked as causal mechanisms. This guilt is often associated with subsequent depression and it is important for those who work with the parents to be aware of any such feelings and to counsel and inform appropriately as to the likely causes in order to remove these guilt feelings. Finally, some parents become embarrassed by the handicap and by what others may think of it. If this persists it may well result in a withdrawal from social contacts and the resultant isolation will bring its own problems.

These reactions to having a baby with a physical handicap, which are summarized in *Table* 6, are not necessarily always found in all parents. The intention of this outline has been to indicate the types of reactions which can be found and the effects which they can have. For many parents these reactions may be relatively transient and they will adapt satisfactorily to the particular demands imposed by the handicap but the reported prevalence of such feelings means that they should not be dismissed or overlooked as their effects can be quite profound.

The stress from the family environment which is engendered by a handicapped child can be seen to stem from three often related sources. These are:

  i. The parent's emotional reactions.
  ii. The parent's failure to understand and accept the problems and implications.
  iii. The difficult physical conditions and extra time which is needed.

Table 6.   Early parental reactions to handicap and their effects on behaviour towards the child

Psychological response		*Effect on behaviour*
i. 'Biological'	→ Protective	→ Overprotection
	→ Revulsion	→ Rejection/dutiful care
ii. Inadequacy	→ Own reproduction	→ Low self-esteem
	→ Child rearing	→ Low self-confidence
iii. 'Bereavement'		→ Anger, depression, adjustment
iv. Shock		→ Disbelief (second opinions, etc.)
v. Guilt		→ Depression
vi. Embarrassment		→ Social withdrawal

The combination of these factors is likely to create a relatively tense and insecure early environment for the handicapped child. For these children, such stresses usually have their greatest effects during the first 2 years and tend to diminish when they go to school. The importance of this early period in personality development has been discussed in Chapter 8 and alluded to in other sections. This inevitably means that a serious secondary consequence of physical handicap is that children may well grow up in a problematic environment, which in turn can have adverse effects on emotional development.

There are marked developmental changes in the child's awareness and reaction to his or her own handicap. Early on there does not appear to be a specific awareness of the handicap *per se* but there are reactions to the demands of such procedures as clinical investigations, physiotherapy and the application of remedial techniques, many of which may involve discomfort and being handled by unfamiliar people. Moreover there are increased chances of hospital admissions and the attendant psychosocial disruptions which these can bring.

By the age of 5 or 6 years, physically handicapped children seem to develop a rather practical awareness of their disabilities and refer to them as a nuisance rather than anything else. At this age, parents also appear to notice that their children know they are handicapped and accept it as part of themselves. From this age onwards, children start to become more aware of themselves in relation to others and once such comparisons are made, emotional reactions to the handicap became more common. Studies of child development indicate that adolescence is generally a time of greatly increased self-awareness and this can be a crisis time for the handicapped when the full implications of their disability really become apparent. This can be expressed in a number of ways but it is not uncommon to find that a stage of denial occurs, sometimes accompanied by the expression of unrealistic ambitions, before a final acceptance is achieved.

Approaching adulthood can present a number of quite specific problems including difficulties associated with sexual maturation and the limited possibilities for emotional and sexual expression. Leaving school often necessitates major adjustments to new circumstances which may be less tolerant than those in a special school. There is an obvious paradox here in that while special schools meet the particular needs of the handicapped child and are protective in many ways, the subsequent shock of dealing with the outside world may be quite marked. In this context it is interesting to note that there are increased attempts to integrate handicapped children into ordinary schools either directly into normal classes or by setting up special units within the school. Even this can create specific problems and there is clearly no easy solution to this question. Finally, finding employment may also be difficult and although firms are encouraged to employ a quota of handicapped staff this is still a pervasive problem.

The pattern of social reactions to the handicapped person in the community will also be likely to have psychological effects. Physically able people often report feelings of discomfort and uncertainty when interacting with a handicapped person. Goffman's description captures these feelings when he describes the signs of this discomfort: 'The guarded references, the common everyday words suddenly made taboo, the fixed stare elsewhere, the artifical levity, the compulsive loquaciousness, the awkward solemnity' (Goffman, 1964).

Since it is known that many of these non-verbal aspects of social interaction are readily perceived and interpreted by the recipient, the handicapped person will become very aware of the abnormal social response to him or her. It has been suggested that a great deal of unease results which will make handicapped persons self-conscious and calculating about the impression they are making. These suggestions have been borne out in observational studies of interactions between normal and handicapped people. These have shown that the patterns of eye-contact, smiling and proximity are all consistently different and that these differences are readily detected by the handicapped (Comer and Piliavin, 1972). Paradoxically the handicapped person will be faced with these situations more often and will tend to become better at managing them whereas the dealings of most people with the handicapped are limited and no adaptive changes are likely to occur. It is only those people who have frequent contact or those with similar disabilities who do not show these differences in non-verbal communication and it is not surprising that many handicapped people only feel they can relax and be themselves in such company.

These distortions in social interaction provide a very clear indication of what is entailed by the secondary consequences of disability. The reactions to the stigma of the disability can create quite specific social problems which reflect the importance of the social context in determining the effects of physical handicap. With handicap as well as with physical illness, there are undoubted biological changes which create specific difficulties and concerns for the person concerned. But, as was discussed at some length in the section on pain in Chapter 1, the final impact of these changes will depend as much on the individual's perceptions and on the social consequences as on the actual severity of the changes themselves.

- ## Recommended reading

Burish T. G. and Bradley L. A. (ed.) (1983) *Coping with Chronic Disease*. New York, Academic Press.

Moos R. H. (ed.) (1984) *Coping with Physical Illness, Vol. 2: New Perspectives*. New York, Plenum.

13

Psychosocial aspects of hospitalization

In recent years there has been an increasing trend towards hospital treatment for all but psychiatric problems. Clearly this has brought many advantages for the patient, who can benefit from the collected expertise which is present in hospital. For the staff, the aims of hospital work are primarily based around the detection of patients' problems and the selection and application of the most appropriate treatment. For the patient, the experience of being in hospital may be much more complicated. The psychosocial disruption and limitations encountered in hospital life can produce a range of psychological responses, some of which can be severe enough to warrant psychiatric help. Lengthy stays in hospital may result in withdrawal, inertia and an inability to cope with life outside. Moreover, there are particular psychological problems associated with the hospitalization of younger children, where this involves separation from the home. Finally, particular hospital treatments such as intensive care and haemodialysis can produce specific emotional reactions due to the limitations and demands they impose on patients. Similarly, many medical procedures are found to be painful or distressing and a number of psychological interventions have been devised to help patients cope with these.

●   **13.1. The psychological effects of hospitalization**
There is an enormous range in the age and length of stay of hospital patients. Also the problems which they experience will vary greatly in all sorts of ways and this inevitably means that there are difficulties in attempting a general discussion of the impact of hospital admission. Some specific issues concerning children and long-stay patients are presented separately but the following account is intended to convey some of the more general factors which have been identified. A second cautionary point for the reader is that some of the psychological reactions which are described may reflect not only a response to hospitalization but also to the illness itself, as was outlined in the previous chapter.

a. The physical environment

One obvious feature of hospital life which will be quite a change for the patient is the physical environment. Strangely there are relatively few studies which have directly investigated how the physical environment of the hospital affects the patient's condition. It is still an unfortunate truism that architects and designers concerned with hospital building are mainly guided by a combination of financial limitations and enlightened guess-work. The least likely person to be consulted for information to determine hospital design characteristics is the patient, who coincidentally is the person who spends the most concentrated period of time in the building. Hospital personnel are increasingly consulted but they do not have to spend their whole day in the building nor do they remain in one place. In hospital, patients are likely to be anxious and in many ways more sensitive and more readily disturbed by changes in the physical environment. However, it is sad to note that more is known about the spatial needs of animals in zoos and circuses than about the spatial needs of people, particularly those who are suffering. For example, it has been shown that the animal which has been given too much or too little space can become quite disturbed and in some cases may become sick and even die.

b. The social environment

In hospital individual privacy is intruded on in a way which might be found intolerable in normal life. The hospital environment is frequently seen to be drab, clinical, impersonal and cold by patients. Usually patients are confined to bed and allow a large number of strange people to observe, move and quite often cause pain to various parts of their bodies. Whereas in the outside world the individual operates with a strong sense of personal space, which is the amount of space necessary for optimal social behaviour, in hospital this space is being constantly invaded as part of the daily routine. The daily routine itself is one which is very likely to be very different from life at home and therefore may require considerable adjustment. Not surprisingly, then, studies which have compared home-treated and hospitalized patients have shown less psychosocial distress in those remaining at home.

The patient's life outside the hospital consists of a fairly well-defined world of people, places and habits which provide an order and consistency necessary for day-to-day living. Admission to hospital obviously removes the individual from this familiar, well-ordered world and places him or her in an environment which is different in every respect. Whereas people can normally come and go as they please, in hospital they are likely to be totally dependent on others for most basic functions such as washing and feeding. Usually they will be restricted to one place, surrounded by new sights, sounds and smells and above all by totally new people, whose skills and interests are now of vital importance to them. The whole of their lives in hospital, their eating, sleeping and their suffering is carried out in the presence of others.

c. Psychological reactions

Looked at in these terms it can be readily seen that admission to hospital is both an uprooting and a dislocation in psychosocial terms. For the patient this inevitably involves the following social changes:
  i. Invasion of privacy.

ii. Loss of independence and individualism.

iii. Reduced opportunities for social contact.

From the few studies which have been carried out it is therefore not surprising to find that for many people, going to hospital is an event of considerable emotional significance. Rachman and Phillips (1975) note that 'at least five manifestations of distress are commonly encountered: fear, increased irritability, loss of interest in the outside world, unhappiness and a preoccupation with one's bodily processes'. They also suggest that, common with other stressful events, there is a sharp increase in the need for social reassurance from both relatives and professional personnel.

It seems most probable that some of the fear and anxiety which is found in many hospital patients is related to the uncertainty and ignorance they have concerning the nature of their illness and its prognosis. There are a number of studies of hospital patients, which show clearly that they are greatly dissatisfied with the communications aspect of hospital life. In contrast they rate the technical skills of medical personnel most highly.

From the studies which have been carried out, it would appear that in the region of 40–50 per cent of all hospital patients are critical of the communication aspects of their stay. As this issue was dealt with in some detail in Chapter 10, the particular communication problems encountered are not described again here. One somewhat depressing aspect of these studies is that in surveys of patients whose doctors felt that they had made special efforts to inform their patients, the dissatisfaction rates were just as high. It is, of course, possible that although doctors had attempted to provide information, this was not expressed in a manner which could be understood or remembered by the patient. Indeed the evidence cited in Chapter 10 which showed the communication 'gaps' and misunderstandings between doctor and patient is consistent with this. However, what also comes out of the studies of hospital patients is that they are diffident in this respect and are unwilling to ask for information. A range of reasons for this diffidence has been found and of these the following were most common:

i. Fear of ridicule or reprisal.

ii. Feeling that nothing would be done.

iii. Not wanting to cause trouble.

iv. Not knowing how to complain.

v. A feeling that complaining or requesting more information was inappropriate behaviour.

Fortunately these problems do not appear to be insurmountable. For example, Ley et al. (1976) conducted a study of hospital patients on three wards of a general hospital. In one ward there was an extra visit made to patients every 10 days, in which attempts were made to ensure that they had understood what they had been told. These visits were relatively brief and only concerned with clarifying existing information rather than raising new issues. The second ward essentially comprised a control group, who received an extra visit to discuss their welfare, food and so on and not to clarify information. Patients in the third ward in the study received no extra visits. The results showed that patients in the first ward showed approximately twice the level of satisfaction with communication as compared with the other two groups. The actual results were:

i. 'Information' ward—80% satisfied with communication.

ii. 'Control' ward—41% satisfied with communication.

iii. 'No information' ward—48% satisfied with communication.

These and similar results from the other studies have shown quite clearly that it is not too difficult to improve communication by attending to the needs of the patient. The benefits from these improvements were indicated in Chapter 10 and include positive changes in compliance rates and general responsiveness to a whole range of treatments and instructions.

One of the particularly valuable advantages of good communication is that it can help to minimize the uncertainty that many patients have in regard to what is wrong with them and what will be happening to them while in hospital. There are a number of well-validated studies, mainly carried out in the USA, which have demonstrated that supplying and clarifying relevant information can be very useful in helping patients in both preparing for admission to hospital and in adapting to painful treatments such as surgery. This work builds on many findings which have shown that the amount of fear generated by a stressful event can be reduced by appropriate verbal preparation based on a description and discussion of the event before it happens. For example, it has been found that patients, who had been well-informed prior to surgery and were appropriately concerned about the impending pain, showed much better postoperative morale and cooperation than those who were ill-informed and hence unrealistically optimistic and unconcerned beforehand.

Research of this type indicates that supplying clear preparatory information which arouses a certain amount of anticipatory anxiety acts as a form of psychological inoculation against a stressful event such as a very painful treatment procedure. It may be that such preparation allows the patient to think about and in some ways rehearse for the impact of the stressor. This is likely to be of value to the patient since this type of mental rehearsal seems to work by reducing two important components of fear and anxiety, namely novelty and suddenness.

The value of improvements in communcation on these lines may even have a significant influence on the patient's physical recovery from surgery. The comparative study of surgical patients, cited in Chapter 1 on 'pain', in which some patients were prepared for surgery with appropriate information, provides a clear example of this since the prepared patients required significantly less postoperative analgesia and were discharged earlier. Above all, what this shows is that there are dangers in 'splitting off' bodily and mental functions in the patient. The patient's psychological state can exert a considerable influence over bodily processes. Since there is likely to be a range of psychological reactions associated with admission to hospital and the associated stressors, failure to recognize and deal with these psychological changes can affect all aspects of patient care. The comments of Rachman and Phillips (1975) are appropriate here since they 'look forward to the day when greater medical and nursing attention is given to the patient's need for emotional comfort and support and less attention to the vagaries of his bowel movements'.

13.2. Psychological responses to specific treatments

In the same way that physical illness imposes physical and social limitations on the individual which in turn give rise to psychological reactions, some treatments are also very restricting and have been found to cause emotional and behavioural changes. In particular a number of studies have been made of patients kept in intensive care units (ICU), those maintained by haemodialysis and more recently of patients kept in isolation systems which ensure sterile environments.

Obviously patients undergoing such treatments are doubly stressed in that they are likely to show a psychological reaction to the severity of their illness as well as to the restriction imposed by the treatment. One of the most striking earlier observations was of poliomyelitis patients receiving artificial respiration in a tank respirator. Many of these patients were found to have quite marked psychological reactions, which included acute confusional states and hallucinations due to the sensory deprivation of the tank respirator. Fortunately improved designs have taken over this type of treatment and have obviated many of these problems. Even so studies of such patients, in which there is a restricted sensory input, combined with continuous high anxiety levels and probable sleep deprivation, show that major psychological reactions of the psychotic type can ensue.

Experimental work with healthy volunteers has shown that long periods of sensory deprivation or sensory overload will often give rise to a state characterized by increased wakefulness, disorientation and visual hallucinations. These states have also been found in some patients who are being treated in ICUs since they are exposed to long periods of sensory deprivation produced by monotony and immobilization, sometimes interrupted by periods of overstimulation, as well as sleep deprivation. It is claimed that the observed 'ICU psychosis' is the result of all these factors on an individual who is already fearful of his or her life because of a serious physical illness. The following description of the typical features of life in an ICU provides a basis for understanding the psychological disorientation which can follow:

> ICU patients are confined to bed, often immobilized by traction or cardiac monitoring devices or respiratory assisting devices, and exposed to a white sound background of whirring motors or regular blips or bleeps. Lights are kept on all the time, in a room with no windows, clocks or calenders to measure the passage of time, and with no opportunity for conversation with relatives save for five minutes every hour. The doctors and nurses are distracted by their responsibilities of monitoring the complex life-support systems. The patients are afflicted by frequent injections and have tubes in most of their body orifices. The atmosphere is one of monotony interrupted at regular intervals by terror. Without warning alarm bells sound and staff rush to care for patients with cardiac or respiratory arrests. Patients hear and see deaths of other patients and fear for their own fate. (Glickman, 1977)

The speed with which patients begin to hallucinate has been shown to be dependent on the restrictiveness of the environment. For example, in one study of a surgical ICU with no windows and limited visiting, patients who were in neck traction became delirious by the sixth day and those who were not in traction became delirious by the eighteenth day. Typically the condition starts with patients becoming confused as to whether they are asleep and dreaming or awake but initially they are amenable to reassurance. However, soon they become more agitated, confused and hallucinated.

Fortunately these dramatic psychological responses gradually disappear when normal amounts of sensory stimuli and sleep are restored by returning the patient to a normal hospital environment. More important, these changes can be pretty well avoided if the ICU contains a more varied sensory environment and with good contact with visitors and staff.

There have been a number of studies assessing the psychological adaptation to haemodialysis and these show that patients typically go through a series of stages. Initially observers have noted something akin to a honeymoon period, which usually lasts for the first few weeks or sometimes months, and in which the intense dependence on the dialysis machine is accepted by the patients. Although there are stress and anxiety, the mood at this stage is typically one of hopefulness and confidence. However, these positive feelings tend to diminish and patients often begin to feel sad, helpless and depressed. Finally, clinicians have noted a long-term adaptation which is characterized by an acceptance and resignation. Even at this stage patients are found to fluctuate in mood between contentment and depression but the periods of contentment are usually more long-lasting. It is reported that many patients use a denying strategy to cope with the anxiety and the demands of the treatment.

The range of psychological responses which are found in relation to physical illness and which were described in the previous chapter, are also found in patients undergoing these very demanding types of treatment. One study of patients in gnotobiotic isolation noted that all the patients used either a preoccupying or denying type of coping strategy to deal with the limitations of the isolation system (Gordon, 1976). The author in this study also drew attention to the difficulties for staff who work in these highly specialized treatment environments, pointing out that they, too, have to adapt to a combination of complex equipment, serious illness and limited patient contact. All of these factors can create a tense working environment and it has been found that nurses are particularly vulnerable to these demands, which may account for the reported high turnover of staff in many of these units. More recent studies have also shown that it is possible to provide psychological support for patients who experience distress in these very trying treatment environments (Foerster, 1984).

Here again the social context of the treatment environment has been shown to exert a very strong effect on the patient's response. Although all of the treatment procedures referred to here have brought undeniable medical benefits to patients and will continue to do so, the social and psychological costs to the patients must not be overlooked. With appropriate attention to the patients' social and psychological needs, many of these potential problems can be minimized or avoided. The findings which have been described here make it much easier to undertand why one recent report on the treatment of renal failure concluded that many aspects of social rehabilitation are considerably better for those who are treated by dialysis at home compared with those treated in hospital. Obviously such findings will be contaminated by patient selection biases but even so it was felt that the inconvenience and restrictiveness of the hospital environment were major factors here.

13.3. Stressful medical procedures in hospital

In addition to the generally stressful effects of hospital admission, there is a range of medical procedures which can give rise to considerable discomfort and anxiety. These include specific investigative procedures such as barium X-rays, endoscopy and cardiac catheterization which may not only be uncomfortable and sometimes physically distressing but which also carry the threat of uncovering a serious medical condition. The other obvious 'event' in hospital which has been found to produce significant psychological effects is surgery. The psychological impact of surgery will partly depend on the procedure, the condition and the likely outcome as well as on such psychological factors as the patient's expectations and coping style and the quality of communication.

The way in which a patient reacts to a medical procedure can also have a significant influence on the outcome, particularly in recovery from surgery. Patients who show the highest pre-surgical levels of stress response will also tend to experience adverse psychological reactions post-surgically and will be more likely to show poorer physical recovery. These patients will request more analgesia, show more post-surgical complications and tend to recover more slowly with delays in discharge, as compared with less anxious or stressed patients.

Psychological interventions for stressful medical procedures

Since studies have shown a relation between patients' psychological state and their recovery, it has been recognized that there could be considerable gains from providing a psychological intervention designed to reduce or minimize the psychological impact of a medical procedure. Broadly these interventions fall into five main groups depending on the techniques involved and the aims of the intervention:

    i. Psychological support.
    ii. Information provision.
    iii. Skills training interventions.
    iv. Modelling.
    v. Cognitive-behavioural interventions.

i. Psychological support

These interventions are aimed at allowing patients to discuss and come to terms with their fears and concerns about the medical 'event' and any associated issues (e.g. the short- and long-term effects of surgery). The doctor, nurse or psychologist typically allows the patient to talk about particular worries and then attempts to provide support and reassurance. The evidence from the studies of this type of intervention has been mixed, with some studies showing considerable gains in patients receiving psychological support as compared with controls, but others showing little or no effects. However, there are indications that those patients who are particularly anxious can derive significant benefit provided the support is reasonably consistent and particularly if it is combined with the other approaches described below.

ii. Information provision

The importance of providing information has already been discussed in Chapter 10 on doctor–patient communication and in Chapter 12 on psychological aspects of physical illness, as well as earlier in this chapter. A number of studies have evaluated the effects of providing different sorts of information prior to stressful medical procedures. Broadly, the type of information provided tends to fall into two categories, namely information about the likely sensations, including pain, that the patient might expect to feel (sensory information) and information as to what will happen during the procedure (procedural information).

Again there is equivocal evidence as to the efficacy of this type of intervention but many studies have shown positive effects in terms of reduced distress, less analgesia and, where surgery was involved, better recovery. Generally sensory information has been found to produce more beneficial effects, particularly with distressing investigative procedures such as endoscopy. The variation in efficacy of information provision appears to depend on how much detail is given and on individual differences within patient groups. Specific information has been found to be more helpful than general information for most patients but for patients who do not cope in an active fashion or who are more external in their locus of control, the reverse seems to be true. All of this evidence points to the importance of relating the type of information to the needs and personality of the patient.

iii. Skills training interventions

These consist of getting patients to learn specific behaviours to cope with specific medical procedures and for helping postoperative recovery. They have included training in breathing and in other aspects of bodily control which are usually related to a particular investigative procedure. These have been found to be quite beneficial in helping patients cope with a medical procedure and in facilitating postoperative recovery but do not seem to have any specific effects on levels of anxiety and distress.

A more general skills training procedure which has been found to be useful in recovery is relaxation training (*see* Chapter 14), which has proved beneficial in reducing anxiety prior to different treatments and investigations.

iv. Modelling

These procedures consist of allowing patients to see, on film or videotape, other patients undergoing a similar investigative procedure, treatment or surgery. This has been used quite widely as a preparatory procedure for children and is employed on a routine basis in some hospitals. Studies have varied the type of model behaviour shown in the film from those who clearly experience distress but still cope to those who seem to cope well throughout the whole process. Overall these studies have shown very positive effects on both distress and on coping with the medical 'event' although it is worth pointing out that the 'events' were generally of the less severe type. Some of the more general characteristics of modelling and associated treatment approaches are described in Chapter 14 in the section on behavioural theories and treatment.

v. Cognitive-behavioural interventions

These are aimed at modifying or facilitating the way patients think of and cope with the procedure they are about to undergo. The rationale and methods for this approach are described in some detail in Chapter 14 since they have evolved as a treatment approach for a range of psychological and physical problems. As with other standard cognitive-behavioural treatments, patients are initially provided with a rationale which emphasizes the extent to which stress and pain can be influenced by their attitude, cognitions and coping behaviours.

In earlier studies using this approach all the patients tended to be taught the same mode of coping by directing their attention and thoughts to positive aspects of the surgery or investigation. More recent work has tended to move away from teaching all patients the same coping strategy to using the individual patient's preferred strategies for coping. Typically patients are first encouraged to identify which aspects of a forthcoming medical procedure (e.g. cardiac catheterization) they think might be stressful for them. After describing the strategies they typically use for coping with other stressors, the intervention will consist of getting them to apply these strategies to the procedure they are about to undergo.

The evidence to date shows that cognitive-behavioural strategies are very effective in reducing the stress of painful or threatening medical procedures. Controlled outcome studies with surgical patients and with patients undergoing cardiac catheterization both show very positive gains, as indicated by patients' own ratings and by the independent ratings of their doctors and nurses.

In summary, there is now considerable evidence to indicate that different types of psychological preparation can not only reduce the anxiety, stress and pain involved in many medical procedures but also that there are considerable related benefits (e.g. less analgesia, better recovery, faster discharge, etc.). Although the above outline of approaches provided separate descriptions of each, they can easily be used in conjunction and often are. However, it is significant that work in this area has focused on the importance of individual differences in the nature of stressfulness of medical procedures and in ways of coping with these. This is entirely consistent with the current views of pain and stress described in earlier chapters.

• 13.4. Children in hospital

By the age of 7 years, approaching 50 per cent of British children will have spent a period of time in hospital. Since there is evidence that children's reaction to illness and hospital treatment can be quite distinct and that the psychological and social consequences of separation from home can produce quite specific problems, a separate consideration of this whole area now follows.

In 1955 a study of the emotional reactions of children to hospital appeared in the *Lancet* (Illingworth and Holt, 1955) and some of the results from this are shown in *Fig.* 20. An inspection of these results immediately indicates that age, length of stay and visiting are important factors in determining the degree of disturbance. Since that time various recommendations have been put forward and, to some extent, implemented to allow a greater access by parents to their hospitalized children. These have included increased flexibility in visiting arrangements as well as a greater provision of overnight accommodation for parents. In spite of all these changes, more recent evidence indicates that, for many children, a stay in hospital still produces a significant emotional response. In particular this work has focused on the role of the parents in determining how

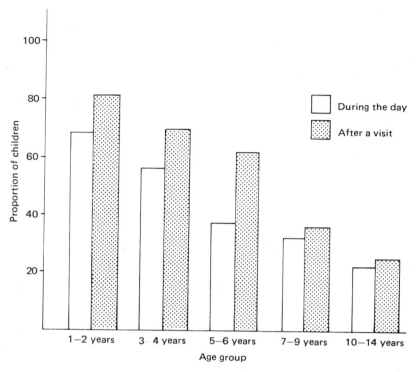

Fig. 20. The proportion of children showing an emotional disturbance on admission to hospital in five different age groups. (Adapted from Illingworth and Holt, 1955.)

their children will respond to stressful events and to hospital admission in particular.

Some accounts of the effects of hospitalization on children can give the impression that children are a homogeneous group in the sense that all the effects are to be found in all children. This is clearly erroneous since adaptation to hospital life will depend greatly on the age and personality of the child as well as on the family and their reaction to the child, to disease and to hospitals. Emotional problems in hospital are much more prevalent in younger children, particularly up to and around the age of 4. Older children are more amenable to explanation and are usually less distressed by separation from home and by being surrounded by strange people doing strange things to them.

The family's attitudes and reactions can be a critical determinant of how the child copes. Where the pre-existing family dynamics are sound, then the parents and family members will typically respond with due concern and cooperation. In less 'healthy' families, the response to the sick child may be distorted by excessive anxiety or guilt on the part of the parents or emotional outbursts in other siblings. In more disturbed family settings, the sick child can become a focus or a scapegoat for pre-existing family tensions. In this situation the response to the child's illness may paradoxically be determined more by the emotional needs of the family members than those of the child. Considerations of this type emphasize the importance for those involved in treating the sick child of accepting the family as much as the child as the essential unit for understanding and treating disease. The illness and hospital treatment of a child both have an effect on and are affected by the family structure.

There are a number of specific psychological problems associated with the hospitalization of children. The problems would appear to stem from three sources:

i. The social separations and disruptions incurred by admission to hospital.
ii. The emotional response to the clinical problem.
iii. The lack of preparation for hospital life and the investigations and treatments to be carried out.

These three problem areas are not usually separate and may often be quite closely inter-related. However, all of them have been shown to have significant effects on the management of children in hospital, particularly among younger children. Fortunately the awareness of these problems has increased greatly in recent years partly as a result of these studies and partly through the action of specific pressure groups. As a result many hospitals do attempt to prepare children before admission and minimize the subsequent separation but the problems still remain in many places.

The more long-term effects of hospitalization on children suggest that some of the traumatic effects may have been overstated. Follow-up studies of hospitalized children indicate that serious problems are only found in children who had psychological problems prior to admission or who come from difficult families (La Greca and Stone, 1985). Recent studies of preparation of children for hospitalization also show that different types of preparation appear to be suitable for children of different ages and with different amounts of prior experience.

● 13.5. The hospital environment: negative and positive aspects

In many ways the various psychological reactions to hospital admission represent an understandable response by patients to the demands and disruptions imposed by their clinical problems and by hospital life. These reactions will usually reduce and disappear on return to home life and on restoration to full health. However, for some patients there may not be a rapid return to home life since their problem may necessitate a much longer stay in hospital. For these patients the stay in hospital may last months, years and in some cases a lifetime. Where this happens, hospital life ceases to represent a temporary dislocation but can become a way of life in itself. The social and physical environment of the hospital will begin to exert very real long-term effects on the patient's behaviour and feelings. Sadly many studies of these effects have been prompted by and concerned with negative aspects of the hospital environment and the effects of so-called 'institutionalization'. However, there has been an increasing realization that there can also be positive relations between the treatment environment and patient improvement. This has led both to studies of different hospital settings and to specific attempts to maximize some of the more positive aspects in situations where the hospital is structured as a therapeutic community. In this section, then, there is a brief account of some of the negative institutional changes which can accompany long stays in hospital and this is followed by a discussion of the relation between the treatment environment and patient's behaviour. Finally, there is a consideration of the concept of the hospital as a therapeutic community.

a. Effects of long-term hospitalization

For a few patients with severe and chronic physical problems but particularly for some psychiatric, geriatric and mentally handicapped patients, hospitalization may continue for long periods of time. It has been noted by many investigators that long stays in an institutional setting will tend to produce a number of detrimental changes in the individuals concerned. Goffman (1968) has used the term 'total institution' to describe residential settings where a group of individuals are cut off from wider society for an appreciable length of time and lead a life which is very much determined by the structure and routine of that institution. Apart from hospitals, other 'total' institutions include prisons, army barracks, boarding schools and monasteries/nunneries. A unifying feature of these diverse organizations is that they all have a characteristic way of life to which the individual has to adhere and that sanctions and penalties are imposed on those who fail to do so.

Older studies of institutionalization tended to describe global changes associated with long stays in hospitals, particularly large psychiatric hospitals. Many of these pointed out the neglect, indifference and dehumanization which the custodial care seemed to result in. Paradoxically it was found that such environments did not necessarily result in positive therapeutic changes but were often counter-therapeutic since they produced behaviour problems that reflected the limitations and monotony of institutional life. Typically it was found that long stays in any such insitution produce social withdrawal, apathy, loss of contact with reality and a resistance to discharge, all of which make it progressively more difficult for the individual to adapt to life outside the hospital.

The terms 'institutionalization' and 'disculturation' have both been used to describe processes associated with the demands of the social systems of some large psychiatric hospitals, which lead to apathy, depersonalization, resignation, dependence, loss of self-esteem and reliance on fantasy in their long-stay patients. These changes can be seen to reflect both the management approach of many long-stay hospitals as well as the influence of a relatively impoverished social and physical environment. On the management side, the prime concern is more often with the smooth running of the organization rather than with particular emotional needs of individual patients. In situations where there is a clash between these two interests, more often than not the organizational rather than individual needs will determine the outcome. The overall effect of such a structure will therefore be to produce a degree of dependence on the institution in the conforming patients which in turn will make those who stay for any length of time less able to return to life outside. With those patients who do not conform to the routine, there will inevitably be problems in management of what is deemed to be obstructive or antisocial behaviour. This will be likely to result in sanctions such as compulsory detention, seclusion and restraints of a social, physical or chemical nature, none of which is noted for bringing about positive therapeutic outcomes for the individual patient.

It is clear from more recent work that these changes in long-stay patients are not necessarily universal nor inevitable but will depend greatly on various aspects of the hospital environment as well as on characteristics of the individual patient. One of the best-known studies of long-stay schizophrenic patients in recent years was that of Wing and Brown (1970) which investigated the effects of many aspects of the patient's environment on the clinical picture.

One of the major findings from the Wing and Brown study was to confirm and document the relation between what they called 'environmental poverty' and the clinical condition of the patient. They found that patients who had the fewest possessions also tended to be occupied in the least interesting hospital activities, were regarded most negatively by the nurses, were least in touch directly and indirectly with the outside world and spent most time doing absolutely nothing. Correspondingly those patients who were better off in material terms were also more favourably rated on the other criteria. These indications of environmental poverty were also strongly related to other important clinical considerations such as social withdrawal, flatness of emotions and poverty of speech. Moreover both environmental and clinical poverty increased as length of stay increased. They were able to demonstrate these relations in three different mental hospitals, which could be differentiated in terms of the quality of their social environments. Hence the hospital with the best rated social environment was found to contain patients with fewest negative symptoms.

From these findings, they were therefore able to show how the social conditions surrounding a patient could actually be responsible for part of the symptomatology. They also found that the longer patients stay in hospital, the more likely they are to want to stay there or to be indifferent about leaving. This increasing resistance to being discharged is one of the primary features of the institutionalization process associated with long stays in hospitals. It appears to be generated by a combination of the patient's 'adaptation' to the hospital routine, increasing apathy and the social attitudes to the patient within and outside the hospital. From this they conclude that indifference and resistance to leaving is the core reason for institutionalism and that, in addition to standard clinical treatment, various measures to prevent the decline in self-respect and self-confidence and to stop the development of institutionalized attitudes are needed.

In highlighting the stultifying and dehumanizing effects of long stays in unstimulating hospital environments, these studies indicate again that human behaviour cannot be fully understood in isolation from the environmental context in which it occurs. The types of behaviour described above appear to be a direct result of various features of the hospital environment. Even so it is probably fair criticism to note that many patients are still kept in environments which, if not directly detrimental to their wellbeing, would not be considered in any way conducive to preparing them for life outside the hospital. This criticism is still particularly relevant to the treatment of mentally handicapped and geriatric patients, for whom resources fall well below the levels found for many other groups. Until changes in priorities come about it may be relatively difficult to do more than scratch at the surface of many of these problems.

b. Treatment environment and patient improvement

The realization that the hospital environment can produce such radical effects on patient behaviour has prompted a great deal of research which has attempted to explore the relationship between the therapeutic setting and both positive and negative aspects of the patient's clinical response. The majority of this work has been carried out with psychiatric patients since changes and effects on behaviour are obviously of direct importance in this group. Typically this research has consisted of attempts to quantify such aspects of the treatment environment as ward size, ward structure and staff attitudes to treatment outcome.

Clinical improvements in patients are affected by various environmental variables. Wards which are characterized by greater staff–patient interaction, less disturbed and bizarre behaviour, larger social clusters and fewer patients produce the greatest patient improvements. In fact most of these studies point to the importance of the quality and quantity of social interaction between patients and staff as one of the strongest predictions of behaviour change, more so than hospital policy variables. Wards which are perceived by patients as having more receptive and involved staff were also found to be those producing the most effective clinical changes. Moreover and possibly more important, it has been found that patients from units where the staff are receptive and accessible show better post-hospital adjustment, as judged by the relatives. Likewise it has been demonstrated that wards which have staff who are perceived as inaccessible or who describe themselves as authoritarian and restrictive seemed to produce less patient improvement.

The degree of control shown by the staff is an interesting variable since high levels of staff control result in a more smoothly running ward but do not appear to promote improvements in the patients' social functioning. The evidence is that on such wards patients became more seclusive and less communicative but were also less hostile and more conforming. In this sense greater control by staff reflects a bias towards smooth management rather than a concern for the therapeutic needs of individual patients and, as such, is not found to be particularly therapeutic. Wards on which emotions, particularly anger, could be expressed openly tended to produce more communicative patients which in turn was associated with greater clinical improvement. Thus environmental acceptance of emotional expression appears to be a therapeutic factor. These findings indicate that acceptance of individual behaviour together with the facilitation of greater social interaction are factors which provide the basis for a therapeutic setting.

All these studies point to the importance of environmental factors in contributing to patient improvement in the hospital and subsequent adjustment in the community. Perhaps the most powerful of these factors is the actual quality of staff–patient interactions. Staff who are perceived as controlling, inaccessible and authoritarian appear to create a social environment which is detrimental to patients, at least as far as hospital adjustment is concerned. On the other hand, staff who mix readily with patients and who are perceived as empathic and supportive create a social atmosphere in which change is more likely to occur.

c. The hospital as a therapeutic community

The awareness that many large psychiatric hospitals are effectively counter-therapeutic together with the realization that the nature of the ward environment can influence clinical improvement has led to an effort on the part of some psychiatrists to develop a therapeutic community treatment approach for patients. The whole notion of the therapeutic community is based on the premise that a ward is a social system which is influenced by both staff and patients. Thus this approach tries to maximize those aspects of the social environment which have been found to facilitate improvement and to minimize those which are counter-therapeutic.

The following characteristics are typical of wards or hospitals which are organized as therapeutic communities:

  i.   Communication is open and direct between staff and patients.
 ii.   Patients are encouraged to participate in their own treatment.
iii.   There are frequent opportunities for patients and staff to participate in administrative and therapeutic decision-making.
 iv.   Although the final authority lies with the staff, much of the operation of the ward is in the hands of the patients.
  v.   The hospital and ward are in close contact with the outside community.
 vi.   Usually the unit has an open door and patients have freedom of movement within the hospital.

Since the community is organized on these lines, the emphasis on the medical model of management is reduced and the model of doctor–patient interaction becomes one based more on mutual collaboration. In this way there is a specific attempt to avoid the social isolation and dehumanization of the 'total institution' and to maximize the involvement of the patients with the staff, their families and the outside community. Obviously this type of approach necessitates some radical changes in traditional patient and staff roles, as seen in more traditional hospital settings. Inevitably staff become much more open, involved with the patients and organized more on multidisciplinary lines with a great deal of role sharing and overlap between different categories of staff. For patients there is an opportunity and encouragement to become more responsible for their current life situations. Moreover there is a greater emphasis on learning about themselves and their relations to others together with the realization that they are responsible for the ward management and hence directly concerned with the therapy of others as well.

The optimal environment for this type of community is in a small- or medium-sized institution which is not removed from the outside community and which is physically pleasant and well organized. Patients keep their own clothes and belongings and have good access to staff and other patients. There should be facilities and space for group meetings since these will form an important part of the running of such a unit. The structure of this type of setting should therefore convey an overall feeling of optimism and positive change to the patients and to the community.

The positive feelings and attitudes engendered by this approach are intended to have an influence on the treatment which takes place. Treatment may well consist of a mixture of individual psychotherapy, group therapy and behavioural approaches based on a system of rewards and sanctions established within the community. The final choice of treatment for any patient will depend on the skills and interests of the staff and on the nature of the problems. There is evidence that different types of patients will benefit from different types of therapeutic settings. For example, one study indicated that patients who were more depressed, anxious and introverted were less able to handle interactions with staff than with other patients. Considerations of this type should therefore be important in determining what happens to any individual patient.

It is not intended to provide all the intricate details of the therapeutic community approach but to present it as one which has grown out of the realization that the hospital environment can have a significant effect on the progress of a patient. For the short-stay patient the impact of hospital admission may be initially disruptive but of no real lasting consequence. For those who are unfortunate enough to need hospital care for a much longer time period, great care must be taken to avoid many of the iatrogenic problems which reflect the influence of a stultifying social environment. It remains to be seen whether the therapeutic community will become the model for the long-stay patient or whether it will lead on to other changes. This type of approach is still being evaluated in order to determine what particular characteristics are of value and to which groups of patients. Whatever the results of these evaluative studies finally show, it must always be acknowledged the treatment environment itself can significantly affect the patient's progress and that a constant awareness of these effects should be second nature to those who work with long-stay patients.

● **Recommended reading**
Wilson-Barnett J. (1979) *Stress in Hospitals*. Edinburgh, Churchill Livingstone.

14

Psychological approaches to treatment

In this chapter there is an outline of some psychological approaches to treatment. Many of these approaches have been developed specifically for the treatment of psychological problems but some have been successfully applied to such physical problems as cardiovascular disorders. A range of procedures is described. These vary in their nature and mode of operation but the unifying theme is that they seek to bring about change by acting on some aspects of a person's behaviour.

It can be argued that any treatment in medicine will embody certain psychological factors and some of these have been alluded to in earlier chapters. The provision of information and the quality of the therapist–patient relationship were both shown to have an influence on the outcome of treatment. Moreover, underlying any treatment there appear to be a number of critical psychological factors, which are usually collectively referred to as the *placebo* components.

- ## 14.1. Placebo effects

Any medication is thought to have a significant 'placebo' component in that some of its effectiveness is due to the expectations of the patient as well as to its chemical properties. Even in a serious organic disease, such as angina pectoris, it has been shown that more than one-third of sufferers may report relief after being given a placebo tablet, which is pharmacologically inert. Moreover, the actions of many pain-killing medications, including morphine, are also held to have a significant placebo component. Interestingly, a reasonable number of patients also show side-effects such as nausea, headache and drowsiness after a placebo dose has been administered.

How such placebo effects work is not really understood. There have been recent claims that they might act through natural opiate mechanisms in the brain. Challenging as such claims are, they are still relatively speculative and by no means account for the many strange properties of the placebo response. There is considerable variability in the placebo response in the same individual in different treatment situations. At least part of this variability will reflect some of the other

Fig. 21. Placebos could be used more routinely in treatment!

important factors, such as the particular expectations which are aroused by the treatment, the behaviour of the doctor and the mode of administration and appearance of the medication.

Greater placebo effects are found when doctors are authoritative, enthusiastic and really believe that a particular treatment will prove valuable. This may explain the 'wonder drug' phenomenon that accompanies many new and heralded medications, the effectiveness of which may strangely decline once the initial excitement has died down. It also makes it easy to understand Osler's insightful remark that doctors should use new remedies quickly while they are still efficacious!

It is clearly important to be aware that placebo effects do exist and can play a critical role in bringing about therapeutic change. A leading article in the *British Medical Journal* (1970) made a plea for the informed clinical use of this effect since it was clearly of such magnitude that it could not be simply ignored or dismissed. Finally, an awareness of these phenomena is of vital importance in evaluating the effectiveness of any treatment and in planning clinical trials. This is true not only in the evaluation of pharmacological agents but also in determining the effectiveness of the psychological treatments which are outlined below. Indeed controlling for placebo responses has been either neglected or found too difficult or impractical in very many evaluative studies of psychological treatments. As a result it is quite difficult to be specific in determining just how effective many of these treatments really are. This should be borne firmly in mind while reading about the different approaches described here.

● 14.2. The behavioural approach

Probably the most widespread psychological approaches to treatment which have been introduced in recent years are the so-called 'behavioural' treatments. They have been given this name since they stem directly from behavioural theories of personality development and dysfunction which were outlined in Chapter 7. One of the claims of some behaviour therapists is that their approach is probably the only one with a clearly defined theoretical and experimental foundation. As we see a little later, this claim may be somewhat misconceived. Even so there can be little doubt that behaviour therapy has made a very significant impact in the treatment of a range of behavioural disorders from quite specific phobias through to more common problems such as sexual difficulties and overeating. In this account there is a brief description of the underlying theory which is followed by an outline of some of the main behavioural treatment methods.

a. Behavioural theory

The central theme of behaviourism is that all human behaviour is acquired or learned by various conditioning processes and for this reason it is very often referred to as 'learning theory'. The main concerns of learning theorists have been to describe the way in which specific stimuli in the environment give rise to specific behaviour patterns or responses. Thus they have been concerned with describing how stimulus–response associations are derived and have sought the answer primarily in terms of two different types of conditioning procedures.

The first of these is usually referred to as *classical conditioning* and is generally associated with the name of Pavlov. Pavlov made the observation that an environmental stimulus, such as a sound or a visual stimulus, could be made to give rise to a response, if it is consistently presented together with another stimulus which normally does produce the required response. The best known example of this is that of a bell causing a dog to salivate. Pavlov achieved this by consistently ringing a bell each time food was presented to the dog. If this is done over a period of time, the animal comes to associate the bell with the food and will eventually salivate to the bell alone. The bell has become a conditioned stimulus which produces a conditioned response of salivation. In this way the animal now produces an entirely new response to a specific stimulus, which is a fairly crude form of learning. During the process of classical conditioning great care must be taken over the timing of the conditioned stimulus, which should occur coincidentally with the neutral stimulus (i.e. the food in the above example) and ideally just prior to it by something like 0·5 second.

Two further characteristics of classical conditioning are worth mentioning. First, the conditioned response is not absolutely specific since it will generalize to similar stimuli. Thus an animal conditioned to salivate to the presentation of a circular shape will salivate in a diminishing fashion as an increasingly elliptical stimulus is presented. Second, the conditioned response will not last for ever and fades out if the original neutral stimulus is not reintroduced.

Using classical conditioning it is therefore possible to link a response to a stimulus not normally associated with it but this response must already be present in the animal, such as the salivation response. It would appear that what has been learned by the animal is an association between a previously neutral stimulus and a response previously made to a quite specific stimulus. Given these basic requirements, it is not surprising to find that classical conditioning only refers to a very simple 'learning' situation where the behaviour consists of fairly simple physiological or reflex responses, which are pretty fixed.

The second conditioning procedure used by behaviourists to account for learning is that of *operant* or *instrumental conditioning* and is particularly associated with the name of Skinner. The essence of this type of conditioning is that all our behaviour is determined by the pattern of rewards and punishments which are generated by the environment. This was put forward by Thorndike (1911) in his 'Law of Effect' which stated that any action which results in a desirable outcome is likely to be repeated in similar circumstances. For example, a hungry animal running around a small cage who finds that accidentally dislodging a lever produces a food reward, will pretty soon learn to pull the lever for food. Alternatively, an animal who receives an electric shock whenever it moves into a certain part of the cage will soon learn to avoid that area. Rewards tend to increase the frequency of a behaviour and punishments tend to have the opposite effect.

This type of conditioning is much more flexible than classical conditioning in that the responses which are conditioned can be infinitely modified as the rewards change. For example, the animal can learn to make a response a certain number of times before a reward arrives or that a certain amount of time has to pass before a rewarded response can be made. As the pattern of rewards becomes more complex, learning also becomes more complicated in that the animal has to find out exactly which features of its behaviour are appropriate by testing the environment and this is often referred to as 'discrimination learning'.

What appears to be learned during operant conditioning is the relation between specific actions and their outcomes. For example, the developing child's behaviour will in part reflect what the child has learned about the appropriateness of his or her previous behaviour. In this case 'appropriateness' reflects the system of parental rewards and punishments. However, learning by children, particularly the learning of social behaviour, may not always arise directly because of specific parental reactions but may involve a third type of learning known as *observational learning* or *modelling*. This involves the learning of behaviour patterns as the result of watching them performed by others such as peers, parents or heroes. Here learning comes about as the result of watching rather than from reinforcements although it is quite possible that the learner anticipates that the new behaviour will ultimately bring certain rewards or benefits. As we noted in Chapter 8 on child development, this process has been invoked to explain the learning of sex roles and of aggressive behaviour in children from parental and other models, including those on television.

From this brief description of learning theory models it can readily be seen that behaviourists seek to explain human learning and behaviour in terms of relations between stimuli and responses. These theories are not therefore concerned with the nature of cognitive processes which are involved in perceiving and storing information from the environment or in problem-solving. The latter processes are outlined in earlier chapters and are necessary to understand *how* learning occurs. Learning theory, then, describes only a relatively limited range of human behaviour and in a rather simplistic and mechanistic fashion. In this context it is worth noting that in experimental psychology, behavioural approaches and models have now been largely abandoned in favour of more complex information-processing models which are concerned with understanding the nature of human cognitions rather than stimulus–response linkages. Even so behavioural explanations are still used to explain the genesis of clinical problems and to provide the basis for treatment, as is now described.

b. Clinical behavioural approaches

i. The behavioural interpretation of problems

Since behaviourists believe that all human behaviours are conditioned or learned in the way described above, it comes as no surprise to find that clinical problems are assumed to originate in the same way and are thought of as learned maladaptive behaviour patterns. Whereas the psychoanalyst will regard a psychiatric symptom as an indication of an underlying, deep-seated problem, behaviourists view the symptoms themselves as the problems and deal with them directly by attempting to make the individual unlearn them or relearn a more adaptive behaviour. Treatment is therefore directed towards the manifested problem and the individual's past history is only considered of value where it throws light on the way the problem has arisen.

Psychiatric problems are thought to come about as the result of both classical and operant conditioning. Many neurotic disorders are considered to arise because a previously 'neutral' stimulus becomes associated with one which normally gives rise to anxiety. Therefore, by the processes involved in classical conditioning, the neutral stimulus is now associated with an anxiety or fear response. For example, someone who has had a particularly unpleasant experience or series of experiences involving injections during medical treatment may eventually become very anxious or even phobic about syringes. This may generalize to other similar situations such as dental treatment or receiving inoculations for visits abroad and may lead to the person taking great pain to avoid any such encounter. Moreover the anxiety response may also generalize to other associated aspects of the original conditioning situation, such as to the smell of the surgery or to people wearing white coats.

In this way, behaviourists claim that many psychiatric problems of the neurotic type can arise. They also maintain that such maladaptive responses do not diminish over time, as one might expect from the basic principles of classical conditioning, because they are maintained by the operant behaviour of the patient. Thus once fear-arousing or phobic responses are generated, patients seek to avoid them wherever possible. Avoidance of this type therefore prevents the fading out or extinction of a maladaptive response from occurring and may actually involve the development of strange behaviours as a result. For example, someone who has developed a specific fear of open places may seek to avoid the anxiety which they create by staying at home all the time and withdrawing from all outside activities. Similarly someone with a particular anxiety about dirt may indulge in repeated hand washing to avoid any possibility of becoming dirty. In this way a compulsive, repeated behaviour, which can cause great interference in daily life, can develop originally as an avoidance behaviour. Obsessive, recurring thoughts are also thought to play a similar role.

ii. Behavioural treatments

Behavioural methods of treatment are also based on operant and classical conditioning principles. An important first step in any of these treatments is to analyse carefully and describe the particular maladaptive behaviour. This behavioural analysis is a critical precursor in the formulation of an appropriate treatment regimen and consists of clearly defining the problem and the various individual and environmental factors that can affect it.

One of the earliest and still most widely used behavioural procedures for anxiety problems is that of *systematic desensitization*. The basic principle of this treatment consists of allowing the patient to gradually come to terms with a particular fear or set of fears by working through various levels of the feared situation from the mildest aspect to the most anxiety-provoking. An important first step in this treatment is for the patient and therapist to devise a graded list or hierarchy of anxiety-provoking aspects of the feared situation from the least to the most fearful aspect. For example, with a spider-phobic patient the hierarchy might range from a picture of a very small spider to being able to pick up a large, moving spider. The hierarchy can consist of actual objects or situations but equally may be based on imagined scenes which the patient can generate and which correspond to the real-life situations. Patients are then usually taught a relaxation procedure and are gradually taken successively through the hierarchy so that each stage can be handled without experiencing anxiety. The goal is therefore reached when patients can face or vividly imagine the most anxiety-provoking aspect of their problem. Systematic desensitization on these lines has been used with a range of neurotic problems but has been particularly successful in the treatment of specific phobias.

In systematic desensitization the patient is gradually allowed to relearn a more adaptive response to a particular situation. In contrast, some other behavioural methods such as *implosive therapy* or *flooding* attempt to rid the patient of an anxiety response by confronting the patient directly with the feared situation. In doing this and not allowing avoidance behaviour to occur, it is hoped that an extinction of the maladaptive response will occur. As with many desensitization treatments the feared situations are often dealt with at the imaginal level but again real-life situations are sometimes used.

With these two types of treatment there is often a well-defined focus or situation which is associated with the patient's anxiety although desensitization is frequently used for general anxiety states. With less well-defined anxiety states, where patients may report being in a state of permanent or semi-permanent tension, the behavioural treatment may consist of *relaxation training*. This consists primarily of bringing about deep muscular relaxation and may take a number of forms. Most of these consist of having the patient tense and then relaxing the major muscle groups of the body in a systematic order. For patients with more localized muscle tension, such as in the head and neck muscles, this type of procedure can be focused on the specific problem areas. This type of relaxation training is a commonly used adjunct to systematic desensitization. An alternative approach to muscular relaxation either for general relaxation or for dealing with more localized areas of the body is that of biofeedback training, which is described in more detail later in this chapter.

Punishment schedules have also been used in classical conditioning-based treatments and these consist of attempts to diminish or eliminate some specific type of behaviour. Often referred to collectively as *aversion therapies* these methods typically consist of pairing an unpleasant stimulus, such as a very loud noise or electric shock, together with some aspect of the behaviour to be modified. Quite rightly many of the crude earlier attempts to change such behaviours as sexual 'deviations' have been the subject of frequent and vocal criticism. More recently there have been attempts to avoid some of these problems by using a technique known as *covert sensitization* in which the therapist gives anxiety-provoking remarks while the patient imagines specific aspects of 'maladaptive' behaviour. Although this removes some of the humanitarian objections to aversion or counter-conditioning treatments, it nevertheless raises the whole question of deciding which behaviours are acceptable or unacceptable, which may ultimately be a social rather than a medical decision.

Operant conditioning procedures are increasingly used to provide the basis for various types of treatment both for individual patients and in a group setting. Typically these comprise systems of rewards or punishments for particular types of behaviour in order to initiate or increase them and correspondingly to reduce or abolish other types. Thus for dealing with a patient with a specific neurotic or habit disturbance, the therapist and patient would get together to define which behaviours were to be promoted (target behaviours) and the nature of the reinforcers to achieve this. They would also have decided on a contingency between the reinforcer and the target behaviour. In the case of somebody with an eating problem (too much or too little) this procedure would consist of deciding on how much should be consumed and the appropriate rewards for doing so.

A popular variation on this approach and which is used in many institutional settings is that of the *token economy*. Here target behaviours such as those which facilitate the smooth running of the institution are rewarded with tokens, which are collected and can be traded in for goods or used to earn privileges, such as visits outside. Antisocial or problem behaviour can correspondingly be dealt with by fining a specific number of tokens. Token economies have been used in a range of settings including attempts to 'normalize' the behaviour of institutionalized schizophrenic patients and in building up basic self-maintenance skills, such as dressing and feeding in severely retarded patients. In nearly all these applications, very significant gains are reported in terms of bringing about and maintaining target behaviours.

It has been argued by its proponents that this scheme allows patients to see that their behaviour has specific consequences and provides an understandable system of motivation. Some critics have raised serious doubts about the intentions of many of these therapeutic programmes, saying that they are intended to create acquiescence rather than to bring about real therapeutic change. In reply to this it can be seen that increasing the self-help of retarded patients frees the staff and patients from many time-consuming, menial tasks and allows for a more productive use of the time gained for both groups. Moreover it is also argued that with schizophrenic patients, such approaches can arrest the social deterioration which is often found in long-stay institutions and which was described in Chapter 13.

Another behaviourally oriented approach which is being increasingly used is that of *social skills training*. These are training procedures which are designed to help people who have problems in social functioning. Thus they might be excessively shy or unassertive or they may lack the skills necessary to engage in meaningful social interactions. A brief mention of this type of treatment was given in the section on non-verbal communication in Chapter 10. Training in assertiveness will usually consist of recreating specific social situations and allowing patients to role play repeatedly through these by building up particular desired responses or skills. These can be built up gradually using videotaped feedback to demonstrate the growing skills and may be enhanced by allowing patients to observe and imitate the way in which socially skilled individuals cope with the same situations (i.e. observational learning).

Observational learning or modelling approaches can be used to treat such problems as excessive fearfulness in specific situations as well as for social skills training (Rosenthal and Bandura, 1978). Research has shown that various characteristics of the model have an important effect on whether the new behaviour is learned. If the observer perceives the model in some way similar to himself or herself and if the model's behaviour can be seen to have positive consequences, then the observer is more likely to try out and acquire the modelled behaviour. Also an important distinction has been made between *mastery* and *coping* models, the former demonstrating flawless, skilled behaviour and the latter demonstrating initial fear which is gradually overcome to produce the desired behaviour. Evidence now indicates that coping models are more effective in producing change, particularly if the coping model can provide a spoken commentary on his or her fearful thoughts and the way in which they change as the behavioural change is accomplished. The value of focusing on the thoughts of an individual while he or she attempts to overcome particular fears or develop new social skills leads conveniently on to the next section and the consideration of cognitive approaches to treatment.

● **14.3. Cognitive-behavioural approaches**
    In more recent years there has been a major change of direction in behaviour therapy since there is now much more emphasis on the role of the *individual's cognitions* or thoughts. Whereas behavioural theories focus on specific behaviours and their relation to specific situations, cognitive-behavioural theories are more concerned with the cognitions (i.e. attitudes, ideas and expectations) that people have about themselves and their situations. Thus the basic assumption here is that these cognitions will determine how people feel and behave. Cognitive-behavioural theories are used not only to explain how such clinical problems as anxiety and depression arise but also to define appropriate approaches to treatment.

a. Cognitive theories of emotional disorders
    As was suggested above, cognitive theories are based on the premise that emotions are determined by individuals' ideas or perceptions about themselves and their environment. For example, if someone is either anxious or depressed, then it is argued that this is not necessarily because his or her situation is intrinsically anxiety making or depressing but because the individual perceives it to be particularly threatening or hopeless, which in turn generates the associated emotional state.

    The best known theory here has been proposed by Beck who has provided a framework for understanding the origins of both depression and anxiety (Beck et al., 1979). Beck's way of explaining depression has some similarity to Piaget's descriptions of children's thinking which were presented in Chapter 8. Just as Piaget was able to say how children of different ages made sense of their world in terms of the concepts or schemas which they held, Beck argues that depressed people have their own characteristic schemas or ways of looking at the world. These schemas provide depressed individuals not only with a globally negative view of themselves, of their experiences and of the future but also have direct effects on the processing of new information. Beck maintains that the depressed person will show depression-related biases or errors in various aspects of information processing from attention through to memory and reasoning. For example, experimental studies have shown that depressed mood can cause individuals to selectively attend to or notice depression-related words or stimuli more than neutral or happy stimuli. Similarly people in a depressed state have been found to selectively recall more negative or unhappy memories, as compared with non-depressed people. These biases or distortions in perception and memory not only occur because of the negative schemas underlying information processing but also serve to maintain the depressive state of the individual by providing a selectively gloomy view of the world.

An obvious question here concerns the origins of these negative schemas and whether they are causes or symptoms of depression. Beck maintains that these negative ways of making sense of the world either tend to be brought about by early experiences, such as a death or loss of an important person, or may reflect patterns of thinking learned in childhood from parents or caretakers. They do not necessarily provide a permanently negative way of thinking and responding but may lay dormant for years and predispose individuals to later depression, which is triggered by a specific event such as a loss, illness or rejection. These events activate the negative schemas which then tend to dominate and influence the individual's way of thinking. The ensuing sad or self-critical thoughts and ideas give rise to feelings of sadness and hopelessness. In mild depression the individual has some control of these negative ways of thinking and may be able to use alternative, less gloomy ways of thinking but, with more severe depression, the negative schemas will tend to dominate. When this happens the individual will not have any control over these patterns of thinking and will become preoccupied with negative thoughts, making it difficult or even impossible to carry out other mental functions.

The cognitive explanation of depression provides an interesting and potentially valuable way of describing the way a depressed person thinks and responds. Research in this area is still fairly recent and it seems too early to say whether the cognitive theory satisfactorily explains the cause of depression or merely describes some of the symptoms. However, this approach has given rise to a very fruitful mode of treatment and this is outlined now.

b. Cognitive approaches to treatment

Cognitive therapies are concerned with getting individuals to identify and alter their distorted and dysfunctional beliefs and thoughts. A range of techniques is used but all tend to involve the following tasks for the patients:

    i. Identify and make a record of the negative thoughts.

    ii. Learn to recognize how these thoughts relate to their depressed feelings and behaviour.

    iii. Be able to look at the evidence for and against the distorted thoughts.

    iv. Replace the negative interpretations with more 'reality-based' and less distorted views.

    v. Learn to identify and change the more deep-seated negative beliefs.

Typically the therapist begins by explaining the rationale for this approach. As a first step patients are required to keep a daily record or diary of the negative or dysfunctional thoughts they experience. The therapist then helps the patient to examine and question his or her own cognitions and this skill can then be used in day-to-day situations.

There have been a number of quite carefully controlled evaluation studies of the efficacy of cognitive therapy for depression and the results are promising (*see* Rush and Giles, 1982, for a review). This type of therapy has been found to be as effective and often more effective than other therapies, including antidepressive medication, in the short term. Perhaps more important is the evidence that, in comparison with drug treatment, cognitive therapy has a better long-term outcome, as measured up to 1 year later. This indicates that for some patients the skills of self-questioning and challenging negative thoughts are maintained and may be of use in preventing or minimizing further depressive episodes.

c. Other applications of cognitive approaches to treatment

Cognitive therapy has also been applied to the treatment of anxiety, very much in the same way as outlined above for depression. Again the results show promise when comparisons are made with other treatments, particularly if relatively focused types of anxiety are involved (e.g. anxiety for examinations or public speaking).

The cognitive approach has been used more widely in recent years and, for example, has been applied to the treatment of pain (*see* Chapter 1), of hyperactive children and people with various sorts of eating disorder. The range of applications has been outlined by Kendall and Hollon (1979) and indicates the extent to which cognitive theories and approaches have become popular. The rapid development of cognitive therapies provides further evidence of the recognition that an adequate understanding of human behaviour needs to be based on the thoughts, perceptions and beliefs which the individual holds.

●   **14.4. Biofeedback**

Biofeedback involves the use of electronic instruments to monitor physiological processes within the body and feed this information back to the individual so that change in a particular direction may be brought about. The processes which are monitored are ones which the individual is not usually aware of and hence are not normally under conscious control. Typically these are under the control of the autonomic nervous system and are therefore subject to continuous and uncontrolled change in most individuals. Although there is good evidence that mystics and yogis are able to control autonomic functions quite dramatically, for most people this is clearly not the case.

The principle underlying biofeedback is a novel yet very simple one. Traditionally when physiological processes, such as cardiovascular activity, are monitored in the medical context, the information is presented to the health professional who is involved in the care of the patient. The novel twist in biofeedback is that this information is not fed back to the 'experts' but to the patient. Thus a patient with tension headache, due to abnormal levels of tension or contraction in the frontalis or occipitalis muscles, only normally knows that the front or back of the head hurts. With biofeedback, the patient can know accurately the level of activity at any time while it is being monitored in these muscles. This information is fed back to the patient in the form of an analogue signal, which is very commonly an auditory or visual signal. Auditory signals may be either clicks or tones and increases or decreases in activity can be indicated by changes in the frequency or intensity of the signal. Common visual signals are dials or lights.

At this point the reader might be slightly bemused by the contention that feeding back this type of information to patients might actually be of some therapeutic use. At a common-sense level it might be expected that patients would get worse rather than better when they are able to 'see' their own abnormal levels of physiological activation. When you are not feeling too well and other people comment on this, this tends to make you feel even worse. So, how does biofeedback produce a therapeutic gain?

The short answer to this is that the clinical importance of biofeedback stems from evidence showing that if appropriate feedback signals are used then individuals are able to gain partial conscious control over a range of autonomic functions and modify the level of activity to reduce their potential harmfulness. In order to understand this more clearly a brief introduction to the general notion of feedback is followed by a description of some specific biofeedback applications.

a. Feedback

The notion of feedback was brought into specific use by Weiner (1948) who defined it as 'a method of controlling a system by reinserting into it the results of its past performance'. It is seen most clearly in the form of the feedback loop, which is shown in a simplified form in *Fig.* 22.

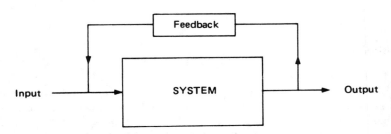

Fig. 22. The feedback loop.

Obviously biofeedback is a special case of this since the system is a biological one for which external feedback is not normally available and thus the feedback is artificial using electrical measuring instruments.

Feedback is an extremely important concept in understanding not only physiological and psychological processes but also many complex man-made systems and is the basis of the science of cybernetics. In considering the role of feedback in controlling our own behaviour, two main types can be distinguished:

i. Internal (or 'intrinsic')

This is information generated by the receptors within the body (i.e. within muscles, tendons, joints, etc.) and which provides feedback information about the relative position, state of tension and degree of movement of various parts of the body. This information is vital in order to sustain smooth coordinated movements and is therefore a natural consequence of any movement since it arises from any motor activity and is not dependent on environmental cues. Certain neurological disorders can disrupt intrinsic feedback by damaging the pathways which carry this information.

ii. External (or 'extrinsic')

External feedback is generated by comparing discrepancies between already executed movements and the desired 'goal' state.

External feedback can be either discrete or continuous depending on the type of behaviour and context it occurs in. Typically discrete feedback is derived from situations where an individual makes successive attempts to meet some defined criterion of performance, receives 'error-information' after each attempt and then tries to use this information to modify the subsequent attempt. A simple example would be that of firing a mortar gun at a fixed target, where the discrepancy between where the mortar shell has landed and the target is used as information to adjust the angle and direction of the mortar. A more familiar and less precise example is that of darts, when a player has to throw at a specific part of the board. In both cases the individual is using a specific (discrete) piece of information as feedback.

In contrast, many tasks are continuous in that information is being fed back to the individual all the time and subsequent performance will be influenced by all this information. Firing a gun at a continuously moving target and driving a car are two situations where external information is continuously sampled and used to determine what will happen next.

Feedback therefore plays a critical role in regulating both internal and external processes. External feedback provides the individual with important information in the form of 'error messages', which help to make performance smooth and accurate. Moreover if this 'error-information' can be used productively (i.e. in reducing and finally eliminating the discrepancy between current and target performance), then it almost always has a motivating function as well. If the individual is able to see performance improving, this provides a strong motivation to continue but if no such information is available or if no improvement occurs then the opposite will be likely. This point emphasizes the importance of not only making feedback clear but also making it realistic to the individual in the sense that he or she is able to make use of the information to move towards the goal state. This latter point is an important consideration in biofeedback, where it has been shown that it is often necessary to progress via a series of small changes in order to attain a particular overall level of change.

b. Applications of biofeedback

A number of reviewers of biofeedback have commented that biofeedback is beginning to resemble some of the wondrous treatments of former times, which were claimed to be panaceas for a range of ills. This is slightly unfair since biofeedback does not comprise one specific procedure but a therapeutic approach, which has many quite different applications. Also each application may utilize quite different instrumentation to monitor the functions which are to be 'normalized'.

In terms of the earlier discussion about general aspects of feedback, it can be readily seen that biofeedback involves the use of external feedback about physiological information, which is normally only subject to internal feedback. Most biofeedback equipment provides the individual with continuous feedback information and efforts should always be made to ensure that target levels are realistic, in the sense which was discussed earlier. Bearing all these considerations in mind, an attempt is now made to outline and evaluate some of the more common biofeedback applications. This outline is not intended to be an exhaustive account of all the applications but to give some idea of the range.

i. Electromyographic (EMG) feedback

The basic principle underlying EMG feedback is that electrodes are attached to chosen muscle groups to detect the firing rates of specific motor neurons. This information is then fed back as either a sound or visual signal to indicate to the person either the actual rate of firing or to provide 'error information'. In the latter situation the feedback signal indicates how close the present level of muscle activity is to some desired state. EMG feedback studies with non-patient volunteers have provided reasonable evidence that a degree of control can be obtained over individual motor units and over whole muscle groups.

The clinical studies have approached a diverse range of clinical problems. One of the earliest approaches involves the use of EMG feedback for direct muscle retraining in patients with diminished or absent muscle activity as the result of strokes, spinal damage or other crippling lesions. A number of studies with such patients have shown considerable gains in muscle activity as the result of including biofeedback as part of therapy (Basmajian and Hatch, 1979). Although it is not usually possible to disentangle the particular contribution of biofeedback, the evidence is still quite heartening and it is significant that physiotherapists are showing an increased interest in the use of biofeedback for work with this type of patient.

In contrast, EMG feedback can also be used effectively to diminish excessive muscle activity such as that occurring in spasmodic torticollis, dystonia and facial spasms. The reduction of frontalis muscle activity is also used to modify tension headaches associated with abnormal levels of frontalis activity.

ii. Cardiovascular feedback

Most of the biofeedback work with the cardiovascular system has been in the control of various cardiac dysrhythmias. Here the patient's heart rate is monitored and feedback is based on an attempt to normalize this in some way, usually to minimize a particular dysrhythmia. A number of studies have investigated patients with premature ventricular contraction who were taught to manipulate their heart rate using biofeedback. Typically these patients are required to increase or decrease heart rate to demonstrate that control can be achieved and then they are required to hold their heart rate steady at a specified level. Generally these studies have revealed significant therapeutic changes but these have been variable. Moreover it is still not entirely clear how well these changes can transfer from the laboratory to the outside world and how persisting these changes are.

There have also been attempts to use biofeedback for the control of hypertension by training patients to reduce their blood pressure. Monitoring blood pressure and supplying usable feedback are quite difficult but some quite sophisticated techniques have emerged in recent years. The evidence from these studies is that normotensives (i.e. people without hypertension) can be systematically trained to increase or decrease blood pressure using biofeedback. Clinical studies also indicate that patients with high blood pressure can be trained to produce reductions in systolic pressure of about 10 per cent. However, it still remains to demonstrate that biofeedback offers anything more than can be achieved by the sort of relaxation procedures described in the previous section.

iii. EEG feedback

In Chapter 4 a brief description was given of the EEG as a method for monitoring brain wave activity. If this information is fed back to an individual, it has been found that it is possible to increase or decrease the occurrence of certain brain wave frequencies. A great deal of commercial effort has been put into developing biofeedback techniques for so-called 'alpha training', which involves biofeedback training for increasing the amount of alpha rhythm in the EEG. It will be recalled from Chapter 4 that alpha waves are present when individuals are in a state of relaxation and so alpha training constitutes a relaxation training procedure. Despite all the publicity given to this approach, it is still really not clear whether producing an abundance of alpha waves offers any advantage to the individual. Moreover it would appear that there are other less cumbersome techniques for relaxation training.

A more specific application of EEG biofeedback has been used with epileptic patients (Sterman, 1973). This has involved training epileptic patients to increase the amount of sensorimotor rhythm found in the EEG. This rhythm is one in the range 12–14 Hz, found over the sensorimotor cortex and has been found to counteract epileptic fits in some way. It is not clear how this comes about but training epileptics to produce this and other rhythms can have beneficial effects on epilepsy. The benefits are seen in terms of reducing both the frequency and severity of epileptic fits.

From this limited account of biofeedback it can be seen that it offers a novel and interesting approach to the treatment of many clinical problems. In particular it seems to be dealing with a number of physiological problems which may be thought of as stress related. One particularly interesting aspect of biofeedback is that the patient plays a very active role in the therapeutic process and is primarily responsible for bringing about the changes. At present there is considerable debate as to the effectiveness and range of application of biofeedback techniques. It is still difficult to establish the extent to which reported changes are due specifically to biofeedback or result from the various placebo effects outlined earlier in this chapter. An increasing number of physiological processes have been found to be amenable to biofeedback control and it remains to see how extensive and successful these will be.

● **14.5. Psychotherapy**

One of the most established but still most debated psychological treatments is that of psychotherapy, a range of procedures which primarily involve the communication and relationship between patient and therapist. This can take many forms depending on the therapist's theoretical orientation, the patient's problems and the aims of treatment. Despite the great range of approaches which are described under the general heading of psychotherapy, perhaps the most universal characteristic is that all make use of the interpersonal situation in which the therapist communicates to the patient that he or she understands, respects and wants to help.

a. Psychotherapeutic procedures

One very broad and misleadingly simple classification of psychotherapeutic procedures can be made into those which are essentially supportive in aim and those which seek to obtain a much deeper understanding of the patient's past and present in order to bring about therapeutic change. This subdivision is misleading because it is far from a mutually exclusive one. Interpretive psychotherapies such as psychoanalysis may be very supportive for the patient and correspondingly a supportive relationship may help to bring about insights and change on the patient's part. However, in this brief account this simple distinction is retained and serves to give some idea of the range of approaches which use talk as the basis of treatment.

i. Supportive psychotherapy

The goals of supportive therapy are fairly limited since it is primarily intended to offer support during a difficult period. In seeing a therapist at regular intervals during such a time, the patient may be able to talk through fears and worries and through this find a way of handling the difficulties. This type of therapy is basically palliative and primarily intended to relieve distress. In some respects supportive help of this type acts as a sort of verbal analgesic since it offers a way of getting through a difficult time but this is a rather negative and limited picture. By providing the patient with regular contact with an accepting authority figure and the opportunity to discuss problems, more positive changes may occur. Some changes may include the restoration or strengthening of coping behaviours which may have been impaired by the stressful situation.

In supportive therapy the role of the therapist is basically that of the accepting empathic listener, encouraging the patient to talk, to express emotions and to help in dealing with guilt, shame or anxiety. Relatively little training may be necessary since the emphasis is more on listening than on skilful guidance or treatment. This may make it easy to understand the success of organizations, such as the Samaritans, who choose appropriate lay people to act as listeners.

Supportive treatment is of particular value when acute stress gives rise to intense worry or anxiety. It tends to be most effective when the patient's personality is basically sound and the stress situation is relatively short-lived. The value of such an approach is also increasingly recognized as part of the treatment of chronic physical illness and in the care of the dying patient. Indeed many general practitioners would now argue that a listening, supportive role is one of their primary functions, as is discussed below.

ii. Interpretive psychotherapy

It is much more difficult to summarize the aims and procedures associated with the more interpretive methods of psychotherapy. These are often collectively referred to as 'insight' or 'reconstructive' therapies since they are concerned with giving the patient increased self-understanding and bringing about changes in attitudes and emotional responses. The best known example here is that of psychoanalysis, which was originally developed by Freud and others towards the end of the last century. Starting from the observation that symptoms could be relieved or removed if earlier painful memories were relived under hypnosis, psychoanalysis developed as a method for uncovering these early memories. Hypnosis was soon discarded in favour of 'free association' in which the patient is required to say whatever comes to mind. In doing this, definite resistances to the return of some memories were noticed and these are pursued since they are deemed to be of importance in understanding the patient's personality and problems.

The main concern of psychoanalysis is the uncovering and working through of childhood memories, which have been repressed and as a result are considered to have interfered with full personality development. Since the gradual integration of this repressed information into the total personality structure is central to psychoanalysis, an important part of the analytical process is concerned with preparing the patient to deal with the information which is unearthed by free association. This can be a very slow and gradual process in which the patient learns how to introspect and to be sensitive to his or her inner thoughts in order to be able to externalize them. There is seldom a direct and logical sequence involved in psychoanalysis since the process is more like one of slowly finding and putting together the pieces of a complicated jigsaw puzzle.

Full psychoanalysis can be a long and sometimes never-ending procedure since there is no clearly defined end-point. As a result inevitably it involves a very large number of meetings between the patient and therapist. Although the therapist assumes a 'neutral' position throughout, a relationship between patient and therapist develops and becomes a central part of treatment. Typically patients will generate intense feelings towards the therapist and these are taken to reflect feelings experienced in childhood, particularly towards their parents. Since these older feelings are stirred up by the psychoanalysis and are now transferred to the therapist, this part of psychoanalysis is usually referred to as the 'transference'.

Originally Freud considered that the transference might hinder the therapeutic process but came to realize that commenting on and interpreting these feelings formed a central part of treatment. Transference turns out to be more complicated than the impression given by this brief description but it is consistent with the general aim of uncovering childhood emotions. Freud's own description provides a clear summary of transference:

> What are transferences? They are new editions or facsimiles of the impulses and fantasies which are aroused and made conscious during the progress of analysis ... a whole series of psychological experiences are revived, not as belonging to the past, but as applying to the person of the physician at the present moment.

Typically this type of psychoanalysis involves frequent meetings between patient and therapist over a long period of time, which can often run into years. It is terminated when patient and therapist feel that a full reintegration of the patient's personality has been achieved or when it is felt that no more progress can be made. There are now many variations on this basic theme with a range of different approaches and underlying theories. More recent evaluations have pointed out the impracticalities associated with such a long and intensive procedure with the result that shorter and more defined treatments have emerged. These are sometimes referred to as psychoanalytic psychotherapies since they borrow from psychoanalytic concepts but are more concerned with current conflicts than with repressed childhood memories. Other more recent developments in psychotherapy include Gestalt therapy, rational–emotive therapy and primal therapy.

b. How does psychotherapy work?

The strange thing about the various psychotherapies is that no one really knows how they work. Different theories have been offered but there is very little in the way of conclusive evidence to substantiate any of these. Such is this uncertainty that some of the stronger critics of psychotherapy, particularly of psychoanalytic approaches, have dismissed the whole process as worthless (Rachman, 1971). They have argued that very many of the problems which are claimed to have been resolved by psychotherapy would have disappeared merely because a certain amount of time had passed and that spontaneous remission occurs with many neurotic problems. They also argue that these treatments are too time-consuming and too ill-defined to be of any widespread value.

While such criticisms should be heeded and have forced a close examination of the aims and modes of action in psychotherapy, there would appear to be little doubt that talk is an important component of treatment for many patients. Indeed evaluative studies of behaviour therapy also indicate that the quality of the patient–therapist interaction is an important determinant of the therapeutic outcome. Thus more recent research in this area has ceased to be primarily concerned with the question of whether psychotherapy works but has looked more directly at what is meant by improvement and how this is affected by patient, therapist and technique variables.

Evaluating improvement or success in psychotherapy will obviously depend on the criteria which are used to assess this as well as on the aim of the treatment. For example, in situations where support is given during a difficult time, a successful outcome may consist of minimizing emotional distress or returning the patient to a previously achieved status quo. In contrast, more interpretive methods seek to bring about changes in self-understanding, personality integration and social adaptation. At a more functional level, symptom relief can be used as a simple operational criterion. From the research on this topic it would appear that change along three dimensions, namely a sense of wellbeing, social functioning and personality integration, are primary considerations of most psychotherapeutic methods. Whether these changes occur separately or in conjunction is not really known but what is clear is that they can be significantly affected by characteristics of both the patient and therapist as well as by the interaction between them.

It is paradoxical and rather sad to note that such an intensive treatment as psychotherapy appears to be most helpful for the least disturbed types of patients. A number of studies have shown that less maladjusted patients or those with shorter psychiatric histories were most likely to improve. By and large it is those patients with milder neurotic disturbances rather than the more violent or deeply disturbed ones who appear to get most benefit. One reason advanced for this is that these patients have the sufficient psychological resources necessary to sustain a long and possibly painful relationship and to tolerate and incorporate all the insights which can result. This is obviously a limiting factor in the applicability of much psychotherapy. Added to this there is also evidence that successful outcome depends to some degree on the patients' motivation in treatment and their willingness to collaborate in the therapeutic process.

The picture that arises from studies of patient characteristics associated with successful outcome is something akin to the inverse care law in that the best results appear to be found with the least needy. As a result of such studies it has been suggested that in order to benefit from psychotherapy, the patient has to be a 'y.a.v.i.s.' person in that it is optimal to be young, attractive, verbal, intelligent and successful. Some cynics have concluded that it is only with such patients that therapists are able to sustain a long and intimate therapeutic relationship. Support for this conclusion has come from recent studies claiming that these patient characteristics are not intrinsically related to successful outcome but reflect the therapist's lack of competence and comfort in dealing with individuals who differ in race or social class from themselves. Indeed there is now good evidence that lower social class patients can benefit greatly if therapists are able to be congruent with patients' personal styles and expectations, which rather contravenes older notions that only middle-class patients are able to benefit from psychotherapy.

Many people now believe that the personality and the behaviour of the therapist are of prime importance in psychotherapy. Although earlier claims that it is only necessary for the therapist to be warm, empathic and genuine have been shown to be rather simplistic, there does appear to be good evidence that personal qualities of the therapist can and do exert a significant influence on the course of therapy. Whether this is because patients can only unburden themselves to people perceived as 'good therapists' or because patients actually identify with the desirable aspects of the therapist's personality is not really clear and may well depend on the type of therapy being pursued. There is also evidence that certain therapist personalities may be more or less successful with different psychiatric problems, particularly when the treatment of schizophrenic and neurotic patients is compared (Razin, 1971).

Perhaps more important than characteristics of patients or therapists which influence therapeutic outcome is the nature of the interaction between the two parties. This can also give some indication as to how psychotherapy might be working. Generally it is those patients who like their therapist who stay in treatment longer and derive more success. Similarly where there is good rapport and open communication, therapeutic outcome is also found to be better but sessions where the therapist is anxious are likely to be stressful for the patient. In common with some of the conclusions reached in Chapter 10 on doctor–patient communication, studies on therapist–patient interaction also show the importance of the patients' own feelings that there is an interest in their problems and that these are fully understood.

Findings of this type add weight to the contention that the primary value of psychotherapy is in providing an appropriate forum for the patient to divulge and talk through problems. It has even been argued that therapy can give some patients the first experience of a real trusting relationship and that this is in itself most beneficial. Hence it would appear to be the supportive elements of psychotherapy which may be of most value for most patients. There is increasing evidence that for many patients supportive therapy may be as valuable and as enduring as more interpretive, psychoanalytic approaches (Gomes-Schwartz et al., 1978). Obviously there are some dramatic examples where interpretive techniques have led to unique and major improvements but these examples appear to be the exception rather than the rule. It still remains to be conclusively demonstrated that what the therapist does has a significant impact over and above the effects of a supportive relationship. Despite these reservations, the value of such a relationship in resolving psychological difficulties or in getting through a difficult time, such as a severe illness, should not be understated. As we have remarked earlier, the best placebo available in medicine is often the doctor.

● 14.6. Counselling: a more general approach to helping

In psychotherapy, the therapist is seen very much as the expert either in interpreting the clients' past or in supporting them through a difficult time. A related but different approach is that of counselling, in which patients or clients are helped to help themselves. Thus the role of the counsellor is to allow the individuals to understand their situation more clearly and to facilitate them in making and taking their own choices for change.

There are many types of counselling and the boundary between counselling and psychotherapy is not very well defined. In this section a definition of counselling is presented and this will be followed by outlining one particular approach which has been found to be valuable. Finally, an attempt is made to look at the use of counselling skills in the health setting.

a. What is counselling?

Counselling has been defined quite simply as 'helping people to help themselves'. Another definition provides a little more detail about some of the processes involved since it describes counselling as 'a relationship through which a person who needs help is enabled to change in ways that the person finds helpful'. There are a number of key words in this definition. First, there is the emphasis on the relationship, since it has been shown that people can be helped best when an accepting and trusting relationship is achieved. As we see below, the early part of counselling is concerned with allowing clients to talk openly about what is causing them concern. It is clearly important that the counsellor establishes a good relationship in order for the client to feel able to 'open up'. There is also the emphasis on someone being enabled to change rather than being treated and on the client's determination of the type of change which should take place.

Counselling is often confused with other sorts of interventions, including ones where people are told what to do or how to view their own situation more 'accurately'. However, the emphasis should be on providing the right sort of relationship to allow people to talk about their problems, make sense of them and identify ways of bringing about change. Although this can be done in groups, it most commonly takes place in a one-to-one setting.

b. A three-stage model of counselling

One of the common difficulties which 'helpers' encounter when they start to counsel someone is that of feeling a bit lost and never quite knowing what interventions work best or why they work well. In recent years a number of psychologists have attempted to put together a structured approach to counselling which can be learned and used in a variety of settings. One approach which is commonly used has been developed by Egan (1982) and this builds on the collected writing and research on counselling and helping. Egan has proposed that there are three broad stages through which counselling should progress and these are now briefly outlined.

Stage I: Exploration

At this early stage the counsellor aims to establish a rapport and create a good relationship so that the client can divulge and explore his or her feelings. The counsellor needs to be attentive, both physically (i.e. good eye-contact, etc.) and psychologically (i.e. listening carefully to what the client is trying to say). Many of the guidelines for opening the interview which were described in Chapter 10 are equally applicable here, particularly the use of open-ended questions, reflections, paraphrases and summaries. However, it is also important to be concrete in the sense of asking clients exactly what they mean when they describe their feelings and reactions. In this way the counsellor, by showing empathy and respect, should be able to allow the client to talk openly and freely in order to provide a clear picture of the problem and to express and share feelings.

Stage II: Understanding

Once the difficulties or problems have been described, it is then necessary for the client to understand why they have occurred by piecing together and making sense of all the data that have emerged in the first stage. Here the task of the counsellor is to get the client to be able to stand back and look at the problem in order to develop more objective perspectives and a better self-understanding. Having got to this point the client should then be able to see the need for change and what direction this should take. The role of the counsellor in this stage is more active than in the first stage and will involve confronting clients and getting them to look critically at the situation and themselves. This can be done in many ways but it is important to tread fairly carefully at first because this is much more demanding for the client than the activities involved in the earlier stage of counselling. Getting clients to look critically at themselves is an important part of the counselling process and will work best if it occurs within the context of a good relationship between counsellor and client.

Stage III: Taking action

Once the client can understand how and why the problems have occurred, the directions for change should then become more apparent. The functions of the counsellor at this stage will be to collaborate in defining realistic (i.e. manageable) goals and to help in implementing change. Part of this will involve the task of agreeing goals and working out how these will be achieved. In doing this it will be necessary to envisage and think through possible difficulties and to ensure that the agreed goals maximize the resources which the client has and minimize possible sources of failure. While the client is in the process of attempting to meet these goals by making changes, it is also vital that the counsellor continues to offer support and challenge.

This stage-by-stage account of counselling makes it sound like a simple unidirectional process but it is intended as a very brief outline rather than a complete description. In reality counselling may proceed in a much less smoothly organized way and may not necessarily involve all the stages outlined above. For example, many patients may find stage I counselling quite sufficient since they find that, having had a chance to ventilate their problems and associated feelings, they will then be able to complete the next two stages on their own. Thus all they need is an opportunity to articulate their concerns and they then have sufficient insight and resources to take effective action. Alternatively someone might get through to stage III and then experience major problems in trying to change his or her situation. The process of taking action might therefore reveal further major difficulties which, in turn, will need to be discussed and dealt with in the process of counselling. Counselling may move between the different stages or phases in many different ways according to the type of problem and the personal circumstances of the person needing help. The value of the 'stages' approach is that it provides a map or guide for the counsellor to know where any counselling relationship has got to and the direction it needs to take.

c. Applications of counselling in clinical practice

It is being increasingly recognized that the component skills involved in counselling are valuable in most areas of clinical work with patients. Listening and attending are fundamental skills in eliciting a history and the addition of warmth and empathy provides a very positive environment for the patient to discuss fears or talk about other problems. There are obviously more specific areas of clinical work where counselling skills are particularly valuable. These include work with dying and chronically sick patients, with people who are bereaved, with parents of very ill or handicapped children and with those who are faced with having to adjust to, or cope with, illness or disability. Some specific types of counselling have been developed for working with particular groups of patients or in particular settings but common to all of these are the general principles outlined earlier. It is also being recognized that many areas of work in the health professions are stressful for those concerned and it is interesting to note that the use of counselling skills and, in some cases, of staff counsellors has been recommended as an essential part of the support needed for health professionals.

One example of these developments has been in general practice and it is noteworthy that the value of counselling was discussed in a fairly recent editorial in the *Journal of the Royal College of General Practitioners* (Murgatroyd, 1983). In general practice, many people present with problems which cannot readily be solved by conventional medical approaches. Some of these will be personal, emotional or social problems while others may consist of chronic physical problems for which no 'cure' is available. Thus when these patients present to the general practitioner it may well be because they are unable to cope with their situation and are directly or indirectly requesting help. The use of counselling can provide a very helpful form of intervention if patients are enabled to express emotion, develop fresh perspectives and take effective action either in terms of changing the way in which they respond or by allowing them to build up new ways of coping.

A frequent objection to this sort of development in general practice has been that there is insufficient time to provide counselling or that it is not really a part of the doctor's job to do so. What exactly constitutes the doctor's job is an open question and one which individual doctors will interpret differently. However, it is often to the doctor that emotional and social problems are first brought and the doctor is therefore in an ideal situation to respond to these. Time is undeniably a problem but counselling does not have to be a long drawn-out process. Basic counselling skills can be incorporated into routine consultations and it is possible to produce beneficial outcomes from a relatively brief and structured use of counselling provided that the attitude and behaviour of the doctor are appropriate (i.e. attentive, empathic, facilitative, etc.). Another important consideration is that although this type of intervention may be initially more costly in terms of time, there is evidence that it may ultimately be more economical since there can be a decreased use of prescriptions and a reduction in further attendances (Hughes, 1983).

Finally, the increasing interest and use of counselling in clinical work raise a more a general issue which is central to this book. The definition of counselling offered here acknowledges patients as experts in terms of their own lives and situations and consequently views the role of the counsellor as one of a facilitator who provides an environment and a relationship from which positive changes can be made. This changing emphasis in the roles of doctor and patient is important for two reasons. For doctors it changes the nature of their task from simply detecting symptoms and providing solutions to one of allowing patients to talk and divulge their own concerns and needs. In this context it is interesting to note that in a recent textbook on the consultation in general practice, the authors maintain that the doctor should be able to achieve a shared understanding of the problems with patients and involve them in an appropriate choice of action (Pendleton et al., 1984). Correspondingly, for patients, becoming a more active participant in their own health care puts them in a situation where they will be able to define their own needs and will have a responsibility for their own treatment.

This theme provides an appropriate finale for this book since it relates to many issues which have been raised in earlier chapters, including the importance of doctor–patient communication in the provision of health care and of psychosocial factors in illness and treatment. Above all, these issues are central to the function of this textbook and in any course which relates psychology to medicine. The function of this book has been to provide a broader perspective or framework for understanding health and disease and to emphasize the role of human behaviour in this. It is hoped that the book has achieved this and, in doing so, has generated a willingness to develop a fuller understanding and to incorporate this into clinical practice.

● Recommended reading

Brown J. and Pedder J. (1979) *Introduction to Psychotherapy*. London, Tavistock.
Kanfer F. H. and Goldstein A. P. (1986) *Helping People Change*, 3rd ed. New York, Pergamon.
Murgatroyd S. (1985) *Counselling and Helping*. London, BPS/Methuen.
Williams J. M. G. (1984) *The Psychological Treatment of Depression*. London, Croom Helm.

Bibliography

Acroyd C., Humphrey N. K. and Warrington E. K. (1974) Lasting effects of early blindness: a case study. *Q. J. Exp. Psychol.* **26** (1), 114–124.

Adamowicz J. K. (1976) Visual short-term memory and ageing. *J. Gerontol.* **31**, 39–46.

Ader R. and Cohen N. (1981) Conditioned immunopharmacologic response. In: Ader R. (ed.), *Psychoneuroimmunology*. New York, Academic Press.

Anisman H. and Sklar L. S. (1984) Psychological insults and pathology: contribution of neurochemical, hormonal and immunological mechanisms. In: Steptoe A. and Mathews A. (ed.) *Health Care and Human Behaviour*. London, Academic Press.

Baddeley A. D. (1976) *The Psychology of Memory*. New York, Harper & Row.

Baddeley A. D. (1978) The trouble with levels: a re-examination of Craik and Lockhart's framework for memory research. *Psychol. Rev.* **85**, 139–152.

Baddeley A. D. (1983) Working memory. *Phil. Trans. R. Soc. Lond.* **B302**, 311–324.

Banks M. H. and Jackson P. R. (1982) Unemployment and risk of minor psychiatric disorder in young people: cross sectional and longitudinal evidence. *Psychol. Med.* **12**, 789–798.

Banks M. H., Beresford S. A. and Morrell D. C. (1975) Factors influencing the demand for primary medical care in women aged 20–44 years. *Int. J. Epidemiol.* **43** (3), 189–195.

Barlow S. M. and Sullivan F. (1976) Behavioural teratology. In: Berry C. L. and Poswillo D. E. (ed.) *Teratology: Trends and Applications*. Berlin, Springer-Verlag.

Basmajian J. V. and Hatch J. P. (1979) Biofeedback and modification of skeletal muscular dysfunctions. In: Gatchel R. J. and Price K. P. (ed.) *Clinical Applications of Biofeedback: Appraisal and Status*. New York, Pergamon.

Baumrind D. (1971) Current patterns of parental authority. *Dev. Psychol. Monogr.* **1**, 1–103.

Beck A. T., Rush A. J., Shaw B. F. et al. (1979) *Cognitive Therapy of Depression*. New York, Wiley.

Beecher H. R. (1959) *Measurement of Subjective Responses*. Oxford, Oxford University Press.

Blank M. and Solomon F. A. (1968) A tutorial language program to develop abstract thinking in socially disadvantaged preschool children. *Child Dev.* **39** (2), 379–389.

Blundell J. (1975) *Physiological Psychology*. London, Methuen.

Bolles R. C. and Fanselow M. S. (1982) Endorphins and behaviour. *Ann. Rev. Psychol.* **33**, 87–101.

Bond M. R. and Pearson L. B. (1969) Psychological aspects of pain in women with advanced carcinoma of the cervix. *J. Psychosom. Res.* **13**, 13–19.

Bower T. G. R. (1977) *A Primer of Infant Development*. San Francisco, Freeman.

Bower T. G. R. (1979) *Human Development*. San Francisco, Freeman.

Bowlby J. (1951) *Maternal Care and Mental Health*. Geneva, WHO.

Boyle C. M. (1970) Differences between patients' and doctors' interpretations of some common medical terms. *Br. Med. J.* **2**, 286–289.

Brindley G. S. and Lewin W. S. (1968) The sensations produced by electrical stimulation of the visual cortex. *J. Physiol.* **196**, 479–493.

British Medical Journal (1970) Editorial: Placebo effects. May, 437.

Brown G. W. (1976) Social causes of disease. In: Tuckett D. (ed.) *An Introduction to Medical Sociology*. London, Tavistock.

Burish J. G. and Bradley L. A. (ed.) (1983) *Coping with Chronic Disease*. New York, Academic Press.

Burt C. (1966) The genetic determination of differences in intelligence: a study of monozygotic twins reared together and apart. *Br. J. Psychol.* **57**, 137–153.

Butterworth G. (1978) Thought and things: Piaget's theory. In: Burton A. and Radford J. (ed.) *Thinking in Perspective*. London, Methuen.

Byrne P. S. and Long B. (1976) *Doctors Talking to Patients*. London, HMSO.

Carruthers M. (1969) Aggression and atheroma. *Lancet* **2**, 1170.

Central Statistical Office (1986) *Social Trends No. 16*. London, HMSO.

Claridge G. (1972) *Drugs and Human Behaviour*. Harmondsworth, Penguin.

Cohen F. (1979) Personality, stress and the development of physical illness. In: Stone G. C., Cohen F. and Adler N. E. (ed.) *Health Psychology*. San Francisco, Jossey-Bass.

Coltheart M. (1978) Lexical access in simple reading tasks. In: Underwood G. (ed.) *Strategies of Information Processing*. London, Academic Press.

Comer R. J. and Piliavin J. A. (1972) The effects of physical deviance on face-to-face interaction: the other side. *J. Pers. Soc. Psychol.* **23** (1), 33–39.

Conrad R. (1979) *The Deaf School Child: Language and Cognitive Function*. London, Harper & Row.

Cooper J. (1976) Deafness and psychiatric illness. *Br. J. Psychiatry* **129**, 216–226.

Cox T. (1978) *Stress*. London, Macmillan.

Craig T. K. J. and Brown G. W. (1984) Life events, meaning and physical illness: a review. In Steptoe A. and Mathews A. (ed.) *Health Care and Human Behaviour*. London, Academic Press.

Craik F. I. M. and Lockhart R. S. (1972) Levels of processing: a framework for memory research. *J. Verb. Learn. Verb. Behav.* **11**, 671–684.

Curtiss S. (1977) *Genie: A Psycholinguistic Study of a Modern-day 'Wild Child'*. New York, Academic Press.

Dobbing J. and Smart J. L. (1974) Vulnerability of developing brain and behaviour. *Br. Med. Bull.* **30**, 164–168.

Egan G. (1982) *The Skilled Helper*, 2nd ed. Monteray, Cal. Brooks/Cole.

Ekman P. and Friesen W. V. (1977) Non-verbal behaviour. In: Ostwald P. F. (ed.) *Communication and Social Interaction*. New York, Grune & Stratton.

Fletcher C. M. (1973) *Communication in Medicine*. London, Nuffield Provincial Hospitals Trust.

Foerster K. (1984) Supportive psychotherapy combined with autogenous training in acute leukaemic patients under isolation therapy. *Psychother. Psychosom.* **41**, 100–105.

Folkard S., Glynn C. J. and Lloyd J. W. (1976) Diurnal variation and individual differences in perception of intractable pain. *J. Psychosom. Res.* **20**, 289–301.

Frankenhaeuser M. (1975) Sympathetic-adrenomedullary activity, behaviour and the psychosocial environment. In: Venables P. H. and Christie M. J. (ed.) *Research in Psychophysiology*. London, Wiley.

Friedman M. and Rosenman R. (1974) *Type A Behaviour and Your Heart*. New York, Knopf.

Friedman M., Thoresen C. E., Gill J. J. et al. (1984) Alteration of Type A behaviour and reduction in cardiac reoccurrence in post-myocardial infarction patients. *Am. Heart J.* **108**, 237–248.

Frisby J. P. (1979) *Seeing*. Oxford, Oxford University Press.

Frith C. D. (1979) Consciousness, information processing and schizophrenia. *Br. J. Psychiatry* **134**, 225–235.

Furth H. (1973) *Deafness and Learning: A Psychosocial Approach*. Belmont, Wadsworth.

Gelman R. (1979) Preschool thought. *Am. J. Psychol.* **35** (10), 900–905.

Geschwind N. (1979) Specializations of the human brain. *Sci. Am.* **241** (3), 180–201.

Glickman L. (1977) The organic brain syndromes. In: Simons R. C. and Pardes H. (ed.) *Understanding Human Behaviour in Health and Illness.* Baltimore, Williams & Wilkins.

Goffman E. (1964) *Stigma: Notes on the Management of Spoiled Identity.* Harmondsworth, Penguin.

Goffman E. (1968) *Asylums.* Harmondsworth, Penguin.

Gomes-Schwartz B., Hadley S. W. and Strupp H. H. (1978) Individual psychotherapy and behaviour therapy. *Ann. Rev. Psychol.* **29**, 435–471.

Gordon A. M. (1976) The effect of treatment environment. *J. Psychosom. Res.* **20**, 363–366.

Gottesman I. I. (1968) Biogenetics of race and class. In: Deutch M., Katz I. and Jensen A. R. (ed.) *Social Class, Race and Psychological Development.* New York, Rinehart & Winston.

Greer S. (1974) Psychological aspects: delay in the treatment of breast cancer. *Proc. R. Soc. Med.* **67**, 470–473.

Groen G. J. and Patel V. L. (1985) Medical problem-solving: some questionable assumptions. *Med. Educ.* **19**, 95–100.

Gross C. G., Rocha-Miranda C. E. and Bender D. B. (1972) Visual properties of neurons in inferotemporal cortex of the macaque. *J. Neurophysiol.* **35**, 96–111.

Hackett T. P., Cassem N. H. and Wishnie H. A. (1968) The Coronary Care Unit. An appraisal of its psychologic hazards. *New Engl. J. Med.* **279**, 1365.

Hartmann E. L. (1973) *The Functions of Sleep.* London, Yale University Press.

Hawkes C. (1974) Communicating with the patient—an example drawn from neurology. *Br. J. Med. Educ.* **8**, 57–63.

Hearnshaw L. (1979) *Cyril Burt: Psychologist.* London, Hodder & Stoughton.

Henry J. P., Ely D. L., Watson F. et al. (1975) Ethological methods as applied to the measurement of emotion. In: Levi L. (ed.) *Emotions—Their Parameters and Measurement.* New York, Raven.

Heron A. and Chown S. M. (1967) *Age and Function.* London, Churchill.

Hersov L. (1976) Emotional disorders. In: Rutter M. and Hersov L. (ed.) *Child Psychiatry, Modern Approaches.* Oxford, Blackwell.

Hodgkin K. (1973) *Towards Earlier Diagnosis*, 3rd ed. Edinburgh, Churchill Livingstone.

Holmes T. H. and Rahe R. H. (1967) The social readjustment rating scale. *J. Psychosom. Res.* **11**, 213–218.

Hubel D. H. and Wiesel T. N. (1979) Brain mechanisms of vision. *Sci. Am.* **241** (3), 150–162.

Hughes D. (1983) Consultation length and outcome in two general practices. *J. R. Coll. Gen. Pract.* **33**, 143–147.

Ikeda H. and Wright M. J. (1974) Evidence for sustained and transient neurones in the cat's visual cortex. *Vis. Res.* **14**, 133–136.

Illingworth R. S. and Holt K. S. (1955) Children in hospital. *Lancet* **2**, 1257–1262.

James W. (1890) *The Principles of Psychology.* New York, Holt.

Janis I. L. (1958) *Psychological Stress: Psychoanalytic and Behavioral Studies of Surgical Patients.* New York, Wiley.

Jefferys M. (1978) The elderly in society. In: Brocklehurst J. C. (ed.) *Textbook of Geriatric Medicine and Gerontology*, 2nd ed. Edinburgh, Churchill Livingstone.

Jenkins C. D. (1976) Recent evidence supporting psychologic and social risk factors for coronary heart disease. *New Engl. J. Med.* **294**, 987–994.

Jensen A. R. (1969) How much can we boost I.Q. and scholastic achievement? *Harvard Educ. Rev.* **39**, 449–483.

Johnston D. W. (1984) Biofeedback, relaxation and related procedures in the treatment of psychophysiological disorders. In: Steptoe A. and Mathews A. (ed.) *Health Care and Human Behaviour.* London, Academic Press.

Jones D. and Weinman J. (1973) Computer-based psychological assessment. In: Elithorn A.

and Jones D. (ed.) *Artificial and Human Thinking*. Amsterdam, Elsevier.

Kamin L. (1974) *The Science and Politics of I.Q.* London, Wiley.

Keele S. W. and Neill W. T. (1978) Mechanisms of attention. In: Carterette E. C. and Friedman M. P. (ed.) *Handbook of Perception, Vol. IX.* London, Academic Press.

Kelly G. (1963) *A Theory of Personality.* New York, W. W. Norton.

Kendall P. C. and Hollon S. D. (1979) *Cognitive Behavioural Interventions. Theory, Research and Procedures.* New York, Academic Press.

Kornhuber H. H. (1974) Cerebral cortex, cerebellum and basal anglia: an introduction to their motor functions. In: Schmitt F. O. and Worden F. G. (ed.) *The Neurosciences: Third Study Program.* Cambridge, Mass., MIT Press.

Korsch B. M. and Negrete V. F. (1972) Doctor–patient communication. *Sci. Am.* **227**, 66–72.

Krashen S. D. (1976) Cerebral asymmetry. In: Whittaker H. and Whittaker H. A. (ed.) *Studies in Neurolinguistics, Vol. 2.* New York, Academic Press.

Kubler-Ross E. (1969) *On Death and Dying.* New York, Macmillan.

Lader M. (1979) Emotions, physiology and stress. In: Elsdon-Dew R. W., Wink C. A. S. and Birdwood G. F. B. (ed.) *The Cardiovascular, Metabolic and Psychological Interface.* London, Academic.

La Greca A. M. and Stone W. (1985) Behavioural pediatrics. In: Schneiderman N. and Tapp J. T. (ed.) *Behavioural Medicine: The Biopsychosocial Approach.* Hillsdale N. J., Erlbaum.

Langosch W. (1984) Behavioural interventions in cardiac rehabilitation. In: Steptoe A. and Mathews A. (ed.) *Health Care and Human Behaviour.* London, Academic Press.

Lazarus R. S. (1976) *Patterns of Adjustment.* New York, McGraw-Hill.

Leaper D. J., Gill P. W., Staniland J. R. et al. (1973) Clinical diagnostic process: an analysis. *Br. Med. J.* **4**, 569–574.

Leventhal H. and Tomarken A. J. (1986) Emotion: today's problems. *Ann. Rev. Psychol.* **37**, 565–610.

Leventhal H., Nerenz D. R. and Steele D. (1984) Disease representations and coping with health threats. In: Baum A., Singer J. and Taylor S. (ed.) *Handbook of Psychology and Health: Vol. IV.* Hillsdale, N.J., Erlbaum.

Levine S. (1975) Psychosocial factors in growth and development. In: Levi L. (ed.) *Society, Stress and Disease, Vol. 2.* New York, Oxford University Press.

Ley P. (1974) Communication in the clinical setting. *Br. J. Orthod.* **1**, 173–177.

Ley P., Bradshaw P. W., Kincey J. et al. (1976) Increasing patients' satisfaction with communication. *Br. J. Soc. Clin. Psychol.* **15**, 403–413.

McFarlane A. H., Norman G. R., Streiner D. L. et al. (1980) A longitudinal study of the psychosocial environment on health status. *J. Health Soc. Behav.* **21**, 124–133.

McGeer P. L., McGeer E. G. and Suzuki J. S. (1977) Ageing and extrapyramidal function. *Arch. Neurol.* **34**, 33–35.

McIntyre N. (1973) The problem oriented medical record. *Br. Med. J.* **3**, 598–600.

Mackworth J. (1976) Development of attention. In: Hamilton V. and Vernon M. D. (ed.) *The Development of Cognitive Processes.* London, Academic Press.

Mackworth N. H. and Bruner J. S. (1970) How adults and children search and recognise pictures. *Hum. Dev.* **13**, 149–177.

Maclean P. D. (1975) Sensory and perceptive factors in emotional functions of the triune brain. In: Levi L. (ed.) *Emotions—Their Parameters and Measurement.* New York, Raven.

MacWhinney D. R. (1973) Problem-solving and decision making in primary medical practice. *Proc. R. Soc. Med.* **65**, 934–938.

Maffei L. and Fiorentini A. (1973) The visual cortex as a spatial frequency analyser. *Vis. Res.* **13**, 1255–1267.

Marks I. M. (1969) *Fears and Phobias.* London, Heinemann.

Marks M. and Folkard S. (1984) Diurnal rhythms in cognitive performance. In: Nicholson J. and Beloff H. (ed.) *Psychology Survey 5*. Leicester, British Psychological Society.

Marr D. (1980) Visual information processing: the structure and creation of visual representations. *Phil. Trans. R. Soc. Lond.* **B290**, 199–218.

Mason J. W. (1968) Organisation of psychoendocrine mechanisms. *Psychosom. Med.* **30** (5), Pt II.

Masterton R. B. and Berkeley M. A. (1974) Brain functions: changing ideas on the role of sensory, motor and association cortex in behaviour. *Ann. Rev. Psychol.* **25**, 277–312.

Melzack R. (1973) *The Puzzle of Pain*. Harmondsworth, Penguin.

Melzack R. and Wall P. D. (1965) Pain mechanisms: a new theory. *Science* **150**, 971–979.

Mischel W. (1969) Continuity and change in personality. *Am. Psychol.* **24**, 1012–1018.

Money J. and Ehrhardt A. A. (1972) *Man and Woman, Boy and Girl*. Baltimore, Johns Hopkins University Press.

Moos R. H. and Schaefer J. A. (1984) The crisis of physical illness: an overview and conceptual approach. In: Moos R. H. (ed.) *Coping with Physical Illness. Vol. 2. New Perspectives*. New York, Plenum.

Murgatroyd S. (1983) Counseling and the doctor. *J. R. Coll. Gen. Pract.* **33**, 323–325.

Nathan P. W. (1976) The gate control theory of pain: a critical review. *Brain* **99**, 123–158.

Newell A. and Simon H. L. (1972) *Human Problem Solving*. Englewood Cliffs, Prentice Hall.

Nicholls K. (1984) *Psychological Care in Physical Illness*. Beckenham, Croom Helm.

OPCS (1978) *Occupational Mortality, 1970–1972*. London, HMSO.

OPCS (1983) *General Household Survey*. London, HMSO.

Parkes C. M. (1975) *Bereavement*. Harmondsworth, Penguin.

Patel C., Marmot M. and Terry D. J. (1981) Controlled trial of biofeedback-aided behavioural methods in reducing mild hypertension. *Br. Med. J.* **282**, 2005–2008

Pendleton D., Schofield T., Tate P. et al. (1984) *The Consultation: An Approach to Learning and Teaching*. Oxford, Oxford University Press.

Perenin M. T. and Jeannerod M. (1975) Residual vision in cortically blind hemifields. *Neuropsychologia* **13**, 1–7.

Pettigrew J. (1972) The neurophysiology of binocular vision. *Sci. Am.* **227**, 84–95.

Powell G. E. (1979) *Brain and Personality*. Farnborough, Saxon House.

Rabkin J. G. and Struening E. L. (1976) Life events, stress and illness. *Science* **194**, 1013–1020.

Rachman S. (1971) *The Effects of Psychotherapy*. Oxford, Pergamon.

Rachman S. and Phillips C. (1975) *Psychology and Medicine*. London, Temple Smith.

Razin A. M. (1971) A–B variable in psychotherapy: a critical review. *Psychol. Bull.* **75**, 1–21.

Rosenman R. (1979) Personality, type A behaviour pattern and coronary heart disease. In: Elsdon-Dew R., Wink C. and Birdwood G. (ed.) *The Cardiovascular, Metabolic and Psychological Interface*. London, Academic Press.

Rosenthal T. and Bandura A. (1978) Psychological modelling: theory and practice. In: Garfield S. L. and Bergin A. E. (ed.) *Handbook of Psychotherapy and Behaviour Change*, 2nd ed. New York, Wiley.

Ross M. and Olsen J. M. (1982) Placebo effects in medical research and practice. In: Eiser J. R. (ed.) *Social Psychology and Behavioural Medicine*. London, Wiley.

Rotter J. B. (1966) Generalised expectancies of internal versus external control of reinforcement. *Psychol. Monogr.* **80** (1), 1–28.

Rush A. J. and Giles D. E. (1982) Cognitive therapy: theory and research. In: Rush A. J. (ed.) *Short-term Psychotherapies for Depression*. Chichester, Wiley.

Rutter M. (1972) *Maternal Deprivation Reassessed*. Harmondsworth, Penguin.

Rutter M. (1976) Infantile autism and other child psychoses. In: Rutter M. and Hersov L. (ed.) *Child Psychiatry: Modern Approaches*. Oxford, Blackwell.

Rutter M. and Yule W. (1976) Reading difficulties. In: Rutter M. and Hersov L. (ed.) *Child Psychiatry: Modern Approaches*. Oxford, Blackwell.

Rutter M. Graham P. and Yule W. (1970) *A Neuropsychiatric Study in Childhood*. Philadelphia, Lippincott.

Rutter M., Graham P., Chadwick O. F. D. et al. (1976) Adolescent turmoil: fact or fiction. *J. Child. Psychol. Psychiatry* **17**, 35–36.

Schacter S. (1975) Cognition and peripheralist-centralist controversies in motivation and emotion. In: Gazzaniga M. S. and Blakemore C. (ed.) *Handbook of Psychobiology*. London, Academic Press.

Schmale A. H. (1972) Giving up as a final common pathway to changes in health. *Adv. Psychosom. Med.* **8**, 20–40.

Seligman M. E. P. (1975) *Helplessness: On Depression Development and Death*. San Francisco, W. H. Freeman.

Selye H. (1956) *The Stress of Life*. New York, McGraw-Hill.

Selye H. (1979) Stress, cancer and the mind. In: Taché J., Selye H. and Day S. B. (ed.) *Cancer, Stress and Death*. New York, Plenum.

Singer J. E. and Lord D. (1984) The role of social support in coping with chronic or life threatening illness. In: Baum A., Singer J. E. and Taylor S. (ed.) *Handbook of Psychology and Health: Volume IV*. Hillsdale, N.J., Erlbaum.

Sobel H. (1981) Towards a behavioural thanatology in clinical care. In: Sobel H. (ed.) *Behavioural Therapy in Terminal Care: A Humanistic Approach*. Cambridge, Mass., Balinger.

Sperling G. (1960) The information available in brief visual presentations. *Psychol. Monogr.* **74**, No. 11.

Spirduso W. W. (1975) Reaction and movement time as a function of age and physical activity level. *J. Gerontol.* **30**, 435–440.

Spirduso W. W. and Clifford P. (1978) Replication of age physical activity effects on reaction and movement time. *J. Gerontol.* **33**, 26–30.

Sterman M. B. (1973) Neurophysiologic and clinical studies of sensorimotor EEG biofeedback training: some effects on epilepsy. In: Birk L. (ed.) *Biofeedback: Behavioral Medicine*. New York, Grune & Stratton.

Terenius L. (1978) Significance of endorphins in endogenous antinociception. In: Costa E. and Trabucchi M. (ed.) *Advances in Biochemical Pharmacology. Vol. 18*. New York, Raven.

Thomas A. J. (1984) *Acquired Hearing Loss*. London, Academic Press.

Thorndike E. (1911) *Animal Intelligence*. New York, Macmillan.

Triesman A. (1966) Human attention. In: Foss B. M. (ed.) *New Horizons in Psychology*. Harmondsworth, Penguin.

Tuckett D., Boulton M., Olson C. et al. (1985) *Meetings Between Experts: An Approach to Sharing Ideas in the Consultation*. London, Tavistock.

Tulving E. (1972) Episodic and semantic memory. In: Tulving E. and Donaldson W. (ed.) *Organization of Memory*. New York, Academic Press.

Turner J. A. and Chapman C. R. (1982) Psychological interventions for chronic pain: a critical review. I. Relaxation and biofeedback. *Pain* **12**, 1–21.

Vygotsky (1962) *Thought and Language*. New York, Wiley.

Wall P. D. (1978) The gate control theory of pain mechanisms: a re-examination and re-statement. *Brain* **101**, 1–18.

Wallston B. S. and Wallston K. A. (1978) Locus of control and health: a review of the literature. *Health Educ. Monog.* **6** (2), 107–117.

Wason P. C. (1974) The psychology of deceptive problems. *New Scientist*, 15 August, 382–385.

Weed L. L. (1969) *Medical Records, Medical Education and Patient Care*. Cleveland, Case Western Reserve University Press.

Weiner H. (1977) *Psychobiology and Human Disease*. New York, Elsevier.

Weiner N. (1948) *Cybernetics*. New York, Wiley.

Weiss J. M. (1972) Influence of psychological variables on stress-induced pathology. In: Porter R. and Knight J. (ed.) *Physiology, Emotions and Psychosomatic Illness*. New York, Elsevier.

Wilkinson R. T., Tyler P. D. and Varey C. A. (1975) Duty hours of young hospital doctors: effects on quality of work. *J. Occup. Psychol.* **48**, 219–229.

Williams P. L. and Warwick R. (1975) *Functional Neuroanatomy of Man*. Edinburgh, Churchill Livingstone.

Wing J. K. and Brown G. W. (1970) *Institutionalism and Schizophrenia. A Comparative Study of Three Mental Hospitals*. Cambridge, Cambridge University Press.

Yarbus A. L. (1967) *Eye Movements and Vision*. New York, Plenum.

Zborowski M. (1952) Cultural components in response to pain. *J. Soc. Issues* **8**, 16–30.

Zeki S. M. (1978) The cortical projections of foveal striate cortex in the rhesus monkey. *J. Physiol.* **227**, 227–244.

Index